THE
ALCHEPEDIA

SECOND EDITION

BY

ERIK P. ANTONI

*"If you see nothing here,
you will not be able to seek further.
You will be blind, even though you are in the midst of light."*

*— Daniel Stolz von Stolzenberg —
Viridarium Chymcium — 1624*

*The Alchepedia is dedicated
in loving memory of my father
who always said I needed to write this book.*

Author
Erik P. Antoni

Cover Designer
Melissa Williams Design

Noetic Press
Text Copyright © 2019-2025 Erik P. Antoni
ISBN: 978-1-7363242-5-7
Second Edition
2.4.5

Alchepedia is a Registered Trademark
Serial Number 88750904

Books Written by Erik P. Antoni

Nonfiction

The Alchepedia
Concerto of the Rising Sun
Song of the Immortal Beloved

Science Fiction
Anthros Galactica (Book Series)

Please visit the author's webpage at:
www.songoftheimmortalbeloved.com

ii
INTRODUCTION

Language is a medium of communication to facilitate the efficient exchange of information. Human beings have a natural built-in ability to speak, listen, and exchange information based on the acoustical vibrations of sound. Through the study of cymatics we've learned that geometric forms arise in nature via the resonance of sound. Sound geometrizes. Long before we knew of cymatics, human beings intuitively assigned geometric symbols to sound with the innate ability to relate signs to particular meanings. It's a cognitive process experts call semiosis. All human languages depend on it. Today, we call individually written geometric symbols representing the shortest measures of sound, "letters." Letters combine into longer units of language called "words." Words are special; they convey meaning. When grammatically combined, words unlock unlimited potential—limited by only the mind—to allow thoughts to rise into expression. Thought development and language development evolve in tandem. Ultimately, what is language? — It is a function of consciousness.

What is consciousness? What is mind?

Is there a language of pure consciousness?

What I've learned through a long alchemical journey is that creation arises out of a source singularity residing in an abstract higher noumenal realm of pure consciousness. It precedes creation, matter, time, and space with an absolute, infinite, eternal existence. It is through an interaction between three special dimensions within the source singularity that all of creation emerges. These three dimensions are Awareness, Life, and Love. When the source becomes aware of its own life—it loves. Because the source is infinite, its life is infinite, and therefore, its love is infinite. The infinite energy of love spontaneously sparks creation into existence. This is the origin of zero-point energy. It didn't do this just once. It does this *ad-infinitum*.

Naturally, the first thing to exist is the most difficult thing to define because nothing precedes it to differentiate it or give it any context.

Consciousness is the first thing. It has always existed. Consciousness doesn't arise from creation. Creation arises from consciousness.

Such a notion of creation is a problem for many mainstream scientists because it suggests the existence of God—and since its inception, mainstream science has sought to explain away God.

When it comes to consciousness, religion is equally challenged. As consciousness expands to compel our thought development, so too does our language expand to express our deeper realizations of consciousness and its ultimate source, and as a result, our view of God naturally evolves. This dynamic challenges pre-existing dogma, for the language of scripture is not allowed to be changed, and the orthodox interpretation of meaning is not allowed to be reinterpreted. Yet, scientists and theologians are sworn to the same thing—the truth.

To the second question, "what is mind?" Matter spontaneously arises out of the source singularity of consciousness, but the two circle back together to form the mind. The mind arises when consciousness and matter combine to form a living being.

To the third question, "is there a language of pure consciousness, a language that is beyond the mind—before the emergence of matter?"

Yes, there is. And that's the main subject matter of this book.

The Alchepedia is the product of a lifelong alchemical transformation process I underwent in the process of unifying the human mind, the culmination of which is mythologized as the philosophers' stone. In the third stage of a three-stage process of unifying the mind, which in hermetic lore is famously called the Three Mountains, we learn how to communicate empathically with a set of living forces underlying the universe which give rise to and organize the process of creation. I call these forces the cosmic quanta.

During the universal alchemical process of unifying the mind, the cosmic quanta relay the story of creation directly to the Human Soul, beyond the mind, via the language of pure consciousness.

The reason it does this is that creation initially bursts forth spontaneously out of an overabundance of energy (love)—from within the source. Because creation arises spontaneously, it initially arises outside the awareness of the source singularity of consciousness.

It is only out of our willingness to return to the source and realize how everything came forth that the universe can integrate the mind and complete the process of creation within the human being.

The intercession of a conscious mind is required to complete the process of creation. As creation is sparked unconsciously into existence, it can only achieve completion through a conscious return to the source from which it sprang. A sustained dual reflection between the mind of creation and the source is essential to the process.

Many of the archetypal characters, in many of humanity's most popular religions, mythologies, and fabled stories, are all representing an underlying set of divine principles and organizational constructs of energy and consciousness residing at the quantum level of existence which give rise to consciousness and all of creation. These same forces—called the cosmic quanta—are attempting to speak to us through our stories via the dynamics of the collective unconscious by utilizing the language of pure consciousness.

At this point, it is necessary to define the term—*divinity*.

Divinity is that which was never created, but yet still exists. Divinity has always existed as the ultimate source of all things.

Mythologically, the way creation initially arises out of the divine source is allegorized in religion as the great fall, but it's actually a real quantum-based process.

In reality, it is creation itself, which is fallen, not some heavenly deity. But creation has an embedded awareness—and thus ensues all the mythologies of the unconscious to make the ineffable tangible.

Creation initially arises in darkness. Darkness is a metaphor used to describe the initial lack of awareness existing between the source consciousness and creation when creation first emerges.

The source quickly becomes aware of creation, and when it does, it loves it and wills that creation should not perish but should be saved and reintegrated with its eternal being so it can last forever.

Sound familiar yet? When this will arises out of the quantum cosmos, mythologically, this is the light, or Logos. (will = word/logos).

Mirroring the three original dimensions of consciousness, the first born—*darkness*, and the second born—*light*, possess the same three dimensions—just a different permutation of the three.

The first permutation in any trinity is awareness. The awareness in the first trinity (divine trinity) is resonant awareness (Father). It's called the Father because within it is the seed of all of creation. The awareness in the second trinity (Erodonic Trinity), born in darkness, is perspective awareness (IAO). The awareness in the third trinity (Sacred Trinity), born in the light, is reflective awareness (Logos).

The second permutation in any trinity is life. The life force of the first trinity is the Divine Soul—the eternal everlasting life force of the Father. The life force of the second trinity, the life force of IAO, born in darkness, is the Erotic Soul. The life force of the third trinity, the life force of the Logos, born in the light, is the Noetic Soul. The Noetic Soul is the Human Soul within humanity. They are the same. The Noetic Soul is the only soul begotten directly by the will of the divine Father to intervene with and bear the weight of creation— to save the Erotic Soul lost in darkness—so all three souls may unify, and creation may continue onward forever.

The third permutation in any trinity is a form of radiant energy. The radiant energy of the first trinity is love, otherwise known historically as the Divine Spirit and Holy Spirit (or Spirit for short). It arises with the Father and the Divine Soul to form the original Monad—Ain Soph. The radiant energy of the second trinity is the atomic matter-energy of creation which binds to form all things in the universe. It arises with IAO and the Erotic Soul to form the Dyad. The radiant energy of the third trinity is the Numina. She arises immaculately by will of the Father with the Logos and Noetic Soul as the Nuad to save creation and reintegrate the Monad.

Mythologically, the sought after reintegrated Monad is Christ, or the philosophers' stone. It is—the unified mind.

The two conceptions of the source, (1) IAO and (2) the Logos, both have their own trinities which mirror the original divine trinity.

The first conception of the divine source occurs spontaneously outside the will of the Father in darkness in descent from the Spirit.

The second conception of the divine source is the proverbial immaculate conception. It is immaculate because it is conceived directly by the Father's will. It is a process called Thelesis.

In mythology, the forces descending in line of the Spirit (love) are symbolized by the feminine because the feminine is associated with love, while the forces of will—Logos—are associated with the masculine. Love and will combine to form the universe. The pairing of darkness and light, love and will, IAO and Logos in the universal creation process is the origin of sexuality and duality within all things.

These permutations recounted in order of emergence are:
(1) Father; (2) Divine Soul, (3) Spirit, (4) IAO, (5) Erotic Soul, (6) Matter-Energy, (7) Logos, (8) Noetic Soul, and (9) Numina.

These are the nine cardinal permutations of consciousness with the first three being uncreated and the following six being created. The number six appears repeatedly in mythology relative to the process of creation, such as the six days of creation in the Book of Genesis.

There are two more permutations that extend beyond the forces of consciousness into the mind: (10) Idamus, and (11) the Gorgon. Idamus and the Gorgon form the two polar sides of the Id-complex. Idamus is the beast of the sea. The Gorgon is the beast of the earth. They're significant and arise unconsciously into world mythology.

"The dragon stood on the shore of the sea. And I saw a beast coming out of the sea. It had ten horns and seven heads, with ten crowns on its horns, and on each head a blasphemous name."
—The Book of Revelation - 13:1.

"After this I saw in the night visions, and behold a fourth beast, dreadful and terrible, and strong exceedingly; and it had great iron teeth: it devoured and brake in pieces, and stamped the residue with the feet of it: and it was diverse from all the beasts that were before it; and it had ten horns."—The Book of Daniel-7:7.

ii - Introduction

These two versus above refer to Idamus—the tenth permutation, symbolized by ten horns. Let's continue with the Book of Daniel-7:8.

"I considered the horns, and, behold, there came up among them another little horn, before whom there were three of the first horns plucked up by the roots: and, behold, in this horn were eyes like the eyes of man, and a mouth speaking great things."

The little horn is the eleventh permutation rising with the tenth permutation within the human psyche. It is the Gorgon. It blocks our inner sight of the first three forces. Unintegrated and left in darkness and chaos, the Gorgon gives rise to what is worst in human beings. One of its prominent features is *narcissism* (speaking great things).

Narcissism is a psychosomatic disease of the mind that begins forming in childhood due to an inability to process and resolve emotions. As part of the disease, the mind offers delusional constructs of self and reality to compensate, and the brain further rewires to reinforce the disease. It typically gets worse throughout life. All sociopaths and psychopaths are narcissistic, but not all narcissists are sociopathic or psychopathic. The difference between sociopaths and psychopaths is that sociopaths are made, psychopaths are born.

Revelation-13:18: "Then I saw another beast that rose out of the earth (the Gorgon); it had two horns like a lamb and it spoke like a dragon. It exercises all the authority of the first beast (Idamus) on its behalf, and it makes the Earth and its inhabitants worship the first beast, whose mortal wound had been healed [..] This calls for wisdom: let anyone with understanding calculate the number of the beast, for it is the number of a man. Its number is six hundred and sixty-six."

The repeating number pattern, 666, refers to the repeating compounding processes of creation. This indicates that the beast of the earth, the Gorgon, is a product of creation. The reason six is used in the repeating number series is because the beast of the earth is the product of matter-energy compounding in on itself within the mind.

Again, all of this is a natural quantum-based process between consciousness and matter whose interaction is known as—*alchemy*.

It is a process I believe quantum physicists will one day be able to witness, measure, study, and explain with their own language. Why? Because the process of creation is not a one-and-done process. It continues to this day and will continue forever, *ad infinitum*.

The alchemical process plays out in scales. The three major scales are the cosmic, planetary, and individual. On a cosmic scale the process has already completed itself because it happened "outside" of spacetime. The completion of the process on a cosmic scale is what caused the known universe to emerge—within which all the laws of physics came into existence. However, the planetary and individual scales are attempting to reconcile "inside" of spacetime—driven by the law of one—the law of unity.

Because the ultimate source of all things is absolute and infinite, the process is playing out inside spacetime within fractal scales in an attempt to square the circle. However, it's a divine paradox.

Because the ratio of Pi has a never-ending integer, the expansion of the universe and the reconciliation of the "inner" scales is forever. The expansion of the universe is driven forever by an unresolvable divine paradox. The beauty in the divine paradox is that creation has infinite runway, and therefore its potential—is unlimited.

The will of the original source consciousness, which some call the cosmic consciousness, whose original unity—or original Monad, which the kabbalists call, Ain Soph, gives rise to what is called the Alpha principle. The Alpha principle cannot be averted.

The Alpha principle is that all things must eventually achieve a unity with the source from which all things originally emerged via a harmonic sympathetic resonance—to fulfill the law of one. It is this will that immaculately conceives the Noetic Soul—a sacred spark residing behind all the ego defense mechanisms of the human mind with the innate capacity to reconnect the mind and body of its creation back to the source. It is the prime directive of the Noetic Soul.

This will generates a force in the universe to guide everything back to that eventual unity. I call this force Alpha. The ancients also recognized this force. Depending on the tradition, they called it Kundalini, the Great Dragon, the Serpent, Destiny, even Grace itself.

To this day, early 2023, physicists still cannot yet explain how the universe expanded so quickly during what they call the *big bang*. They also cannot yet adequately explain its continued expansion— what they call *dark energy*. And they cannot yet explain a large unobservable pulling force in the cosmos they attribute to *dark matter*. This force is so powerful on a large scale that physicists say that its dark matter must comprise 85% of the total matter of the universe, yet its matter is undetectable. Most likely, this force exists outside the bounds of creation and does not arise from an invisible dark matter.

The pulling force that physicists attribute to an unseen dark matter is most likely not due to any matter at all. Alpha is the most likely candidate and should be explored as a developing hypothesis.

All of these mysteries correspond to the alchemy of creation. Physicists are doing well in explaining the physics "within" creation, but they're not even scratching the surface yet in understanding the physics that "drives" its emergence into existence, or the physics "acting upon" creation to steer it to higher and higher levels of reality. These two other types of physics form a higher physics involving the interaction of matter and consciousness, otherwise known as alchemy.

Why are the forces of the cosmic quanta trying so hard to communicate with us?

And what are they trying to tell us?

The cosmic quanta are continually broadcasting that there's a special reason to the origin and purpose of sentient humanoid life. Sentient humanoid life is not unique to just the planet we call Earth. It is spread throughout the cosmos with one universal prime directive. What this prime directive is, the story of its discovery, and the saga that came to unfold between worlds in an attempt to fulfill it, deny it, or steer it, becomes the greatest story of the cosmos. Its story is being told and retold, time, and time again, by the collective unconscious until this one universal prime directive is finally fulfilled within us.

One of the principal rules of the collective unconscious is that the further historical figures recede in time, the more their characters take on mythological parallels to the various forces of consciousness. I call this dynamic "Theopomorphism" as a direct mirror opposite effect to "Anthropomorphism" where human attributes are added to the forces of consciousness. Anthropomorphism and Theopomorphism are dualistic and work in tandem with each other. It's how the universe speaks to us. This dynamic doesn't lessen the reality of various historical figures, it's just that their stories echo more than actual history, they also echo the forces of consciousness.

Admittedly, the dynamic of unconsciously attributing human qualities to the forces of consciousness (anthropomorphic) and or attributing godly or angelic natures to various historical figures (theopomorphic) has been a source of great confusion among the masses throughout history. To unconfuse, untangle the web, and clarify the stage, the real history of various ancient religious figures should be reexamined in a purely mundane context, and the nature of consciousness and the story it's trying to tell us should be deciphered and made known.

The Alchepedia clarifies how theopomorphic principles are applied and where they arise out of. They arise out of the universal story of consciousness and creation—and the need for these forces to speak to us—to compel us in the work to reintegrate the Monad.

For clarifying the true nature of the historical figures that have been theopomorphized, modern scholars are busy at work unraveling this mystery. Indeed, reading the Bible, for example, from the basis of pure literal history reveals a completely different story than the interpreted meanings of mainstream religion. But note, as the true nature of the historical figures in the Bible are eventually revealed, this does not necessarily undermine the universal story of creation and consciousness that the cosmic quanta have overlayed upon these historical figures in an attempt to speak to us and reveal the purpose and prime directive of the Noetic Soul. Knowing this dynamic, however, helps to clarify all of it, including real history, the forces of consciousness and the process of creation. Ironically, by clarifying the real history of figures that have been reimagined by religion as something divine, aids us in seeing a clearer picture of the story of creation and consciousness that the forces of the cosmic quanta and the collective unconscious are trying to tell us.

The Noetic Soul within humanity has a divine mission, or prime directive. We all have the same mission. Whatever earthly purpose we think we have in this world, it's all secondary to this prime directive.

Fragments of this long forgotten cosmic story have been unconsciously sown into most of the Earth's mythologies by human beings themselves via the dynamics of the collective unconscious.

"Until you make the unconscious conscious, it will direct your life and you will call it fate," —Carl Jung.

The unconscious is the sphere of the mind that the conscious mind is not yet aware. The collective unconscious is a transpersonal source of shared information stored collectively between all human beings within the unconscious recesses of the psyche. All human beings continuously upload to and download from the collective unconscious.

The greatest mysteries of existence await to be discovered within the eternal depths of the unconscious mind of the human being and the collective unconscious of humanity as a whole. It is from within the depths of the unconscious that we endeavor to fathom the very existence of God.

It is for this reason that Jung said an enlightened person is someone who had been swallowed by the unconscious. The universal story the collective unconscious has been sowing into the myths and legends of world mythology via motif and symbolism has an element of actual truth and history behind it.

It is the story of consciousness, it is the story of creation, it is the story of humanity, it is the story of us. It is the greatest story ever told. In context of this cosmic story, the Alchepedia reexamines "words." And being based on words, we now proceed into the index of terms.

iii
INDEX OF ALCHEMICAL TERMS

Absolute, 27

Adam Kadmon, 244

Ahura Mazda, 223

Ain Soph, 28

Akashic Records, 29

Alchemy, 29

Alchemy–Development Stages, 30

Alchemy–Meditation Practices, 42

Alkahest, 257

Alpha, 49

Alpha Convergence, 155

Alpha Principle, 49

Alpha Wave, 50

Ancient Builder Race, 256

Animal Mind, 232

Anthropomorphism, 17

Anti-Christ, 169, 202

Apprentice, 52

Ashmole, Elias, 255

Astral Body, 53

Astral Projection, 275

Astral Projection, The Key to, 276

Astral World, 57

Atalanta Fugiens, 260

Atkinson, William Walker, 209

Atma-Buddhi, 28

Atman, 28

Aurelion, 53

Authentic-Self, 54

Auto-Cognition, 56

Auto-Cognitive Period, 56

Azoth, 261

Bacon, Roger, 261

Bagua, 76

Bandwidths, 57

Bardo, 36

Barstow, 181

Beast of the Earth, 162

Beast of the Sea, 200

Beast with Ten Horns, 202

Being, 58, 330

Binah, 298

Blessed Mother of God, 203

Bodhisattva, 31

Book of Revelation, 170, 294

Boyle, Robert, 58

Browne, Sir Thomas, 257

Buddha, 62, 92

Buddhi, 115

Calcination, 34

iii – Index of Alchemical Terms

Campbell, Joseph P., 57
Candidate, 59
Carmot, 261
Causal 'A', 59
Causal 'B', 60
Causal 'M', 65
Celestial Body, 69
Center Head of Cerberus, 283
Cerberus, 70
Chaos, 71, 170
Chardin, Pierre Teilhard de, 249
Cheirokmeta, 255
Cherubim, 72
Chia, Mantak, 73
Children of the First Light, 72
Chinese Alchemy, 73
Christ, 87
Christic Trinity, 92
Cibation, 37
Cinnabar, 80
Cintamani, 258
Coagulation, 38
Collective Unconscious, 93
Common Human Emotion, 93
Communion Turiya, 350
Conjunction, 35
Conscious Mind, 232
Cosmic Alchemy, 96

Cosmic Christ, 105
Cosmic Consciousness, 100
Cosmic Cultivation, 100
Cosmic Mind, 103
Cosmic Monad, 105
Cosmic Quanta, 106
Cosmic Seal, 106
Creation, 107
Creation Paradox, 210
Crucifix, 217
Dante, 261
Dark Champion, 162
Darkness, 11
David, 111
Dee, John, 177
Deism, 112
Delusion, 202
Demiurge, 194, 220, 223
Demiurgos, 220
Demon, 262
Demonic Possession, 165
Dervish Dances, 102
Devil, 229
Differential Resonance, 113
Din, Gevurah, 299
Dissolution, 34
Divine Soul, 114
Divine Source, 116

Index of Alchemical Terms – iii

Divine Spirit, 322
Divine Trinity, 108
Divinity, 11, 116
Dominion Over Creation, 90
Dominus Turiya, 351
Dyad, 143
Dynamis, 330
Earth Monad Project, 117
Eastern Alchemy, 73
Echelons, 134
Eden, 266
Ego, 135
Eikasia, 203
EL, 229
Elixir, 142
Elysium, 181
Emergent, 135, 136
Emergent Period, 136
Emotion, 137
Empyrean, 138
End of Days, 198
Epsilon, 139
Erawan, 181
Erodao, 140
Erodonic Trinity, 140
Erodysis, 142
Eroplatia, 36
Eros-Dyad, 143

Erotic Soul, 144
Eternal Alchemy, 98
Eternal Sea, 114
Eternal-Primordial Being, 146
Evil, 133
Exaltation, 40
Eyad, 151
False Alchemy, 326
False-Self, 153
False-Selves, 153
Father, The, 154
Fermentation, 38
Ferris, 36
Fibonacci Sequence, 217
First Factor, 154
First Mountain, 155
First Sanctum, 155
First Triumphant, 347
Five Centers, 156
Force of Unity, 330
Force Potential, 330
Foreman, 157
Four Beasts, 170
Four Needs of Divinity, 235
Fourth Triumphant, 348
Fourth Way, 156
Fractured Mind, 232
Gaia, 165

iii – Index of Alchemical Terms

Geber, 256, 261
Genesis–Summary of Creation, 159
Gerishan, 36
Ghost, 263
God, 161
Gog, 198
Golden Ratio, 217
Gorgon, The, 162
Gorgonism, 252
Great Arcanum, 171
Great Work, The, 173
Gurdjieff, 156
Harmonic Bridge, 179
Hayyan, Jabir ibn, 256
Heavenly Realms, 179
Hell, 353
Hermes, 261
Hermes Trismegistus, 92
Hesed, 298
Higher Self, 58
Hod, 299
Hokhmah, 298
Holy Grail, 38, 350
Holy Spirit, 322
Human Being, 182
Human Mind, 232
Human Soul, 243
Hyperborean Mystery, 348

IAO, 183
Id, 195
Id Complex, 195
Ida and Pingala, 311
Idamus, 196
Illusion, 202
Immaculate Conception, 203
Immortal Beloved, 325
Immortal Maxim, 88
Individual Mind, 232
Individuated Mind, 232
Indra, 194
Infiniton Field, 65
Intraspection, 204
Introspection, 204
Jehovah, 184
Jenesis, 181
Johnson, Obed Simon, 73, 362
Journeyman, 205
Jung, Carl, 57, 206
Kant, Immanuel, 207
Keter, 298
Khimmadooree, 181
Kier, 208
Kiraphon, 162
Krishna, 92
Kundalini, 208
Kybalion, The, 209

Index of Alchemical Terms – iii

Lancelot, 221
Lao Tzu, 73, 86
Law of Attraction, 191
Law of One, 211
Law of Unity, 211
Left Head of Cerberus, 170
Light, 12
Lilith, 162
Logos, The, 212
Lord's Prayer, 225
Lu Dongbin, 73
Lucid Dreaming, 275
Lucifer, 228
Magdalene, 92
Magnum Opus, 173
Magnus, Albertus, 257
Magog, 162, 198
Maier, Michael, 260
Majuj, 170
Maub, 229
Maya, 203
Medicine Wheel, 82
Metatronic, 146
Metatronic World, 323
Microcosmic Orbit, 230
Monad, 233
Morality, 207
Morning Star, 218

Mount Elohim, 239
Mount Kabbalah, 284
Mount Magia, 336
Mount Sophia, 155
Muhammed, 261
Multiplication, 40
Mutus Liber, 257
Narcissism, 296
NDE, 149
Neidan, 73
New Father, 92
New Heaven, 154
New Thought, 209
Nexus, 243
Nezah, 299
Nirvana, 181
Noetic Soul, 243
Noosphere, 93, 232
Norton, Thomas, 260
Noumenon, 207, 245
Number 666, 167, 170
Number 777, 217
Numina, 247
Old Father, 154
Old Heaven, 154
Omega, 249
Omicron, 250
One Cloud, 74, 79, 83

iii – Index of Alchemical Terms

Orial, 37
Osiris, 223
Ouroboros, 69
Ouspensky, 156
Parabinlaya, 37
Paracelsus, 178
Pazuzu, 200
Personality, 253
Perspective Awareness, 254
Phi, 217
Philosophers' Stone, 254
Philosophical Trinity, 337
Planet Lifting, 36
Planetary Alchemy, 262
Planetary Group Mind, 232
Plato, 256
Poltergeist, 262
Prelescent Period, 56, 264
Prima Materia, 264
Primations, 347
Prime Directive, 110
Primordial Alchemy, 97
Primordial Being, 146
Primordial Body, 146
Primordial Earth, 265
Primordial Universe, 267
Prometheus, 132
Psychological Elements, 153

Psycho-Sexual Dynamic, 268
Ptah, 184
Putrefaction, 36
Q Level, 269
Qigong, 74, 271
Quantum Meditation, 272
Quetzalcoatl, 92
Recycled Return, 31, 278
Red Sulfur, 257
Reflective Awareness, 277
Refracted, 269
Reincarnation, 277
Religio Medici, 257
Resonance, 280
Resonant Awareness, 280
Right Head of Cerberus, 202
Rubicon, 280
Rupescissa, 260
Sacred Fire, 208, 281
Saint Jnaneshwar, 258
Sanctum of Magia, 282
Satan, 283
Satanism, 252
Sea of Chi, 317
Sea of Eros, 114
Second Death, 250
Second Factor, 284
Second Mountain, 284

Index of Alchemical Terms – iii

Second Sanctum, 285
Second Triumphant, 348
Sefirot, The, 285
Self-Actualization, 309
Self-Observation, 44
Self-Realization, 309
Semiosis, 9
Sentience, 309
Separation, 35
Seraphim, 150
Seraphina, 37
Sexual Cultivation, 309
Shadow Scout, 85
Shah, Indries, 261
Shakti, 49
Shamanism, 80
Shambhala, 266
Shekhinah, 299
Shiva-Lingam, 220
Short Path, 320
Sigma, 321
Simmatuu, 181
Singularity Wall, 146
Snake in Garden of Eden, 170
Source, 116
Spiral Path, 321
Spirit, The, 322
Spiritual Group Mind, 322
Spirituality, 324
Squared Circle, 258
St. Germain, Count of, 176
Stone of the Wise, 260
Straight Path, 326
Sublimation, 38
Sufis, 156
Sumerian Mythology, 186
Super Cognitive Emotion, 328
Super Ego, 327
Super Meta, 329
Symphysis Turiya, 350
Tantra, 309
Tao Te Ching, 86
Taoism, 73
Taoist Sexual Yoga, 309
Tau, 217
Temporal Group Mind, 331
Temporal Physical Being, 333
Terrasumna, 181
Tetragrammaton, 184
The Fourth Way, 156
Theism, 333
Thelesis, 13, 203, 330, 334
Theoflection, 334
Theokinesis, 334
Theopomorphism, 17, 88
Theosis, 120

iii – Index of Alchemical Terms

Theosphere, 335
Theta, 335
Third Factor, 336
Third Mountain, 336
Third Sanctum, 337
Third Triumphant, 348
Thirumoolar, Siddhar, 258
Thoth, 223
Three Factors, 337
Three Mountains, 342
Tiferet, 299
Time Paradox, 210
Tirumandhiram, 258
Tithing, The, 38, 344
Tracker, 85
Transformation On-The-Go, 48
Transmigration, 277
Treasuries of Light, 345
Treasury of Souls, 346
Triad, 246, 347
Triumphants, 347
Triune, 78, 211, 233
Turiya, 349
Turiya Faculty, 351
Typhon Baphomet, 219
Unconscious Mind, 232
Valhalla, 181
Vampirism, 252

Vaughan, Thomas, 256
Virgin Mary, 247
Vishnu, 214
Vishu, 37
Void, The, 353
Vritra, 194
Waidan, 73
Whore of Babylon, 170
Will of the Father, 356
Winn, Michael, 73
Wuji, 357
Wundt, Wilhelm, 156
Xerion, 256
Yahweh, 292
Yajuj, 199
Yaldabaoth, 184
Yang, 358
Yesod:, 299
YHWH, 184
Yin, 358
Yoga Vasistha, The, 258
Yuan, 358
Zen Buddhism, 359
Zero-Base-Prime, 330
Zeus, 92
Zietgeist, 359
Zoroaster, 360
Zosimos, 255

Absolute, The

As a noun, the Absolute is the infinite, abstract, uncreated realm from which all of creation comes forth. It is said to be the ultimate reality —or only true reality—which precedes all of creation. Everything else is a shade of gray or distortion of that ultimate reality. The absolute always was and always will be. It is absolute because it has no correspondence or relativity to anything within creation. Only the original divine Monad, or cosmic singularity, from which all things come forth, resides in the Absolute abstract space. The original divine Monad has many names depending on the philosophical source. In western alchemy, and the Kabbalah, one such name for the original divine Monad is the term Ain Soph.

Similar or Equivalent Terms:

George Hegal:	Absolute, The
Erik P. Antoni:	Causal 'A'
Mahayana Buddhism:	Ārūpyadhātu (Formless Realm)
Hasidic Judaism:	Dwelling Place of Atzmus, or Atzmut
Hinduism:	Brahmaloka, Bramapura, Satyaloka
Sufism:	Noor-e-Ahadi, Haqiqa, or Haqiqat
Taoism:	Wuji
Theosophy:	Realm of Atma-Buddhi, Atman
Zoroastrianism:	Domain of the One Eternal Light

A - Ain Soph

Ain Soph – or Ein Sof, Eyn Sof

Ain Soph is the original unity of forces which precede all of creation. It is the original divine unity of God. It is the original divine Monad. Ain Soph is the God particle within the quantum cosmos. It is divine. Divinity, by its very nature, is paradoxical. The definition of divinity is that which was never born, procreated, or permutated. Ain Soph always was, and always will be. It has an absolute eternal existence and is indestructible and untarnishable. Ain Soph is the cosmic consciousness expressed in unity. There are three dimensions within the unity of Ain Soph which are (1) Awareness, (2) Life, and (3) Love. Ain Soph precedes creation and all permutations of consciousness, mind, or matter. Ain Soph is absolute because there is nothing which precedes it to limit it or define it. The domain of divinity in which Ain Soph exists is called "Causal 'A'" or the "Absolute." The word Ain Soph, or Ein Soph, traces back to the Kabbalah and generally means endless one, eternal one, or infinite one.

Similar or Equivalent Terms:

Mahayana Buddhism:	Tathagatagarbha (Womb of all Buddhas)
Hasidic Judaism:	Atzmus, or Atzmut
Hinduism:	Brahma (Godhead within Ain Soph) (See: Father, the)
Sufism:	Ruh, Batin, or Qalb (Innermost Hidden Self)
Taoism:	Wuji
Theosophy:	Atma-Buddhi, Atman
Zoroastrianism:	The One Eternal Light. Some may attribute Ahura Mazda in Zoroastrianism as equating with Ain Soph but if studied carefully, Ahura Mazda aligns with the Logos. (See: Logos).

Akashic Records *[a-ka-shic]*

The akashic records are the memories of the cosmos embedded in the underlying abstract of the universe that can be accessed by a conscious mind. The term akashic stems from the Sanskrit term akasha which means aether, sky, or atmosphere. In theosophy and anthroposophy, the akashic records were more closely equated with the collective unconscious or noosphere in its entirety. In other schools of thought, the akashic records are purely the memories embedded in the collective unconscious but is not the collective unconscious in its entirety. It is widely believed that Nostradamus and Edgar Cayce accessed the akashic records and saw memories of the future embedded in non-linear time.

Alchemy *[Al-che-my; Al-Keh-mee]*

Alchemy, as a word, essentially means transformation. As a subject, alchemy has a broad history dating back many thousands of years to before recorded history and has both eastern and western traditions. The eastern traditions are centered in China. Western alchemy is centered in Egypt and is integral to hermetic philosophy involving spiritual transformation and the elevation of the human condition. It is legend to be the first of two original philosophies, or natural sciences, with its twin sister being astrology. Both western and eastern alchemical traditions have similar aims, immortality, longevity, and overall wellbeing. Later, the term alchemy became associated with the pursuit to transform base metals into gold such as with medieval European alchemy where many of its metallurgic processes were adopted as metaphors for the deeper spiritual alchemical process. The real-world pursuit to alchemically transform metal into gold eventually gave rise to modern chemistry. In the realm of spiritual alchemy, alchemy is the interaction of matter and consciousness. It is a psychosomatic process that rewires the brain and unifies the mind until reaching a self-actualizing state of being. Various traditions have different methods to achieve the same aim.

A – Alchemy – Developmental Stages

Alchemy – Developmental Stages

One of the primary premises of the spiritual alchemical process is that the human being is born incomplete. The human mind arises and develops in a highly fragmented condition between all the nature instilled programs, ego defense mechanisms, super-ego scripts, learned personality traits and subconsciously adopted social behaviors with only a small percentage left for a clarity of mind and freewill. That small degree of free will and clarity are often lost below the turbulent sea of the human mind during the course of life.

The Human Soul, also known as the Noetic Soul, rises within the psyche within that narrow space of freewill as the authentic self. It has a universal prime directive to harmonize, integrate, and unify all the constituent parts of the mind, but is often lost and suppressed behind all our ego defense mechanisms and programed scripts with few moments of free expression throughout a person's lifetime.

The sheer presence of the Noetic Soul within the mind has a gradual lifting and integration effect as long as it does not lose control of the mind to the forces of the id complex. But left to its own process without any intentional cooperation of the conscious mind, the natural lifting and integrating effect of the Noetic Soul on the psyche does not unify the mind within the course of a single human lifetime. The slow resonant interactive effect of the Noetic Soul on the mind and body is a larger operating function of human evolution as an entire species over the long course of planetary time.

This alchemical evolution of matter and consciousness toward a synchronized unity of mind, driven by the presence of the Noetic Soul, can be accelerated if we become aware of the dynamic and choose to cooperate with it. This is where we differentiate the natural process of nature and call it "spiritual alchemy," but the truth is, everything in nature is already alchemical. The natural course of evolution is already following an alchemical process of higher and higher grades of transformation leading toward a more self-actualized human being.

Alchemy – Developmental Stages – A

To speed up this process demands self-awareness and conscious effort, and for this reason alone, most human beings will die without ever completing the unified mind—otherwise known as the Monad. Humanity as a whole is evolving psychosomatically in this direction in group sync over the course of a spiraled evolution through the transmigration of the Noetic Soul through the noosphere of the Earth, organized and directed by Alpha and its law of sympathetic resonance.

There are two types of transmigration of the Noetic Soul: (1) Recycled Return, and (2) Reincarnation.

In a recycled return, the Noetic Soul does not wake-up inside its immortal primordial body in the eternal primordial universe after death of the physical body in the physical universe. Instead, the Noetic Soul remains trapped inside the temporal ethereal bodies belonging to its prior deceased physical body until the temporal group mind (noosphere) enveloping the physical Earth automatically recycles the temporal ethereal bodies of the mind, with the Noetic Soul trapped inside, into a new physical body by means of the law of sympathetic resonance. The temporal ethereal bodies are drawn to the same level of darkness within a new physical body that it had cultivated in its prior existence. Darkness begets more darkness.

Reincarnation is when the Noetic Soul is freed after death from its temporal ethereal bodies, which function as non-physical dimensions of the human mind, and wakes-up inside its immortal primordial body in the primordial universe—an eternal paradisical mother universe to the physical universe that parallel each other and are dual reflecting. While in the primordial, the human being decides where, when, and how to take a new physical body. When a Noetic Soul reincarnates, not just returns, in Buddhist terms, this being is a "Bodhisattva."

We are all participating in a special consciousness project here on Earth in the physical universe. We are all attempting to fulfill the universal prime directive of the human Noetic Soul in physical form.

A – Alchemy – Developmental Stages

It has already been achieved on the primordial level. We are now attempting to achieve it on the physical level.

The Earth is special in that most other worlds with sentient humanoid life are *not* attempting such a feat of creation because it requires the Noetic Soul to endure the darkness of the initial stages of the physical process that the Alpha wave naturally takes us through. Other worlds have genetically severed their minds from the universal process, and by doing so, have set their species to remain eternally mortal in the physical universe. When naturally followed, the Alpha wave mirrors and repeats, as a reverberating echo, the same process the universe went through at the cosmic level at the beginning of time. It is the only way Alpha works—and only Alpha can take us there. And this is the problem that other worlds have with Alpha. These worlds consider the immortal Monad the proverbial "forbidden fruit."

The Alpha wave includes patterns within patterns and cycles within cycles. At the highest level, the Alpha wave pattern unfolds in three major sequences which, mythologically, are referred to as the "Three Mountains." Spanning the three mountains is a series of several alchemical processes, and within each alchemical process, a set of alchemical labors. The medieval European alchemy modelled and labeled the noticeable Alpha sequences and geometric stages of development with its own cryptographic code. It is even possible that they did it unconsciously—steered unknowingly by the cosmic quanta.

Most people studying the alchemical processes via the lens of this cryptographic code assume that the alchemist must discover, understand, and then guide each alchemical process to unfold by employing a unique alchemical formula at each stage. This is wrong. The secret is understanding that the processes are already unfolding on their own in nature and all we need to do is become aware of it and learn how to support the process rather than oppose it. When we do, the momentum of the Alpha wave pattern picks up its pace within you to quicken your own process toward the unification and integration of your mind which mirrors the reconstitution of the Monad at the cosmic level of creation, all in one lifetime. The reconstituted Monad of the integrated unified mind is the self-actualized human being, the mythological Christ being, and the proverbial philosophers' stone.

Alchemy – Developmental Stages – A

The natural rhythm of Alpha is accelerated within you by application of a set of cognitive and psychosomatic practices called the Three Factors. The same Three Factors are practiced at every Alpha interval of the alchemical process. Each interval of the Alpha wave pattern unfolds on its own as long as the Three Factors are continuously practiced in earnest. Alpha directs the inward focus of the conscious mind on the different areas and levels of the psyche, and the various forces of the cosmic quanta, at the time and place of its own choosing. The conscious mind of the alchemist only cooperates and supplies energy to the Alpha wave via the Three Factors. It does not lead the process. Alpha leads the process.

The conscious mind is able to observe and discern the different stages of the Alpha wave unfoldment. Each pattern and sub-pattern are different. These differences give way to the differences portrayed in the mythological representations of each alchemical process. Depending on the level of nuance observed and differentiated by an alchemist, this creates a variation in the number of recorded stages between different alchemists. This is not a problem to be studied and solved. It is purely academic. The reason being is, the alchemist does not initiate each stage of the alchemical process, and it does not guide each stage (Alpha does) and nor does the alchemist devise the methods. All the alchemist does is accelerate the process based on a few universal principles inherent to the operation of the universe.

Spiritual alchemy unfolds organically through the force of Alpha. Any attempt to synthesize the unified mind would lead to failure. The re-unified mind cannot be engineered. In stark contrast to spiritual alchemy, this would be considered a method of dark alchemy. It would compel the de-evolution of the species.

All that being said, it is quite interesting to compare what has been written and recorded by alchemists of the naturally occurring patterns of Alpha both in their mythological and purely expressed forms. On the next page is a comparison between each stage of the alchemical process I observed, experienced, and recorded when traversing the three mountains alongside some popular descriptions of the stages found in the study of European alchemy.

A – Alchemy – Developmental Stages

1st Alchemical Process (1st Mountain) The acceleration of the force of Alpha. This happens in twelve consecutive stages with each stage corresponding to one of the twelve bodies of the human being. The twelve bodies must be consumed by the sacred fire of Alpha. This turns the temporal ethereal bodies from bodies of darkness into bodies of fire.	**Calcination** Sometimes represented by the constellation of Aries. Modern Definition of the Word: To convert into calx by heating and burning. Calx is the oxide or ash substance which remains after metals, minerals, etc., have been thoroughly roasted or burned.
2nd Alchemical Process (2nd Mountain) The transformation of the "false-selves" via differentiation with the "Spirit." This process consolidates the authentic-self within the noetic sphere of the mind. This process occurs across 9 alchemical labors with each labor corresponding to a deeper level of the human psyche. Each level is represented by one of the major celestial bodies of the solar system.	**Dissolution** The process of dissolving a solid material in a liquid solution; the reduction of a dry substance in water. Sometimes represented by the constellation of Cancer. Modern Definition of the Word: In chemistry, the process by which a solid, gas, or liquid is dispersed homogeneously in a gas, solid, or, especially, a liquid

Alchemy – Developmental Stages – **A**

3rd Alchemical Process (2nd Mountain) The silencing of the temporal ethereal bodies. This occurs over the course of four alchemical labors with each labor corresponding to one of the temporal ethereal bodies: (1) Temp. Emotional (Jupiter); (2) Temp. Mental (Saturn); (3) Temp. Instinctive (Uranus); (4) Temporal Vision (Neptune). This stage does not involve the temporal ethereal vital body which is a hyper extension of the physical body. Each body is alchemically stigmatized or crucified thereby separating the bodies from their innate auto-cognitive programming which suppresses the natural expression of the authentic-self.	**Separation** The process of separation is often symbolized by swords, scythes, arrows, knives, and hatchets. The operation is represented by the constellation of Scorpio. Modern Definition of the Word: To set apart, disconnect, dissociate.
4th Alchemical Process (2nd Mountain) The first work inside the "Void." In this process the conscious mind develops its profound capacity for super cognitive emotion while inside the void. We learn to communicate with the cosmic quanta, most importantly, the	**Conjunction** Often symbolized by the coming together of the opposing forces of the Sun and Moon or the king and queen. Modern Definition of the Word: In astronomy, the coincidence of two or more heavenly bodies at the same celestial longitude.

A – Alchemy – Developmental Stages

cosmic quanta of the "Divine Soul." In this process we begin filling the void residing at the center of all creation, with the light of the non-created divine source.	In astrology, this is characterized by a unification of the planetary energies.
5th Alchemical Process (3rd Mountain) The conscious mind is tasked by Alpha to differentiate the causal influences rising out of the darkness of the temporal group mind and rise above them. The conscious mind must rise above the influences of the temporal group mind thereby elevating the levels within the individual mind to a closer resonance with the Divine Soul. This process is called "Planet Lifting." The 5th alchemical process involves the first 4 levels of planet lifting corresponding to the first 4 levels of the eight levels of purgatory called: (1) Bardo; (2) Eroplatia; (3) Gerishan; and (4) Ferris	**Putrefaction** Considered by some to be the first stage of the fermentation operation. Putrefaction is a digestion process in which decomposing essences are reabsorbed. The process is represented by the constellation of Leo. Modern Definition of the Word: The process of causing something to decay or breakdown.

Alchemy – Developmental Stages – A

6th Alchemical Process (3rd Mountain) The 6th alchemical process involves the second four levels of planet lifting corresponding to the second four levels of the eight levels of purgatory called: (5) Vishu; (6) Orial; (7) Seraphina; and (8) Parabinlaya. In the 6th alchemical process, the main stressor is the automatization of the individualized lifeform compelled by an underlying broadcast within the temporal group mind to automatically steer the evolution of the species. The conscious mind must break free and rise above the temporal group mind's effort to control human evolution. In this way, our alchemy begins directing our evolution rather than our evolution directing our alchemy. This is accomplished through a differentiation with the "Divine Soul." The mind becomes free of the forces of evolution allowing it to follow Alpha back to the divine source.	**Cibation** Cibation is a process involving the addition of new material to the contents of the crucible. It requires adding liquid to the desiccated matter at precisely the right moment. Modern Definition of the Word: The act of taking food. The operation of feeding the contents of the crucible with fresh material.

A – Alchemy – Developmental Stages

7th Alchemical Process	**Sublimation**
(3rd Mountain) The process of planet lifting continues. Here the alchemist focuses on and differentiates the resonance between his or her temporal bodies and the deeply profound spiritual resonance of the divine Father. This process lifts the vibrational resonance of the temporal bodies of the alchemist's being into consecutive levels of higher resonance with the heavenly realms of the spiritual group mind of the Earth, one heaven at a time. This process concludes with a profound realization of the divine trinity.	The first stage of what some alchemists call "coagulation," in which the vapors solidify. This stage is represented by the constellation of Libra. The vaporization of a solid without fusion or melting, followed by the condensation of its vapor in the re-solidified form on a cool surface. The elevation of a dry thing by fire, with an adherence to its vessel. Modern Definition of the Word: The transition of a substance directly from a solid to the gas phase without passing through the intermediate liquid phase.
8th Alchemical Process	**Fermentation**
(3rd Mountain) Awareness of the eighth alchemical process is suppressed and made secret by the forces of darkness, not by God, and therefore its knowledge is revealed inside of what is called the great arcanum. Primordial alchemy is the eighth alchemical process. It occurs at final stage of the	Represented by the constellation of Capricorn. It is a two-stage process which begins with the 5th alchemical process of putrefaction. Fermentation is said to be the fifth alchemical process, but it depends how someone differentiates the processes. It is more accurate to separate the first stage of fermentation into

Alchemy – Developmental Stages – A

third mountain when the alchemist enters the third sanctum. In this process, the bond of resonance (love) between the human Noetic Soul and the Father is tested by the forces of eros. This testing period is called "The Tithing." When the bond of that resonance (love) is tested and confirmed, the covenant of the Father's love is restored within the matrix of creation. At this point, the forces of heaven (the Father) now have an avenue and a means to bring the forces of the Earth (creation) into harmony with its Spirit via its unbreakable bond with the human Noetic Soul. This is the holy grail. The holy blood symbolizes the resonance of the Father running through the veins of creation. This process brings the alchemist's physical body of creation into unity with the divine source. This is the Christ Monad.

the alchemical processes of putrefaction, cibation, and sublimation and make fermentation the label for its own second stage.

Modern Definition of the Word: Derived from the word "Ferment" which is agitation, unrest, excitement, commotion, tumult. An organized ferment can bring about "fermentation." Fermentation among yeast enzymes converts grape sugar into ethyl alcohol – ultimately wine.

A – Alchemy – Developmental Stages

Completion of the Monad The completion of creation via the reconstitution of the Monad which is symbolized in mythology as Christ. Christ is the reconstituted Monad within the human being. This stage is not an alchemical process in and of itself. It is the completion milestone and manifestation of a new heaven and a new earth within the unified human being.	**Exaltation** The alchemical stage where the substance is raised into a purer and more perfect nature. (This is the philosophers' stone) Modern Definition of the Word: To glorify, or elevate in rank or character
9th Alchemical Process. (Mount Elohim) The 9th alchemical process is the continuous never-ending expansion of the Christ Monad called "eternal alchemy." The Christ Monad (philosophers' stone) is achieved but not perfected with completion of the 8th alchemical process. The 9th alchemical process emerges after the completion of the Christ Monad to perfect it. However, a new paradox emerges. The process of perfecting the Monad is never completed. It's eternal. This is why this level of alchemy is called eternal alchemy. The	**Multiplication** The stage employed to increase the potency of the philosophers' stone, elixir or projection powder. It occurs near the end of the magnum opus in order to increase the gains in the subsequent projection. Modern Definition of the Word: The process of repeated addition, growth, and inflation.

Alchemy – Developmental Stages – A

cosmic level of the physical universe is now engaged in its own 9th alchemical process of eternal alchemy. At an individual level, humans are being led by Alpha to eventually enter into the process of eternal alchemy. The straight path (three mountains) takes us there in one lifetime. The spiral path takes us there over many lifetimes. In the eternal alchemy practice, the alchemist brings into differential resonance:
(1) The infinite depth of the awareness of the Father, with
(2) the infinite depth of the forces of darkness within matter. In the eternal alchemy practice, the awareness of the Father lines-up behind the self-observing awareness of the conscious mind via the intercession of the Noetic Soul. This compels the Father to observe and realize the body of creation of the human being and for the darkness in matter to continuously rise-up into unity with the Father. This drives the eternal expansion of the Monad (Christ Monad).

A – Alchemy – Meditation Practices

Alchemy – Meditation Practices

<u>Alchemical Meditation - Level 1 Practice</u>

The meditation practices an alchemist uses to transform and integrate the mind are introduced in levels as it takes consistent daily practice to develop the inner cognitive faculties to engage in the more advanced practices. The level one meditation practice orients a person in how the mind is structured. With this practice, we begin to learn how to (1) self-observe, and (2) develop a means of gaining self-knowledge. The meditation practice and orientation are as follows:

1. Sit in a comfortable position.

2. Quiet your mind for a few minutes with a breathing exercise where your mind is focused on your breathing.

3. As your mind wanders, bring your focus back to your breathing. Inhale through your nostrils in moderate deep breaths and then exhale through your mouth. Once you are relaxed and more focused, go to the next step.

4. Focus on the heart area of your chest. While your mind is focused on this area of your body, recall a past emotional experience.

5. Now notice the feeling, the mood, the flavor, the quality of energy, of this emotion in the heart area of your chest.

6. Now focus on a completely different emotional experience from your past and recall the emotion.

7. Notice how the feeling, the mood, the flavor, the energy, of this emotion changes in the heart area when you change to a different memory of a different emotional experience.

8. While you are in a seated meditation, shift the focus of your mind back to the first emotional experience you recalled when you were studying your emotional center.

Alchemy – Meditation Practices – **A**

9. Now with this mood firmly in your mind, shift your focus to your mental center in your head, and take notice of the flavor of the same mood in your mental center and the types of thoughts running through it.

10. Once you have captured this mood in your mental center, and you have understood it the best you can, shift to the second experience you recalled while studying your emotional center.

11. Now with this mood firmly in your mind, shift your focus to your mental center in your head, and take notice of the flavor of the mood in your mental center and the types of thoughts running through it.

12. Now contemplate how each mood from the two experiences which you were recalling had a different expression or flavor in the mental center.

13. Switch between the moods a couple of times to realize this.

14. Also notice that the same mood has a different expression between the emotional center and the mental center, yet you still know it is the same mood. This is an innate realization.

15. Just as you used the two different life experiences with different corresponding moods to learn about the emotional and mental centers, you must now repeat this practice with your instinctive center (instinctive temporal ethereal body) felt in your abdomen.

16. Then repeat this practice with your motor center (corresponding to the physical body) felt between your shoulder blades.

17. Then repeat this practice with your sexual center (corresponding to both your physical body and vital temporal ethereal bodies) felt in your genitals.

A – Alchemy – Meditation Practices

Self-Observation

Before we proceed into explaining levels two and three of the alchemical meditation practice, the practice of "self-observation" is explained as it serves as an extension of the level one practice.

When we are not meditating, we need to take our developing inner senses and learn to keep an inner eye on our moods while we go about the day. When going about the day, we can narrow our inner focus to just our emotional, mental, and instinctive centers. When self-observing and going about the day, we are just taking self-reflective mental snapshots of our inner moods.

Later in the day, when we can meditate, we should enter seated meditation and retrospectively go back to the moments during which we had observed certain moods. Allow the memory of these moods to bring back the mood itself. Once the mood has returned, we should focus on the mood in all five centers of the mind, one center at a time.

Alchemical Meditation - Level 2 Practice

There are two key differences between the level one and level two meditation practices:

Difference 1:   In the level two practice, we incorporate prayer into the meditation practice.

Difference 2:   In the level two practice, we go beyond observing, feeling, and understanding the moods to actually transforming them.

As we practice alchemical meditation every day - for at least one hour per day – our inner sense of self-observation will become so acute that the moods will subdivide into very distinct individual formations of the mind called "false-selves." We see or sense the false-selves with our inner cognitive feelings. It is essential in alchemy that we learn to see with our inner feelings rather than to see visually with the mind's eye. In this practice, the eyes of the mind will deceive you, but the heart will always tell you the truth.

Alchemy – Meditation Practices – A

1.) During the level two alchemical meditation practice, when we are focused on the specific mood we wish to transform – after having reached a deep level of understanding of the mood in each of the five centers – we should pray to the Spirit for the mood to transform. (Pray from your heart. No script is necessary.)

2.) This prayer should be made repeatedly in a state of meditation while focused on the mood, shifting your focus on the mood between each of the five centers. Each center of the mind reveals a different dimension of the same mood.

3.) Once the false-selves become visible to our inner sense of cognitive feeling, the alchemist must focus on only one false-self at a time, otherwise, transformation will not occur. You cannot kill two birds with the same stone.

4.) During the alchemical meditation practice, when we focus on a false-self, and when we are praying to the Spirit for a particular false-self to be transformed (there are many within the psyche), we should be watchful with our feelings for a change in energy of the targeted false-self where the targeted false-self starts losing its power and form.

5.) When we see the targeted false-self within us losing form, we should pray to the Spirit to reveal the authentic-self being trapped by the false-self.

6.) When we witness a new aspect of the authentic-self, we must focus on it in all five centers, one center at a time. We will notice something very unique about the authentic-self versus the false-selves. The liberated aspect of the authentic-self has an even quality of energy or feeling between all five centers. There is no variation between the centers. This is how we know the difference within us between our authentic-self and a false-self.

A – Alchemy – Meditation Practices

Alchemical Meditation - Level 3 Practice

The level 3 alchemical meditation practice includes all the same components and methods as the level 2 practice but adds a new force of consciousness which catapults the alchemical practice to an entirely new stage of development. This new force is the Spirit.

1.) During the meditation practice when the alchemist is focused on a false-self, and he or she has gone beyond the intellectual understanding of the false-self, the alchemist should pray to the Spirit to reveal (help to feel) both the authentic-self trapped by the false-self as well as the light of the Spirit itself.

2.) The observer first feels the false-self. Then during prayer, the Spirit emerges. The observer then holds the inner feelings of both the false-self and the Spirit together in contrast within his or her mind, and then finally the authentic-self emerges out of a transformed false-self.

3.) When the observer holds both the higher feeling of the Spirit and the lower feeling of the false-self in the mind in the very same moment, the law of sympathetic vibrations goes into motion (Alpha) to correct the disharmony between the two. This is *"Differential Resonance."*

4.) The result of differential resonance is the liberation of the aspect of the authentic-self which was trapped by the targeted false-self.

5.) This practice is repeated thousands of times for every false-self discovered within you, and subsequently for every automatic program found within the deep cognitive sphere of your mind.

> *"The wound is the place where the light enters you."*— Rumi

Alchemy – Meditation Practices – A

*** The practice of differential resonance within alchemical meditation is the grand alchemical key. It has either been lost for thousands of years or held secret by a few overzealous alchemists. Without this key, the alchemist would struggle endlessly and ultimately end up nowhere. ***

It was thought by some that the sexual practices of the Second Factor formed the lost key. This is wrong. The sexual practices only support the alchemical process, they do not lead the process. Differential resonance leads the alchemical process. The Three Factors lead us to the moment of differential resonance in the alchemical meditation practice but when we arrive at this moment, the triangulation of the observer in conjunction with the Spirit and a targeted element of the mind, is the grand alchemical key which brings everything into fruition. When the Spirit and a false-self (an element of the mind) are held in contrast in a state of differentiation, transformation occurs.

Transformation occurs due to the false-self being compelled by the law of sympathetic vibrations to collaborate its resonance with the resonance of the Spirit triggered by the intervention of a conscious mind observing the two in contrast simultaneously. This is differential resonance. Its principle is the foundation of alchemy. The observer must gain a higher emotional knowledge of all three observed components during the meditation process. By higher emotional knowledge, this means, we must sense and realize the knowledge beyond thought and contemplation.

The three observed components are: (1) False-Self, (2) Spirit, and (3) New Aspect of the Authentic-Self.

Knowledge of the Spirit is beyond the range of common human emotion and therefore is beyond anything the temporal mind can imagine. However, it first emerges only the size of a mustard seed. As we transform one false-self after another – within the contrasting light of the Spirit - our relationship with the Spirit grows - and we are led deeper into the mystery of the Third Factor.

A – Alchemy – Meditation Practices

<u>Transformation On-The-Go</u>

A common response I hear from those contemplating doing the alchemical work is, "I don't have time."

The truth is—the alchemical work does not require much time. The work is done in parallel to all your everyday life activities. Initially, there is a concerted effort required with the First Factor to develop the mind's ability to transform, but this training period does not last long until the mechanics of the meditation practice can be performed with quick inner focuses while you go about your day. Other people will not even be aware of your alchemical work.

Once the alchemist is well on the way, the alchemist will only occasionally need seated meditation to transform something large he or she is working with. Most of the psychic mass of the mind, however, is transformed while we go about the day. We can transform while we drive, walk, or work. Differential resonance on-the-go becomes the most common of all alchemical practices.

There is no separate instruction for performing the practice on-the-go. The alchemist just needs to self-experiment and attempt the practice while not in seated meditation. In brief time, the alchemist will learn to walk. It is important that the First Factor practice of transformation, transition from a meditation practice requiring a seated position, to a practice of transformation we practice while in motion (on-the-go). Being able to transform on-the-go is more efficient as we lose fewer opportunities to realize and transform.

The entire transformation process can happen while we are working, driving, walking, etc. The alchemical practice is repeated non-stop as we move from one life moment to the next (on-the-go). We must always remain vigilant and present in order to capture each automatic reaction of our mind attempting to disrupt our natural center of gravity. We must learn to live in the "Now."

Therefore, a person cannot say they do not have time to practice alchemy. In fact, alchemy creates more time in your life because it makes you more present, and therefore more efficient, and by being more efficient, you gain more time.

Alpha

Alpha is the operating force of the law of sympathetic resonance. Alpha continually raises and reorganizes creation to increasingly higher levels of existence until reaching a point where all the forces become harmonized into a new singularity or reconstituted Monad (unity). Alpha emerges as a force driven by a will expressed within the original divine Monad of Ain Soph to reconstitute the unity between all things which the process of creation initially multiplies. In the process of integrating and unifying the human mind, Alpha emerges as the guiding force in directing the unification process. The force of Alpha rises to a higher tempo within the human being when the conscious mind becomes aware of the unification process and decides to cooperate with it. This cooperation is "spiritual alchemy."

Similar or Equivalent Terms: Grace, Presence, Shakti (Hindu) Shen (Chinese), The Spirit moving within all things (Lipan Apache), etc.

Alpha Principle – Law of One

The Alpha principle is an underlying law in the universe driving all things within creation toward an eventual re-unification with the divine source (original Monad) from which all things emerged. Because creation emerges spontaneously and automatically out of the source, it initially emerges in chaos and darkness. A will/word (light/Logos) emerges out of the divine source to reunify creation with the source to bring all things out of darkness. The force of this will is Alpha. Alpha is the operating force of the law of sympathetic resonance. In a re-unified state, where creation is brought into a new unity with the divine source, the mind internally reflects an awareness of the Father (The godhead of awareness within the source possessing the seed of creation). The Alpha principle is a fundamental law in the universe superseding all other forces to carry-out the will of the Father to reunify creation with the divine source.

A – Alpha Wave | Angel

Alpha Wave

When the force of Alpha emerges to impose its force upon creation to re-organize it and lead it toward a re-unification with the divine source, this re-organization unfolds as a noticeable geometric pattern. It repeats among all scales and objects of creation. This geometric pattern is the Alpha Wave. The Alpha Wave is what caused matter to organize and the atom to form. The Alpha Wave is the undercurrent directing the formation of the galaxies and all the laws of the universe. Alpha could very well be the force behind what physicists call "dark energy." Physicists call it "dark" because they don't understand it. They don't understand it because they are searching for only a mechanical explanation for it. The Alpha Wave emerges as a result of the source consciousness expressing a will to re-unify creation. To date, modern physics has been unwilling to formulate a system within which consciousness by itself is a key causal factor.

Angel

In various theistic traditions, an angel is a supernatural spiritual being who serves God. The angel is a universal symbol arising out of the collective unconscious to manifest in Earth mythology. Angels represent a few different phenomena:

1.) Angels in clouds playing musical instruments represent the very real supernatural phenomenon of the spiritual group mind enshrining the primordial Earth. The hierarchy of angels symbolizes the gradient levels of resonance our temporal mind ascends while harmonizing with the life, love, and awareness of the divine Father. Each gradient level of resonance aligns with each bandwidth of the spiritual group mind of the Earth.

Angel – **A**

2.) All life in the physical universe, including every human being, has both a physical side and a primordial side. The primordial side of every human being is angelic in comparison to the physical side. Upon physical death, the human Noetic Soul is recalled by its primordial being to re-awaken in its primordial body. Upon reawakening, it reassumes its same primordial life in the eternal realm of the primordial universe. It picks up where it left off before living a physical existence. Every human being living on Earth in the primordial universe plays a critical role in managing the Earth Monad project ongoing on Earth in the physical universe. Human beings in the primordial are constantly reaching out to human beings in the physical, including our deceased family and ancient ancestors. In this context, angels represent the primordial side reaching out to the physical side.

3.) The cosmic quanta are the super intelligent forces of consciousness underlying our known reality within the pantheon of cosmic forces. They collectively form the noumenon. The conscious mind of the human being has the innate ability to communicate with these forces through super empathic resonance. The practice of quantum meditation teaches and trains the conscious mind to communicate with the forces of the cosmic quanta. The cosmic quanta can be interpreted as angels when they're passing information to the conscious mind.

4.) Many of the characters in the bible identified as angels may very well have been physical sentient beings from other planets visiting the humanity on Earth in the ancient past. They could very well have been our own ancient ancestors and progenitors helping us and guiding us during the cradle period of our human civilization. A popular title for this is, "ancient aliens."

A – Apprentice

Apprentice

An alchemist in the first mountain is an apprentice. The main objective of the apprentice in the first mountain is the acceleration of the force of Alpha within. This acceleration occurs over the course of twelve developmental stages spanning all twelve bodies of the temporal-spiritual anatomy of the human being.

The self-organizing force of the universe (Alpha) is directing all human beings to develop a harmonious unification of mind with the divine source. Alpha is driving everyone to rebuild the Monad within creation. When people cooperate with this force in a subconscious manner, they continue to reincarnate life after life in lockstep with the rest of humanity on the planet to achieve the same goal. This slow, many lifetime approach, is called the spiral path.

When people wake-up to the process Alpha is guiding them upon, and decide to cooperate with it, the process speeds up within them and they can complete the Monad in one lifetime. This accelerated approach is called the straight path. When the straight path emerges, Alpha directs the conscious mind of the person through three major stages in development of the Monad, which in hermetic lore are called the three mountains. As stated, an alchemist in the first mountain is an apprentice. An alchemist in the second mountain is a journeyman. An alchemist in the third mountain is a foreman. (See Three Mountains).

When on the spiral path, the human being traverses all three mountains simultaneously. We experience flashes of each mountain throughout the course of our life. This occurs over many physical existences in lockstep with all other human beings on Earth. When on the straight path, the three mountains separate and we climb each mountain sequentially, one after one. Ironically, climbing the mountains sequentially is faster than climbing them all together. The later in life that we begin the three-mountain journey, the faster we move through them due to the accumulation of our current life experiences and realizations.

Astral Body

The astral body is a generic term for any one of the ethereal bodies. There are five temporal ethereal bodies corresponding to the temporal hemisphere of the mind and the physical body, and five spiritual ethereal bodies corresponding to the spiritual hemisphere of the mind and the primordial body. All together the human being has twelve bodies. The ethereal bodies are all instruments of the mind. They are not part of the soul. The soul is the lifeforce associated with any function of awareness.

Aurelion *[Aur-li-on; Or-Lee-On]*

The Aurelion is a vision held within the Cosmic Mind of a human being's ultimate created form that the human being is slowly evolving toward life after life in the physical universe. Upon physical death the mind recoils up inside the primordial hemisphere of the human being and is then re-projected into a new physical life. The best qualities and realizations of the temporal mind are saved by the primordial being and are re-used within each new physical existence until eventually achieving a likeness of the vision held within the Cosmic Mind. This vision is the Aurelion. Only the aspects of the temporal physical being which resonate with the divine source are kept and saved by the primordial being after physical death.

Mythological Equivalencies: The Golden Fleece

A – Authentic-Self

Authentic-Self

The Authentic-Self is a term applied to the Noetic Soul (Human Soul) when viewed as a component within an overall psychological model of the human mind. It is necessary to differentiate that which is authentic within the mind versus that which is false. That which emerges from the Noetic Soul is real and is called the authentic-self when viewed as the natural governing principal of the psyche. There are other constructs of the mind which originate from the automated programs left over as artifacts of human evolution which suppress the clear expression of the authentic-self. These constructs are considered false. The conscious mind has the ability to differentiate the authentic-self from that which is false by utilizing the energy of the Spirit to differentiate that which is false from authentic. The process for facilitating this differentiation is done through alchemical meditation. The most important aspect of the authentic-self— alternatively called the Noetic Soul or Human Soul—is that it functions as the "observer" within the human being and within all realms of creation. It is the intercessor between divinity and creation whose mission and prime directive is to reconcile creation and the divine source to reconstitute the Monad.

In the alchemical meditation practices, the mind is split into the observer and the observed, to ultimately transform the observed psychic material in the process of unifying the human mind. The authentic-self should not be confused with the personality or the id. The personality and the id have different origins. Their functions within the mind are ultimately transformed, elevated, and integrated through the alchemical process. *See Alchemy – Meditation Practices.*

Authentic-self – A

The ultimate goal of the alchemical work is to achieve a unity between all dimensions of mind, body, and consciousness made possible through the innate latent ability within all things to achieve a sympathetic resonance between all things.

Alpha is the momentum of the universe reorganizing in response to a greater harmony being realized between two or more bodies of nature. These bodies can be either animate or inanimate. This is the self-organizing alchemical principle of the universe. The process of applied alchemy is all about learning how to leverage and accelerate this universal principle.

Alpha is elevated to increasingly higher degrees of amplification within the mind-body system of the alchemist when we are properly working with the Three Factors. Alpha is accelerated when a conscious mind fixes its internal observation on two or more elements within the mind-body system which should be in resonance but are not. These elements are observed with our inner cognitive awareness, or in other words, with our feelings. It is a faculty of higher emotional intelligence.

When observing the psychic elements of the mind within us, it is not our conscious mind which decides which elements are in resonance or not in resonance. Alpha measures and determines this. We only need to become conscious of the lower elements within us which suppress the free expression of our authentic-self and then introduce the higher forces of the Spirit which each lower element will transform its resonance to harmonize with. This process frees our authentic-self and allows our mind to consolidate and unify. This practice is repeated over and over moment-to-moment unseen by the outside world. This is how we come to know the authentic-self.

Similar or Equivalent Terms:

Noetic Soul, Human Soul, Essence, True-Self, The Observer.

Auto-Cognition; Auto-Cognitive

Auto-cognition is when the cognitive functions of perception and instinct are led into perceiving, feeling, and responding in an automated way based upon an innate programing of the mind whose basis is found in the neurological wiring of the brain. The auto-cognitive mind functions robotically. The robotic program is an artifact of evolution instilled in the species to promote and guide the survival and reproduction of the species.

Auto-Cognitive Period

The auto-cognitive period is the first of three major periods in the development of how consciousness emerges and functions within the mind. In the auto-cognitive period the conscious mind has not yet grown to question its own existence. It operates purely under the direction of the automated programs wired in the neurological systems of the species. The automated systems guide the animal's perception, instincts, and choices in order to guide the natural selection and evolution of the species. Most lifeforms on Earth exist at some level within the auto-cognitive period.

When sentience begins to develop within a species, reflective awareness emerges faster than the autonomic programs of nature can recede and switch off. The autonomic programs of nature become a form of evolutionary baggage disproportionately influencing the human mind in direct conflict with the human being's emerging reflective awareness of the original source consciousness thereby forming the disorder. This disorder is a critical catalyst which propels a human species through a major period in the evolution of consciousness called the Prelescent Period. Our humanity on Earth is currently in its prelescent period. There are three major periods in the development of reflective awareness within a species with minor levels or degrees within each period. The three major periods are identified as: Auto-Cognitive, Prelescent, and Emergent.

B

Bandwidths

The word "bandwidth" is a term used to describe the levels of mind within us individually and surrounding the planet globally. There are two spheres within us and all about us. The two spheres are the temporal and the spiritual. The temporal sphere bounds and envelopes the physical Earth and is called the temporal group mind. The spiritual sphere bounds and envelopes the primordial Earth and is called the spiritual group mind.

The physical Earth and the primordial Earth co-exist in the same location just at different wavelengths. The nine highest frequency bandwidths of the spiritual group mind are the nine heavens of the Earth which historically have inspired much of humanity's mythological folklore.

The planetary group mind as a whole, both temporal and spiritual, forms and gives rise to the collective unconscious studied by Carl Jung and Joseph P. Campbell.

The planetary group mind is also known as the Noosphere.

The astral world made popular by many metaphysical schools is really the planetary group mind. The ethereal bodies of the human being, which are organs of the human mind, interact and correspond to the bandwidths of the planetary group mind.

When the physical body of the human being is asleep, the ethereal bodies interact with the planetary group mind in an immersion mode much like inside a virtual-interactive theater. Depending on the level of interaction, these interactions give rise to our dreams and our spiritual visions. The emerging data is real. It only needs to be decoded.

Being

The term "being" can have different meanings depending on the context. In a metaphysical context, when someone refers to the "being" as an entity beyond the "self," then it is referring to the higher-self of a person. There are multiple tiers within the higher self. When the term "being" is used in context of the higher self, it can refer to any of these tiers. The highest tier would be the being of the original divine Monad, Ain Soph, which is the God particle existing at the center of all things. It can also refer to the primordial being which is the immortal twin being to the mortal physical being. It may also refer to forces of the cosmic quanta which correspond to our own being such as the Logos, the Numina, and even the Cosmic Monad. The term "being" is also the name of the second divine principle in a series of divine principles called the "super meta." The second super meta called, "being," is the intrinsic lifeforce of awareness itself. Awareness corresponds to the first super meta called Force Potential. The third super meta is the called the Force of Unity. The super metas continue beyond three. (*See Super Meta*)

Boyle, Robert

Robert Boyle (25 January 1627 – 31 December 1691) was an Anglo-Irish natural philosopher, chemist, physicist, alchemist and inventor. Boyle is largely regarded today as the first modern chemist, and therefore one of the founders of modern chemistry, and one of the pioneers of the modern scientific method. He is best known for Boyle's law, which describes the inversely proportional relationship between the absolute pressure and volume of a gas, if the temperature is kept constant within a closed system.

His work, *The Sceptical Chymist*, is viewed as a cornerstone book in the field of chemistry. He was a devout Anglican and is noted for his writings in theology. Boyle incorporated his scientific interests into his theology, believing that natural philosophy could provide powerful evidence for the existence of God.
(Sourced from Wikipedia 2023)

Candidate

A person attempting to enter the first mountain and become an apprentice in the alchemical process of re-building the Monad within creation is a candidate. The main objective of the candidate is learning and beginning to practice the Three Factors. When the Three Factors are practiced consistently, this compels Alpha to begin rising within the alchemist. When Alpha begins rising to a faster rhythm within the alchemist, the candidate has become an apprentice.

Causal 'A'

Causal 'A' is the non-created non-local realm of divinity. It is the eternal absolute domain of Ain Soph which precedes all of creation. Ain Soph is the "God particle" residing at the center of all things at the quantum level of existence. It is the chief force particle within the pantheon of the "cosmic quanta." The cosmic quanta are all the force particles of consciousness residing beneath the fabric of reality.

Causal 'A' and Ain Soph are one and indivisible. Causal 'A' has no dimensions of time or space. However, it has three dimensions of consciousness, which are Awareness, Life, and Love. Within Causal 'A' of Ain Soph, the awareness is the Father (called such because it holds the seed of creation). The life is the Divine Soul. The love is the Spirit. All three dimensions produce their own unique force. All three forces resonating as one is Ain Soph, the original divine Monad.

All three forces within Causal 'A' of Ain Soph are considered "divine" because all three forces precede creation. Divinity is that which was never created. It always was and always will be. The forces of divinity are "absolute." They do not take form within creation. For this reason, Causal 'A' is also called "the Absolute."

C – Causal 'A' | Causal 'B'

There are three forms of awareness. The original form of awareness is the awareness within Causal 'A' of Ain Soph which is "Resonant Awareness." Resonant awareness is the state of pure consciousness. Its awareness is the infinite Father. Its lifeforce is the infinite Divine Soul. Its energy is the infinite love of the Spirit. "Perspective Awareness" collapses the infinite non-local wave function of Causal 'A' to give birth to the created cosmos. Perspective awareness is the mind. All of creation is embedded in some level or expression of mind. Reflective awareness rises within the mind via the human Noetic Soul to enable the mind to reconnect back to and realize the divine source of Ain Soph (Causal 'A'). Perspective awareness and reflective awareness originally emerge from resonant awareness.

Similar or Equivalent Terms:

Erik P. Antoni:	Causal 'A'
George Hegal:	Absolute, The
Buddhism:	Ārūpyadhātu
Hasidic Judaism:	Dwelling Place of Atzmus, or Atzmut
Hinduism:	Brahmaloka, Bramapura, Satyaloka
Sufism:	Noor-e-Ahadi
Taoism:	Wuji
Zoroastrianism:	Domain of the One Eternal Light

Causal 'B'

Causal 'B' is the realm of creation existing outside the non-created non-local realm of divinity (Causal 'A'). There are two universal carrier waves within Causal 'B' that overlay and parallel each other at different wavelengths. The first is the primordial and the second is the physical. Human beings oscillate between the primordial and physical between physical lifetimes. Our physical universe is nested up inside a singularity within this higher, mother, primordial universe.

Causal 'B' – C

The primordial universe is based in eternity. The physical universe is based in time. Both universes have their own hyperspace extensions which emerge when the laws of that universe become stretched by individuals, vehicles, or planetary bodies inhabiting or traversing these universes.

The primordial universe was the first universe within Causal 'B' to emerge and therefore it is called the "primordial" universe. The word "primordial" refers to "the first." Some may say that the realm of divinity within Causal 'A' came first, however, Causal 'A' never came or emerged and was never created therefore its place is more correctly "zero." It precedes the first. The first is the first in a series, and the only series is the compounding processes of creation. The first of creation is the primordial universe.

The parallel universe concept many mainstream physicists are currently contemplating today (early 21st century) is a model where each universe is a bubble existing side by side in a sea of bubbles and the energy that sparks the creation process within a bubble universe is when the bubbles collide. This is a horizontal model of creation. The model alchemy reveals is a vertical model where the universes overlay each other in the same location of space but at different frequency wavelengths. The bubbles described in the horizontal model may still exist as part of the vertical model. In context to the alchemical process, the vertical model is more relevant due to the drive within the universe to reconcile and vertically integrate the two via the conscious mind while reconstituting the Monad.

Ain Soph is the original Monad (old heaven). Christ is the new Monad (new heaven and new Earth) which reconciles and integrates creation (old Earth) with the original Monad (old heaven).

Ain Soph and Christ are organizational constructs of energy. The mythological references to Christ, Ain Soph, Eloah, Logos, Buddha, and the like, are all artifacts of human evolution in our growing ability to understand these forces. Most of the archetypes and mythological figures in much of our literature are all metaphorical

C – Causal 'B'

references to forces of consciousness and energy organizing and reorganizing at the quantum level of reality. It all emerges via the collective unconscious existing as part of the planetary group mind of a planet. The stories of these quantum forces all emerge unconsciously into all our arts and literature.

The primordial universe, and all scales within it (cosmic, planetary, and individual), have already been fully reconciled with the divine source (Ain Soph – Causal 'A') from which all things emerged. We already have a reconstituted Cosmic Monad or Cosmic Christ Monad. Any realm of creation sustained in an organized state, exists within a reconstituted Christ Monad.

The physical universe has already been reconciled and organized at the cosmic level. The cosmic level of the physical universe encompasses both the world within the atom and the furthest reaches of the universe. It is a cosmic loop or a serpent swallowing its tail. The physical universe is nested inside a black hole or cosmic singularity within the primordial universe.

The primordial universe is the mother universe from which the physical universe emerged. The physical universe is still undergoing the reconciliation process at the planetary and individual scales of creation. That brings us into the whole purpose of alchemy which seeks to complete the reconciliation process (Christ Monad).

The reconciliation process itself is the universe reconciling and completing its own process of creation. Until the reconciliation is complete, creation remains incomplete. In order for the process of creation to reach its goal, the conscious mind must insert itself. It is the conscious mind which reconciles the spontaneous emerging processes of creation (darkness) with the eternal divine presence of the original divine Monad. This is done via the human Noetic Soul and its Logos (light). Christ is the completion of the creation process. It is the eternal form which all things are driving toward. Christ and Buddha represent the same pinnacle state of completion.

Summary of the Creation Process – How Causal 'B' Emerged

A popular theological belief in religion is that the original unity of God (Ain Soph) created the universe because he or it was alone. Meditation on the quantum forces within us reveals that this was not the original cause. Quantum meditation reveals that the original act of creation occurred in three primary stages:

Stage 1: Creation was originally sparked (see Dynamis) into existence spontaneously and unintentionally by the force of love (the Spirit) produced by the awareness of Ain Soph (the Father) being aware of his own living lifeforce (the Divine Soul).

Stage 2: The Father became aware that the Spirit of his love had sparked creation into existence, but that creation was stuck in darkness because this spark of creation happened unintentionally without his awareness.

Stage 3: The Father's realization of his creation compelled (Thelesis) a love for his creation to arise (Numina) and a will (Logos) to save it. The living lifeforce of this will is the human Noetic Soul. The creation process unfolded in a repeating pattern of fractal scales. The first scale to emerge was the cosmic.

The cosmic scale of creation was saved, or reconciled, at the beginning of time. A new unity emerged between Ain Soph and creation. This new unity is a new union between divinity and creation on the cosmic scale. It is a living conscious mind that bounds the entire universe. The organized universe emerged inside a literal Cosmic Mind. It is the Cosmic Christ—known in religion as Eloah or Allah. When the new unity was finally realized and achieved, sexuality emerged within all living things as a reflection of the original coupling of love and will in the alchemical creation process.

All duality is a reflection of the original creation process and the Father's will (Logos) to bring creation back into unity with his divine source. Darkness-light, odd-even, hot-cold, female-male, negative-positive, are all a reflection of the original cosmic creation process.

C – Causal 'B'

This process is now repeating on the individual and planetary levels of creation. It's repeating in scales. The Father sent the human Noetic Soul into the world by force of his will to lift up creation back into unity with his original divine being. Your creation is your mind and body. Your Noetic Soul will keep coming into the world until you fulfill the will of God (the Father). See "Theokinesis" for a detailed explanation of the creation process. Also see "Chaos."

<u>Causal 'B'</u>

The physical universe is a denser, darker, mirror image of the primordial universe. They are dual reflecting of each other.

Causal 'M'

Causal 'M' is the third of three causal realms to emerge in the theokinetic process of creation. Causal 'M,' or the 'M' Causal, emerges as a reconciliation between the first two causal realms, Causal 'A' and Causal 'B.' It is the realm of immortality. All levels of creation on the primordial side of the Causal 'B' are already sunk within Casual 'M.' The physical side of Causal 'B' is already sunk inside Causal "M' on a cosmic level but is a continuous work in progress on the planetary and individual scales of creation. In this model the stars exist on the planetary level, not the cosmic level.

It is part of the grand design of creation, that entire worlds, and individual people, in the physical universe, which have achieved the reconstitution of the Monad, eventually sink bodily in physical form within Causal 'M' to continue to exist forever while still appearing in both the physical and primordial sides of creation (Causal 'B'). This reorganization of creation is the celestial body of light which is an integration of all twelve bodies of the human being. The twelve bodies consist of the physical body (central temporal body), primordial body (central eternal-spiritual body) and five satellite ethereal bodies corresponding to each central body.

The letter 'M' is used to designate the third causal realm because the third causal realm re-establishes the "Monad" within creation. The letter M also refers to "Metatronic" which is the integrated matrix between the primordial and physical sides of creation.

The 'M' Causal is a singularity. The 'M' Causal organizes creation. It facilitates the organization of the atom and all the star systems. It facilitates the emergence of the laws of physics within Causal 'B.' Without Causal 'M', Causal 'B' would remain in darkness in a disorganized state of chaos emerging spontaneously and automatically out of the infinite force of the Spirit in Causal 'A.' Causal 'M' is the "Theosphere" as coined by Teilhard de Chardin and is known as "The Great Cinnabar Field" by the Taoists. It also forms the Infiniton Field in quantum physics.

C – Causal 'M'

Many physicists now believe that when energy achieves "uniformity" this reverses gravity and instead of gravity being attractive, it flips over and becomes repulsive. Furthermore, repulsive gravity can literally expand a particle of energy at the atomic scale to something the size of the observable universe in less than a blink of an eye. The mainstream scientific theory correlating the "uniformity" of energy with repulsive gravity elegantly aligns with the hypothesis that when creation and divinity reconcile to achieve unity (uniformity – Christ Monad) this causes matter and the laws of physics to organize and a new universe to emerge.

The mythological and religious label "Christ' is used because the mythology of Christ arising out of the collective unconscious is the story of the reconciliation of divinity with all of creation. The collective unconscious is repeatedly broadcasting the story of creation across all spheres of mind and space because the process of creation continues, and remains to be completed, on an individual level and on a planetary level within the physical universe. In the process of reconstituting the Monad within creation on an individual human level, the conscious mind must relive and witness the process of creation within itself, and come to know, on a super cognitive emotional level, all the primeval forces involved.

By getting to know all the primeval forces through an emotional resonance, the mind coalesces into a reintegrated Monad. This same process has already completed itself on a cosmic level allowing the atoms and galaxies to organize. This same process is now trying to complete itself on a human individual level and on a planetary level.

When the process completed itself on a cosmic level, the reconciliation process refracted itself into fractal spheres. The three major fractal spheres are the Cosmic, Planetary, and Individual. When the process completes itself on all three levels, a Super Monad emerges incorporating all three levels. The Super Monad has already completed itself on all three levels in the primordial universe and is slowly swallowing all three levels within the physical universe.

The physical universe has already been reconciled on a cosmic level. All that remains are the planetary and individual levels of creation in the physical universe. The process of reconciliation on the planetary and individual levels of creation in the physical universe is never-ending due to the fact the physical universe is based in time, not in eternity, such as the primordial universe. The cosmic level of the physical universe achieved the reconstitution of the Monad because it emerged "with time" rather than "within time." Its reconciliation actually created time. The dynamic that this creates is that all planetary realms, and all lifeforms with a noetic consciousness, must undergo their own separate integration processes. Time spreads out the process horizontally within the physical universe rather than vertically as within the primordial universe of eternity.

The primordial universe was destined to complete itself on all three levels. The physical universe is destined to continue the process *ad-infinitum*. This is why we see separate singularities throughout space in the physical universe. The specialness of the physical universe is that it gives the never-ending process of creation infinite runway because the theokinesis within Ain Soph will never end.

This is why there are two universe types within Causal 'B' – Primordial (Eternal) and the Physical (Temporal). There are only two universe types because that is all that is needed to satisfy and reconcile the process of creation. However, fundamental to this reconciliation is Causal 'M' which functions as a hyperspatial seat between Causal 'A' and 'B.' Causal 'M' allows Causal "B' to continue forever. Eventually, the mainstream scientific community will include a model of consciousness and the process of theokinesis within its mainstream cosmology to complete its understanding of the universe. At this point, a unified theory of everything will emerge.

Similar or Equivalent Terms: Great Cinnabar Field (Taosim); Theosphere (Teilhard de Chardin); Supermentalised (Sri Aurobindo); Infiniton Field.

C – Causal 'M'

Causal 'M' - Analysis of the Squared Circle

The outer circle is Causal 'M,' New Monad, Christ, New Heaven, New Earth. The Triangle is the Sacred Trinity, Logos, Noetic Soul, Numina. The square is Causal 'B,' – Creation and the Mind. The inner circle is Causal 'A,' Original Monad, Ain Soph, Old Heaven.

Causal 'M' - Super Monad

All three levels of the Christ Monad superimposed:

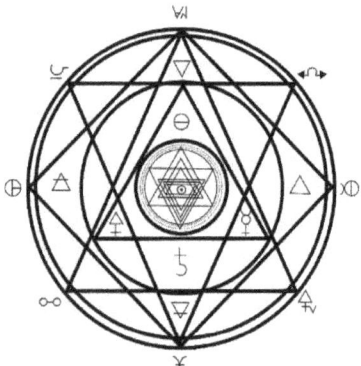

Causal 'M' - Ouroboros

The serpent swallowing its tail is a popular motif arising out of the collective unconscious. In alchemy, it has more than one meaning.

1.) The inner and outer cosmos reconnecting.
2.) The return to unity.
3.) The accomplishment of the Great Work.
4.) Eternity.
5.) The cycle of creative destruction.

Celestial Body

The ultimate goal of the alchemical work is to achieve a unity between all dimensions of mind, body, and consciousness. This is made possible through the innate latent ability within all things to achieve a sympathetic resonance between all things. In alchemy, this unity brings all the bodies of our physical creation into sympathetic resonance with all the bodies of our primordial creation. Once full resonance is achieved, all 12 bodies of our being become unified within one great body called the "Celestial Body." The celestial body is the wedding garment of the human Noetic Soul. The wedding is a marriage between divinity and creation.

C – Cerberus

Cerberus *[Cer-ber-us; Surr-burr-uhs]*

In the alchemical process of the legendary Three Mountains of Hermetic lore, Cerberus symbolizes the third and final guardian of the three Guardians of the Threshold. As tenebrous as the symbol of Cerberus may be, the symbol is only a mild indication of its true nature. Cerberus guards the human Noetic Soul's entrance into the Eternal. The central head of Cerberus is Set, the right head of Cerberus is Idamus, the left head of Cerberus is Chaos (The Gorgon). His body is the mind. His animal form is a symbol of creation. In the 8th alchemical process, while under vicious assault by Cerberus, we must quickly learn how to become his owner without hurting him. If we hurt him, we will not become his owner, but if we do not move quickly, he will devour us and destroy us.

Hercules (the alchemist) and Cerberus pictured above. The cosmic temple of IAO in the rear. The nine gates of the temple of IAO are shown. The nine gates symbolize the nine principal permutations of consciousness. The temple in its totality, beginning with the 10th permutation, is the mind. The land is in ruins during the reconciliation. The fourth cardinal force (IAO) is symbolized by fire.

Chaos

The modern definition of the word "Chaos" is "disarray; disorder; the state of utter confusion." An older Greek definition of the word Chaos is "the infinity of space or formless matter preceding the existence of the ordered universe." Chaos is a "disordered" formlessness of "matter." In alchemy, there are two states of formlessness. Chaos corresponds to only the second of these two states of formlessness. The two states of formlessness are:

(1) The "ordered" formlessness in the original divine source of Ain Soph called the Absolute or Causal 'A.' There is no chaos in Causal 'A.' The formlessness in Causal 'A' is "ordered" through sympathetic resonance. It exists in a state of sublime peace and divine bliss. Secondly, there is no "matter" in the formlessness of Causal 'A.' All there is, is "Consciousness." Causal 'A' creates matter, but when it does, that matter immediately emerges inside a new realm called Causal 'B.'

(2) The "disordered" formlessness of "matter" emerging out of Causal 'A' as the initial outpouring of creation. This is the original primordial "Chaos." Matter is a construct of energy emerging with the Cosmic Mind. The Cosmic Mind emerges out of Causal 'A' to form Causal 'B.' What eventually brings order to the chaos of matter is the intervention of the quantum of the Logos and the forces of its Sacred Trinity. The second formlessness is a mirror of the first formlessness but yet, one is ordered and the other is disordered. (See Theokinesis).

The term Chaos also corresponds to the 11th permutation of consciousness called the Gorgon. The Gorgon emerges out of the "disordered matter" of creation. The Gorgon (Chaos) is also the left head of Cerberus. The center head is Satan or Set. The right head is Idamus. The Gorgon (Chaos) is also Magog whose twin helper is Gog. Mythologically, Gog and Magog (or Goth and Magoth) are the twin helpers of Satan or Set. *See Gog and Magog, Satan, and Gorgon.*

C – Cherubim | Children of the First Light

Cherubim [Che-ru-bim; Cheh-ruh-bm]

The heavenly realm of Jenesis is the sublime Earth plane of the cherubim. It is one of the highest vibrating bandwidths of the spiritual group mind enveloping the Earth in the primordial universe. The cherubim represent a high order of sympathetic resonance between the human Noetic Soul and the Divine Soul. The cherubim also represent the divine language of kier and the many different effervescent intelligent forms of consciousness which dance, play, resonate, and communicate a special form of quantum messaging. This messaging takes place between Ain Soph and the higher and lower realms of the Cosmic Mind, the Planetary Group Mind, and the Individual Mind. *See Kier and Heavenly Realms.*

Children of the First Light

In the planetary group mind (Noosphere) enveloping the Earth, there are two great spheres, the spiritual group mind enveloping the Earth in the primordial universe, and the temporal group mind enveloping the Earth in the physical universe. The temporal group mind is in darkness—meaning, it's asleep. It dreams. When people dream, they dream in concert with the temporal group mind. There is, however, a liberated dimension of the temporal group mind. The intelligence operating on the dark side of the temporal group mind is called Maub. The liberated aspect of the temporal group mind is called Germain. The liberated quantum of the temporal group mind (Germain) shares that once enough people on Earth in the physical universe achieve the reconstitution of Monad within themselves, as part of an initial noetic vanguard, this will lead to the liberation of the temporal group mind and ignite the planetary Monad of the physical Earth. The rest of humanity will then follow with the reconstitution of the Monad. This initial vanguard of souls is called the Children of the First Light.

Chinese Alchemy – Eastern Alchemy, Daoist Alchemy

Chinese alchemy has a lineage and history just as long and old as Western Alchemy. Interchangeably referred to as Eastern Alchemy, Chinese alchemy is studied within the philosophical framework of Daoism (Taoism). Western alchemy originated in Egypt with the writings and teachings of Hermes Trismegistus. The origin of Chinese alchemy is less clear and defined. It recedes far into antiquity. Much of what is known of Daoism and Chinese alchemy stem from the teachings of Lao Tzu (Laozi) and Lü Dongbin.

Like western alchemy, Chinese alchemy has both an outer form dealing with the transmutation of physical elements (Waidan) and an inner alchemy dealing with the transformation of the human being (Neidan). In both eastern and western traditions, the external functions as an unconscious mythological parallel to the real internal alchemy that echoes the natural rhythm and function of the universe.

Both eastern and western traditions have the same goals—wellbeing, prosperity, longevity, and immortality. Just as the external form of western alchemy gave rise to modern chemistry, the external form of eastern alchemy gave rise to Chinese medicine.

Chinese alchemy was initially introduced to the western world by Obed Simon Johnson (May 5, 1881 – October 12, 1970). Obed was an American academic, chaplain, congregational missionary and student of Chinese culture and history. He is known for his book, *A Study of Chinese Alchemy*.

The study of Chinese alchemy can be just as challenging as western alchemy in deciphering the deeper meanings of the texts. Mantak Chia and Michael Winn have produced numerous works and teachings to bridge a deeper understanding with western thinking. To date, no one has gone further than Michael Winn in explaining how to actually implement the inner alchemical process utilizing ancient Chinese methodologies and thought processes. The following composition was written by Michael Winn. It provides an illuminating view into the inner alchemical process from a Daoist perspective, but in a writing style that is easily understood.

C – Chinese Alchemy

<u>How the Alchemist Shapes the Qi Field</u> – *By Michael Winn – 08-Sep-2019*

"My thesis on alchemy as a deep language relies on the premise that the very act of shaping any aspect of the qi field, in any dimension / heaven, by human or non-human intelligence, is best understood as a spontaneous yet recognizable expression of language. The patterns of qi flow or 'wave forms' vibrating between the continuum of *shen* (intelligence) and *jing* (matter) constitute the deep grammar of this universal language. This qi wave language is how the infinite field of spirit / intelligence talks to the finite bodies/particles formed by essence *(jing)*.

"The deep structure of these qi language patterns are embedded in One Cloud's (Daoist Master) *nei dan* formulas as the empty force of *wuji* (the Original unity of jing-qi-shen) and the three primordial forces (yin-yang-yuan). All other 'numbers' are generated by the interaction of the original trinity, including the often-used yin-yang patterns of the micro-cosmic orbit, the five phases [*wu xing*] or eight manifesting forces. The qi field is how the universe both expresses its many functions and remembers its countless experiences. In traditional Daoist cosmology, the qi field defines every possible relationship within both the form and formless worlds. Its coherence allows the movement between chaos and order without losing balance and harmony. *(See Endnotes at the end of this section)*

"Qigong is the language process of using ritual body movement, breath, and mind intent to shape the qi in order to communicate mostly with the 'horizontal' (as humans see it looking forward) or exterior manifest qi field of Earth. *Nei dan* deals more with the 'vertical' (as one looks up to sky and down to earth) and interior communications between Primordial, Early, and Later Heavens. One does not practice qigong or alchemy to GET qi. Rather one already IS part of nature's infinite qi field—and is just learning to recognize the unconscious communication patterns that are always flowing between one's micro-cosmic (personal) qi field and the impersonal macrocosmic qi field.

"At its simplest level, all human sensing, thought, speech, feeling, body movement, breathing rhythm, and visualized image are attempts to 'speak to' or shape this qi field. Whether you scratch your nose or do higher math, both elicit a response from the qi field. The totality of these shapes, the sum of the conversation between Heaven and Earth that is passing through us, is one's experience of physical reality. Our personalities, our bodies, and even our environment, are the moment-to-moment shape of the fluctuations in this superintelligent qi field.

"Within the natural physical world, the movement of the qi field is the hidden language by which the intelligence within atoms, molecules, cells, rocks, plants, animals, young children, mountains, oceans, sun, moon, planets and stars communicate and maintain their rhythm and harmony. Everything, without exception, is alive and communicating something by virtue of the physical and energetic shape given to it by Nature's intelligence. The internal alchemist eavesdrops on this conversation within the qi field, and then from a human perspective, performs alchemical operations to shape the qi field in order to accelerate the unfolding of life's inherent simplicity, wholeness, and aliveness.

"All paranormal abilities in humans - ESP, channeling, clairvoyance, etc. are also communications by human body-spirits (*jingshen*) shaping the qi field, but most are unconscious faculties and thus differ from *nei dan*. Alchemy is not the unconscious channeling of Nature's intelligence. Rather the alchemist attempts to accelerate the conscious unfoldment of Nature's macro-cosmic intelligence through resonance with the adept's personal micro-cosmos.

"How does the *nei dan* adept communicate between heavens, i.e. between Heaven and Earth? It depends on what level of heaven they are communicating with, and the skill level/formula they have achieved in resonating with the qi field. There are many different practices, but all may be categorized as *yang* practice, *yin* practice,

C – Chinese Alchemy

or *wu wei* practice. All three practices require the adept interiorize the outer universe within the adept's body. In yang practice, the adept uses his yi 'mind intent' or 'creative imagination,' the Later Heaven *shen* ruling the earth element/spleen/center direction, to actively communicate with or 'speak to' the qi field in cooperation with the other four elements/body spirits. This effectively involves the use of projection—guiding or shaping the qi field according to the adept's inner will."

The Mystic Tablet

The Lo Shu diagram on the back of a small turtle (in the center),
surrounded by the animals of the Chinese Zodiac and
Eight Yin-Yang Forces known as Bagua.

"In yin practice, the adept 'listens' to the qi field and concentrates on receiving energy patterns or absorbing spiritual qualities from the qi field. This is akin to one's ego-will surrendering to one's higher-will or a more collective level of the self. In this case the five body spirits or eight extraordinary channels act as internal antennae for decoding the qi wave patterns being communicated from the outer qi field to the adept. Any given alchemical meditative operation may involve both yin and yang practices—the choice depending on the season, time of day, the situation in the individual life of the adept. The type of alchemical method may reflect the cycle of events in the life of the greater cosmos—its geomantic and astrological forces.

"The wu wei practice involves the adept cultivating a shift from outer will to inner will, from the struggle amongst the desires of various body spirits (*jing shen*) to the unity of the original spirit (*yuan shen*). Wu wei is translated variously as 'spontaneous action' or 'effortless non-action,' but the practical accomplishment of this requires the cultivation of *yuan qi*, which is the superconductive non-resistant energy of Primordial Heaven. Essentially, wu wei is the fruit of mastering yin and yang practices; the adept evolves to a level of conscious and simultaneous sending and receiving qi, i.e. two way communication between the adept and the mind of nature. Wu wei requires a state of total trust between the adept and the Dao; their *yi*, or will, is gradually aligned as the adept develops trust in the lifeforce and his ability to manage it. The adept grows to receive the full power of the dao needed in any given moment, and the dao trusts the adept to create or express its reality in harmony with the lifeforce.

"This cooperation is made possible because the communications network of qi channels and spirit relations inside a human being are essentially the same patterns as those inside a planetary being or galactic being, the main difference being in scale and specific qualities embodied. This ancient daoist idea is expressed in modern theory by fractals repeating themselves on vastly different scales, i.e. from starscape to mountain shape to internal landscape. The adept is not giving up all individual will to an outside agency that is more spiritually powerful and more intelligent. Rather the adept learns from the macrocosm of Nature how the lifeforce behaves and internalizes that within their personal process. Likewise, human babies learn from their parents how to navigate this reality, but then ideally use that learning to create a life according to their own nature.

C – Chinese Alchemy

"All communications between shen, qi, and jing are ultimately dissolved into the adept's interior cauldron of pre-natal emptiness. Thus, the details of the often elaborate alchemical process are frequently abbreviated to simply '*jing-qi-shen-wu*' — [ed. note: essence-energy-consciousness–undifferentiated void]. The more one practices *nei dan*, the greater one's facility with the qi field becomes, and the more the qi field of Nature recognizes one as a sensitive and available location within the physical plane for expressing itself. The ultimate act of communication with the mind of the dao is to crystallize the *yuan qi* into conscious form on earth, known as the Immortal body." (Michael Winn goes on further to discuss this in *The Cauldron as Portal for Communicating with Original Qi*)

Sidenote:

"Early Heaven acts as a cosmic pre-natal womb where the seed virtues/creative powers of *yuan shen* are gestated before being shaped in the human realm into more defined spiritual qualities such as kindness, trust, love. Since *yuan qi* is the 'unconditioned energy' of the universe, all 'unconditional virtues' of the Original Spirit such as unconditional love, unconditional truth, unconditional acceptance are communicated through *yuan qi*. Early Heaven divides the triune (three-as-one) unity of yuan qi into the five element energy phases (*wu xing*) of cosmic time. This five-phase intelligence shapes the matrix of cosmic space as it unfolds rhythmically on a web of eight yin-yang forces [symbolized by the trigrams of the Bagua]. These sacred directions and time cycles, imbued with their inner powers and spiritual qualities, are symbolically mapped on the ancient Ho Tu and Lo Shu [magic square] diagrams. The symbolic relationships of the Ho Tu and Lo Shu may be seen as deep language communications appearing out of the Qi field; as simple numeric expression of the eight channels and five elemental cycles through which Nature communicates with itself." (*Daoist Cosmology as Nature's Deep Grammar*, by Michael Winn.)

Chinese Alchemy – C

How the Alchemist Shapes the Qi Field - *By Michael Winn – 08-Sep-2019*

Footnotes:

This entry was slightly modified to fit the stylistic requirements of *Qi Encyclopedia* from which it was taken. The original source is from "*How the Alchemist Shapes the Qi Field.*" It is a section of "*Daoist Internal Alchemy: A Deep Language for Communicating with Nature's Intelligence,*" by Michael Winn. http://yang-sheng.com

For further information about Daoist thoughts on the deep structure of qi see:

1. *One Cloud's Nine Tao Alchemy Formulas To Cultivate the True Immortal Self*, by Michael Winn.

2. *Nei Dan Formulas as Stages of Cultivating Original Qi*, by Michael Winn.

3. Further information on the "Three Open Channels" of Reality, Peace, and Spirits see *The Book of Balance and Harmony: A Taoist Handbook*, by Daochun Li, introduction and translation by Thomas Cleary. Shambala Publications, 2003.

4. *Magic Numbers, Planetary Tones and the Body: The Evolution of Daoist Inner Alchemy into Modern Sacred Science,* by Michael Winn.

C – Chinese Alchemy

Chinese Alchemy and Shamanism - *By Carl Joseph DeMarco*

"The origins of Daoist, or Chinese, alchemy are shrouded in the dim unwritten past of shamanism. For most scholars who know only the written word, this fact remains as speculation. To those who are trained and practiced in both Daoist alchemy and shamanism though, the connection is clear.

"Michael Winn has elaborated marvelously on the deep language and grammar of qi that makes the alchemical work possible. Daoist alchemy is concerned mainly with neidan (内丹, literally 'inside cinnabar'). Interestingly 丹 is a pun on 蛋, which means 'egg,' so the inner cinnabar is like the inner egg or embryo that is being cultivated by the alchemist. One of the joys of alchemy is that its terminology and symbolism is infinitely rich and layered such that even proficient and accomplished alchemists can never unwrap all the meanings.

"Anyone who says a certain term, or a certain symbol, has only this or that specific meaning, is not accomplished in alchemy. It may have said meaning, but also more. Thus, Laozi begins the Dao De Jing (道德經):

道可道非常道 (Dao ke dao feichang dao)

铭刻名非常名 (Ming ke ming feichang ming)

This can be summed up as:

'The Dao cannot be known or named.'

"This is why I'm against books about alchemy, and yet, ironically, like Laozi, I'm writing about it. Alchemy is rife with paradox and irony.

Chinese Alchemy – C

"Both Daoist alchemy (I am referring here to the alchemy that descends from the wandering Daoists, not temple or "religious" Daoism) and Shamanism cultivate intimacy with qi. Alchemy does it through internal practice, shamanism through external practice. Stripping both of their cultural trappings, down to the nuts and bolts, is revelatory. In the end, the alchemist becomes a shaman; and the shaman becomes an alchemist. This fact is hidden from scholars and academics who know only form, not substance. They will argue it unto their deaths, intoxicated with their glorious ignorance, blind men describing an elephant.

"At the core of shamanism is awareness. At the most basic level, this is learning the concentric rings of nature. Everything around us has a baseline activity that can be read by anyone who knows how to tune in and pay attention. Every time something changes, it ripples through nature like the concentric rings 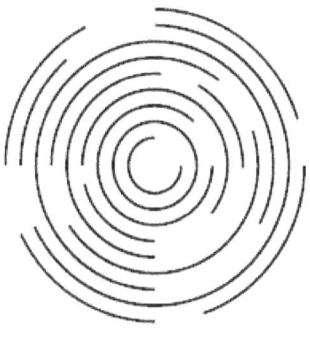 on a pond. For example, if a predator enters a location, birds (or deer, or monkeys) will sound their alarm calls, and those calls will carry in every direction around them, affecting other animals and their activity, gradually dissipating from the center of disturbance. Specific predators or other disturbances (like a tree falling or an earthquake) each have a unique pattern of concentric rings. This is the language of nature, the flow, the flow of qi. Accomplished trackers and shamans can read this language like a book and know what is happening, even many miles away. They can find their cat when it's outside.

C – Chinese Alchemy

"This language is learned by sitting quietly in the forest (or desert, or backyard, etc.) and just observing everything with all your senses, and asking "What does this mean?" A new smell, a sudden noise, birds suddenly dropping from the canopy to the ground, all indicate something. Through diligent and disciplined practice in the same spot every day and at different times of day, you can learn the language of nature through observation. If done properly, observation and understanding become deeper and deeper.

"This practice so far is obviously physical. Eventually, as the practice deepens, you find yourself penetrating new levels of understanding of the language of nature: the force, spirit, and void. These four levels (physical, force, spirit, and void), correspond to what the Daoist alchemist calls jing, qi, shen, and wuji (精, 氣 神, 無極). The difference is that the shaman starts on the outside, and the alchemist starts on the inside. This is the deep language and grammar of qi.

"This brings us to 'surrender.' This is the second critical factor to becoming a shaman. You must surrender to nature. It will flow in and saturate your being, and it will tell you everything you need to know if you surrender to it, and not just energetically. It can tell you what plants and animals are good to eat, what herb will heal what ailment and when and where to collect it, what the weather will do, where to find water, how to build shelter, the stars and the planets, and everything else. This surrender corresponds to the Daoist wuwei (無為). They are the same.

"Even beyond these formless, esoteric structures that endow shamanism and alchemy, we find even formed structures shared by both. In shamanism we have the medicine wheel representing the four directions. This is the exoteric form. As we go deeper, we find that there are really five directions: north, east, south, west, and center. But of course, if we go deeper, we find that there are really nine directions: north, northeast, east, southeast, south, southwest,

Chinese Alchemy – C

west, northwest, and center. But of course, if we go deeper, we find that there are really eleven directions: north, northeast, east, southeast, south, southwest, west, northwest, up, down, and center. And so on, just in case you were thinking it ends there. Each direction has its own attributes and powers. The shaman stands at the center.

"This is the same as the Daoist bagua. The Daoists elaborated and articulated it more. Perhaps as alchemy evolved and humanity sank deeper into unconsciousness, this became necessary. It is certainly useful.

"We see more similarities. In One Cloud's first alchemical formula, we find animals. The shaman communicates with animals and takes on their forms in order to help his people and advance his own state of being. Often this is done by moving around a circle, that is, the medicine wheel. It is also done by replicating the concentric rings of the target animal. If one could reproduce the concentric rings of a fox, would not one then be perceived as a fox? It's all about the flow of qi.

"In One Cloud's formula we use the six healing sounds and five animals to prepare our inner energies for the alchemical work. The exercise is done around a circle, as in the bagua or medicine wheel, combining the sounds with the movements of animals. It's all about the flow of qi.

"Looking at the legends of the immortals of the East, many of them are associated with animals. A famous example is Laozi riding his buffalo or ox. Here we see the alchemist in union with an animal power in nature. This symbol can mean many things, about Laozi or the alchemical work that are worthy of study, but here the purpose is to point out how the great alchemist worked in harmony with nature. He didn't need a nose ring and a leash. Other animal "powers" important in Daoist alchemy are the crane, the deer, the monkey, the tiger, the bear, and the dragon, among others. Note how the animals are specific to the ancient shamans of the East's environment, just as the totem animals of the North American Indians are taken from their local environment. Eastern shamanism is not different from New World shamanism because they use different animals, the principle is identical.

"The Primordial Qigong, also known as Wuji Qigong (無極氣功) is another superb example of the shamanic origins of Daoist alchemy. It wasn't invented until the 12C, and yet preserves the shamanic origins. The practitioner stands at the center of an imaginary bagua. Wherever you are when you do it, whether it's the local park or your own living room, you envision the bagua around you, and go through the circular movements of the exercise. You invoke the "powers" of the direction you are facing as you go. Typically, you start facing east, but you can change the starting position depending on intent and purpose. You make quarter turns, alternately facing East, South, West, and North. In each direction you invoke the powers or attributes of that direction, including the animals associated with them. Does this not recall the medicine wheel or the Great Circle of Life?

"The idea of Primordial Qigong is to cultivate yuan qi (元氣). This is neutral qi, the space between yin and yang, the empty space, original qi. There is more than one way to describe it. The neutral space is neither yin nor yang, neither male nor female, neither dark nor light. It is primordial; impenetrable; the beginning, mother, and key to all things. Laozi says in the Dao De jing:

无 , 名天地之始 (Wu ming tiandi zhi shi);

有 , 名万物之母 (You ming wanwu.zhi mu).

And later,

玄之又玄 (Xuan zhi you xuan),

众妙之门 (Zhong miao, zhi men).

"We can interpret the first two lines as 'The Unnamable is the origin of Heaven and Earth; Named it is the Mother of all things.' The third and fourth lines we can interpret as 'The Mystery of mysteries is the gateway to all creation.'

"The alchemist who successfully cultivates original qi and unifies with the Dao (the one that can't be known or named) achieves what is called the union of Dao and man. He is immortal.

"In some shamanic cultures we find shadow scouts. These are people who live in the shadows, neither light nor dark, in the neutral space (they call it "dead space"), in the space between yin and yang. They are trained from a very early age and through sufficient achievements in awareness and surrender, become shadows, the perfect blend of yin and yang, neutral. Not all shamans achieve this, just as not all alchemists achieve the union of Dao and man.

"It can be said that the career of a shaman begins as a tracker. Awareness (which includes reading both footprints on the ground and concentric rings) is exactly what a tracker (in primitive societies anyway) uses to track and find game, interpret animal behavior, find water, and keep tabs on enemies or rival clans. In fact, we might say that both shamanism, and therefore Daoist alchemy, have their origins in tracking. Deep in the primordial, impenetrable past of Man, some tracker crossed a threshold in awareness and was buffeted by the sublime wave of qi that inundated him, he surrendered to it, and shamanism and alchemy were born."

C – Chinese Alchemy

Lao Tzu

Lao Tzu (Chinese: 老子 / laʊdzə / Laozi) was a legendary ancient Chinese Taoist philosopher credited with writing the Tao Te Ching. Lao Tzu is a Chinese honorary title, generally translated, "Old Master." Although modern scholarship mostly regards him as a fictional person, traditional accounts say he was born as Li Er in the state of Chu in the 6th century BCE in China's "Spring and Autumn Period," [770 to 481 BCE] and served as the royal archivist for the Zhou court at Wangcheng (modern Luoyang), met and impressed Confucius on one occasion, and composed the Tao Te Ching in a single session before retiring into China's western wilderness.

A central figure in Chinese culture, Lao Tzu is generally considered the founder of Taoism (Daoism). He was claimed and revered as the ancestor of the 7th–10th century Tang dynasty and is honored in modern China with the popular surname Li. In some sects of Taoism and Chinese folk religion, it is held that he then became an immortal hermit or a god of the celestial bureaucracy under the name Laojun, one of the Three Pure Ones. His work had a profound impact on subsequent Chinese religious movements and philosophers.
(Source: Wikipedia 2023)

Tao Te Ching

The Tao Te Ching is one of the most significant treatises in Chinese cosmogony. Although the identity of its author(s) or compiler(s) has been debated throughout history, it has regularly been identified with the name Lao Tzu (Laozi). The text itself is often called the Lao Tzu.

The Tao Te Ching describes the Tao *[dao, dow]* as the source and ideal of all existence. It is unseen, but not transcendent, immensely powerful, yet supremely humble, being the root of all things. People have desires and free will (and thus are able to alter their own nature). Many act "unnaturally," upsetting the natural balance of the Tao. The Tao Te Ching intends to lead students to a "return" to their natural state, in harmony with Tao (Dao).
(Source: Wikipedia 2023)

Christ – C

Christ *[Kryst]*

Christ is the highest and most exalted permutation of God, for Christ is everything reconciled to one, including divinity and all of creation. Ain Soph is the original Monad (old heaven). Christ is the new Monad (new heaven and new earth) which reconciles and integrates creation (old earth) with the original Monad (old heaven).

Revelation 21

"1 And I saw a new heaven and a new earth, for the first heaven and the first earth were passed away, and there was no more sea. 2 And I John saw the holy city, new Jerusalem, coming down from God out of heaven, prepared as a bride adorned for her husband. 3 And I heard a great voice out of heaven saying, Behold, the tabernacle of God is with men, and he will dwell with them, and they shall be his people, and God himself shall be with them, and be their God. 4 And God shall wipe away all tears from their eyes; and there shall be no more death, neither sorrow, nor crying, neither shall there be any more pain, for the former things are passed away. 5 And he that sat upon the throne said, Behold, I make all things new. And he said unto me, Write, for these words are true and faithful. 6 And he said unto me, It is done. I am Alpha and Omega, the beginning and the end. I will give unto him that is athirst of the fountain of the water of life freely. 7 He that overcometh shall inherit all things; and I will be his God, and he shall be my son."

Alchemical Analysis

Verse 1: Christ is the union of creation and divinity, (old earth and old heaven), to form a new union between heaven and earth to fulfill the law of one. "There was no more sea" refers to the formless sea of the cosmic quanta transformed into the resonating form of creation.
Verse 2: "The holy city, new Jerusalem, coming down from God out of heaven, prepared as a bride adorned for her husband" is the matter-energy of creation to become the bride of Christ. Within matter-energy, the sixth permutation of consciousness, there is an

C – Christ

embedded awareness. Left in darkness, this embedded awareness is the Gorgon, but when integrated (prepared as a bride) within the new Monad, it becomes the metaphorical Magdalene, our inner Magis, the bride of Christ. It's referred to in a feminine sense because this force is in direct descent from the Spirit, which is love, universally symbolized by the feminine. Her super-partners are the Spirit and the Numina, the third and ninth permutations of consciousness.

One of the principal rules of the collective unconscious is that the further historical figures recede in time, the more their characters take on mythological parallels to the various forces of consciousness. I call this dynamic "Theopomorphism" as a direct mirror opposite effect to "Anthropomorphism" where human attributes are added to the forces of consciousness. Anthropomorphism and Theopomorphism are dualistic and work in tandem with each other. It's how the universe speaks to us. This dynamic doesn't lessen the reality of various historical figures, it's just that their stories echo more than actual history, they also echo the forces of consciousness.

Verse 3: "Men" refers to all humankind, not only to one sex. "The tabernacle of God is with men" refers to a mind capable of housing the spirit of God, and that human beings in particular, have this special ability. What confers this special ability is the Noetic Soul. Verse 3 is saying that human beings are special, because unlike the rest of creation, human beings have the unique ability to embody the spirit of God (via the Noetic Soul). It is important to realize and understand that the unification between divinity and creation (Christ) is being driven to be completed by Alpha on three fundamental scales within creation—the Cosmic, Planetary, and Individual. The scales are reflected by the words, "And he will dwell with them, and they shall be his people, and God himself shall be with them, and be their God." The scales dwell within one another.

Verse 4 echoes the Immortal Maxim, which is that creation can only survive and last forever when it establishes and maintains a harmonic resonance with the divine soul, the source from which all of creation emerged, otherwise, it will perish. The forces of creation are called to believe in (to resonate with) the Divine Soul. A body of creation that resonates with the Divine Soul by way of the Noetic Soul, will not perish, but will achieve everlasting life. When this is achieved, all tears are wiped away. There is no more death, sorrow, crying, and pain, for all the former things are passed away, and all things are made new.

Verse 5: "And he that sat upon the throne said, Behold, I make all things new. And he said unto me, Write, for these words are true and faithful." Meaning, the unity of Christ makes all things new.

Verse 6: "And he said unto me, It is done. I am Alpha and Omega, the beginning and the end. I will give unto him that is athirst of the fountain of the water of life freely."

"It is done" refers to a work that needs to be done. It is the great work, the magnum opus, the work of unifying creation with divinity. Christ is the Alpha and the Omega, because everything that was in the beginning, and everything that is in the end, are now reconciled to one within the body of Christ. The fountain of the water of life is the Divine Soul of Ain Soph which resides as one at the center of Christ, and because Christ has reconciled Ain Soph with all of creation, Christ now becomes the dispensary of the water of life.

Verse 7: "He that overcometh shall inherit all things; and I will be his God, and he shall be my son."

The Noetic Soul is born immaculately by the will of the Father with the Logos and the Numina to lift up creation and reunify it with Ain Soph. The Noetic Soul is one of three soul types, the divine, erotic, and noetic. The Divine Soul was not begotten because it has always existed. The Erotic Soul was begotten by the love of God, the Spirit, not directly by the Father. Only the Noetic Soul is begotten directly by the Father through the Father's Will/Word, the Logos. Word and Will are one and the same. The Noetic Soul is the only begotten son of God. The son in this context is the soul which has no gender. At the beginning of time, the Noetic Soul on a cosmic scale,

C – Christ

suffered for creation and lifted it up and reunified it with Ain Soph to form the Cosmic Christ (Eloah or Allah). This act is what brought about the organization of the cosmos (Causal 'B') and set off its never-ending expansion in the physical universe. The Noetic Soul that is in every human being today is a refraction of light of the Noetic Soul of Eloah. When the Noetic Soul accomplishes the will of the Father to reunify creation with divinity to become Christ (All in-One), the Noetic Soul fulfills the purpose of the son, and becomes the ultimate realization of the Father's son. This is what is meant in verse 7, "… and he shall be my son." There are two levels of God. The "God-Above-God," which is the Father and his total being which is Ain Soph. The second level of God is just simply "God," which is Christ. It is Eloah or Allah. Eloah is the son of the God-Above-God, the son of the divine source. Its mind bounds the entire cosmos to become the Cosmic Christ. When an individual human being accomplishes the great work, that individual human being joins its consciousness with Eloah, and they come to dwell within each other. "He that overcometh shall inherit all things," refers to the great work and its outcome. The Father, through His will to save creation, and hence the immaculate birth of His only begotten son, the Noetic Soul, to fulfill that will, has given dominion over all of creation to the Noetic Soul, which becomes fully realized in Christ when that will is fulfilled, in other words, "when it is done."

Ain Soph and Christ are both organizational constructs of energy. The mythological references to Christ, Ain Soph, Eloah, Logos, and the like, are all artifacts of human evolution in our growing ability to understand these forces. Most of the archetypes and mythological figures in much of our literature are all metaphorical references to forces of consciousness and energy organizing and reorganizing at the quantum level of reality. It all emerges via the collective unconscious as part of the planetary group mind of a planet (Noosphere). The stories of these quantum forces all emerge unconsciously into all our arts and literature.

Christ – C

The collective unconscious continuously broadcasts and re-tells the story of consciousness. The most important mythological character in the greatest story of the cosmos is the character representing the reconstituted Monad. The reconstituted Monad is "Christ." Christ is a major archetype of the collective unconscious representing something far more profound than what modern day theologians interpret from religious mythology yet far more mundane, logical, and scientific. The reader should not interpret what is being shared through a religious perspective, but rather the religious perspective should be elevated to a higher understanding. The great mystery is all pointing toward a story of consciousness and creation existing at the quantum level of all things.

The religious stories are only echoes and patterns emerging out of the depths of the quantum cosmos. Eventually, science will come to express the most literal and mathematical explanation for the processes of creation and consciousness. In this endeavor, we must explain the emergent mythologies of the collective unconscious so we can resolve them and let go of our religious interpretations. In this way, we elevate our understanding to a higher level of existence.

Everything is leading toward a unity in Christ, the completed universal transcendent human being. When our created being becomes unified through the unity of Christ, we realize that all along, it was the Cosmic Christ who was compelling Alpha and Omega and directing our movement through the Great Work. Christ is the living embodiment of the way, the truth, and life of the Father, and alchemy is his song. For he is, for all eternity, the Immortal Beloved.

The universal fire is the symbol of IAO and the all-seeing eye is the symbol of the Logos. Together, they symbolize the re-unified God (Christ).

C – Christ | Christic Trinity

Similar or Equivalent Terms:

Eloah, Elohim, Allah, Buddha, Krishna, Hermes Trismegistus, Mercury, Shekhinah, Immortal Beloved, Philosophers' Stone, Cinnebar, Quetzalcoatl, God, Zeus, Cosmic Christ, Cosmic Monad, Christ Monad, New Monad, Reconstituted Monad, Re-Unified God, Alchemical Monad, Planetary Monad, New Heaven-New Earth, New Father, Causal 'M, Metatronic World, Complete Being.

Christic Trinity *[Chri-stic; Kri-stik]*

A new trinity emerges within the unity of Christ. Within every unity (or most) there is a trinity. The awareness of Christ is Dominus. The life of Christ is David. The love of Christ is Erodysis.

Dominus is the unity of awareness. It is the unity of
(1) The Father (resonant awareness within the Ain Soph Monad),
(2) IAO (perspective awareness within the Dyad—the mind), and
(3) The Logos (reflective awareness).

David is the unity of life. David is the unity of
(1) The Divine Soul (Soul of the Father), (2) The Erotic Soul (Soul of creation), and (3) The Noetic Soul (Soul within humanity).

Erodysis is the unity of love. Erodysis is the unity of
(1) The Spirit (Love of the Father), (2) Matter-Energy (Offspring of the Spirit's love), and (3) The Numina (Father's love for creation).

Christ is the unity of all. Christ is the unity of
(1) Dominus, (2) David and (3) Erodysis.

The cosmic quanta within Matter-Energy transforms from the Gorgon into a living manifestation of love to become the bride of Christ - our internal Magdalene or inner Magis. This is what is known in alchemy as "The Making of the Rose Diamond."

Our inner Magis has an extraordinary power to literally transform and rewire the underlying construct of reality. It is the destiny of the Noetic Soul to integrate her into the matrix of the unified mind—Christ. Until this is done, the divine mission and prime directive of the Noetic Soul is incomplete.

Common Human Emotion

The term, or phrase, "Common Human Emotion," encompasses all the common everyday emotions arising in the human psyche as a reaction generated through, one, the perception of the mind, and two, a set of innate automated instincts wired in the brain. It's a functional artifact of the evolutionary mechanics programmed in the neurology of the human brain to promote the survival and reproduction of the species. It is a lower manifestation, and echo, of the original system of feeling and resonance (Spirit) within the domain of Ain Soph. Within the domain of Ain Soph (The Absolute, Causal 'A'), the divine awareness within Ain Soph, traditionally called the Father, communicates empathically through a sonar-like sympathetic resonance. This is the origin of what many have come to know as "Emotion." "Common Human Emotion" is a lower manifestation of its original form. "Super Cognitive Emotion" is a faculty which emerges when the human being relearns how to use the original resonance system of consciousness to communicate with the forces of the cosmic quanta which underlie the fabric of reality.

Collective Unconscious

The phrase "Collective Unconscious" was coined by Carl Jung to explain a source of information arising in the human psyche that is evidently not its own, but emerging from an unseen transpersonal source shared by all of humanity. It carries the "unconscious" tag because the conscious mind of a human individual is not aware of its presence or influence on its own psyche.

The Collective Unconscious is the vast collective of psychic information emerging out of the Planetary Group Mind and Cosmic Mind. What Princeton University calls the Noosphere, described by Pierre Teilhard de Chardin, is what others call the Planetary Group Mind and the Collective Unconscious. They are all pointing to the same metaphysical phenomenon.

C – Collective Unconscious

The planetary group mind is a psychic energy field enveloping the entire Earth. It is generated by all the psychic energy (mental, emotional, instinctive, spiritual energy) that all life on Earth feeds. This psychic energy field is inherently intelligent as it is synergistically created via a resonate-field-effect arising between all minds on Earth.

The planetary group mind is divided into two great theaters or cathedrals of the soul. The first is the temporal group mind enveloping the physical Earth, the second is the spiritual group mind enveloping the primordial Earth. The primordial Earth exists in the same location of space as the physical Earth, just at a different space-time frequency.

The temporal group mind has a symbiotic relationship with the temporal dimensions of the mind of all life on Earth in the physical universe. The spiritual group mind has a symbiotic relationship with the spiritual dimensions of the mind of all life on Earth in the primordial universe.

There are some major differences between the nature of the temporal group mind and the nature of the spiritual group mind of the Earth. The spiritual group mind is an awakened being who is reflectively aware of the source (Cosmic Consciousness; Ain Soph). The temporal group mind is a planetary mind - which although intelligent - is profoundly asleep spiritually. The collection, organization, and rebroadcasting of information within the temporal group mind is systematic and automated.

The human mind utilizes its ethereal bodies to interact with the various bandwidths of the planetary group mind. Each ethereal body communicates with a different range of planetary group mind bandwidths within the collective unconscious of our humanity. The language of this communication is the language of universal mythology. When we dream, we dream in concert with the planetary group mind. The intelligence within the planetary group mind co-authors the content of our dreams and spiritual visions.

Collective Unconscious – C

Although our focus of awareness may shift back and forth, the physical world is always present, as is the planetary group mind encompassing it. Whether we are physically asleep or physically awake, our individual mind maintains a direct correspondence to specific bandwidths of the planetary group mind. Every human mind resonates with, and lives in accordance with, a range of planetary group mind bandwidths which the mind is most resonate with based on the nature of the mind's illusions and based on the nature of the mind's realizations of the cosmic consciousness (Ain Soph). The human Noetic Soul mediates the connection between the mind and the cosmic consciousness.

Joseph Campbell researched and wrote extensively about the mythological archetypes of the collective unconscious (the planetary group mind). See Joseph Campbell's book "The Power of Myth."

A study of our planet's mythology unlocks and decodes the language of the planetary group mind of our planet. The system of communication the collective unconscious utilizes is governed by theopomorphic and anthropomorphic principles. Theopomorphism applies attributes of God to historic figures the more they recede in time relative to our observation of them in the present, whereas anthropomorphism applies human attributes to the forces of God while we observe them in the present. The effect is, in the past, certain human beings may appear more god-like, while in the present, the forces of the cosmic quanta appear more humanlike. These principles work inversely while in tandem. An awareness of these principles is critical when deciphering the language of the collective unconscious. A lack of awareness of these principles has greatly confused many while interpreting mythology and scripture, all of which were written by human beings who were unconsciously influenced by the collective unconscious when choosing their words, phrases, and creating their storylines and characters.

The story of creation, consciousness, and the effort to bring it all back into unity, is the story the collective unconsciousness keeps sowing unconsciously into all our myths and religious doctrines.

C – Cosmic Alchemy

Cosmic Alchemy

There are three levels of alchemy: (1) Individual, (2) Planetary, and (3) Cosmic. In order to achieve the integration and unification of the human mind on an individual level, alchemy must be practiced on all three levels. Each stage of alchemy is entered upon in consecutive stages during the Three Mountain alchemical process led by Alpha, the self-organizing force of the universe. The individual mind is an extension of both the planetary group mind and the cosmic mind; therefore, the conscious mind must become aware of the planetary and cosmic forces while undergoing the integration process. When the conscious mind becomes aware of the planetary and cosmic forces, it does so by engaging in the alchemy of these forces. This dynamic is what leads the alchemist into the spheres of planetary and cosmic alchemy.

Cosmic alchemy involves both an awareness of (1) the cosmic forces involved in the creation and maintenance of the cosmos, and (2) the target substance of what is being transformed, reconciled, and integrated. The target substance in cosmic alchemy is matter-energy itself. The alchemist delves into matter-energy by delving into the matter-energy of his or her own physical body and the temporal ethereal bodies which function as satellites of the physical body. Cosmic alchemy has three stages which are (1) Cosmic Alchemy, (2) Primordial Alchemy, and (3) Eternal Alchemy.

1.) <u>Cosmic Alchemy</u>: Stage one of cosmic alchemy is called "Cosmic Alchemy." It is the initial stage of the cosmic alchemical spectrum. Here the human being must continuously raise the vibrational resonance of each of his or her five temporal ethereal bodies. These bodies function as dimensions or organs of the temporal mind associated with the physical body. This is a practice of cosmic alchemy, not individual alchemy, because it's all headed toward the raising of physical matter which comes to us through the greater cosmos. The temporal ethereal bodies must be raised first as the first of two precursors to the direct alchemical work with physical matter itself. The resonance of the temporal ethereal bodies is raised by the conscious mind of the human being becoming increasingly aware of the resonance of the original awareness of Ain Soph. During this process, the conscious mind becomes simultaneously aware of the heavens of the Earth enveloping the primordial Earth in the primordial universe and progressively transverses them. The heavens of the Earth are the spiritual group mind bandwidths of the planetary group mind of the Earth. The process of cosmic alchemy begins in the Third Mountain when the conscious mind of the alchemist ascends and enters the Elysium Heaven of the spiritual group mind of the Earth.

2.) <u>Primordial Alchemy</u>: The second precursor to the direct alchemical work with physical matter itself is the integration of the forces of the Id-complex. The forces of creation and the Id-complex are integrated during the second stage of cosmic alchemy called "Primordial Alchemy." It is called "Primordial," because its alchemical process mirrors the same original alchemical process that the greater cosmos underwent to reconcile the forces of light and darkness before the beginning of time.

The process of primordial alchemy is veiled behind the secrecy of what is known as the "Great Arcanum." The secrecy is imposed by the forces of darkness to conceal from the human Noetic Soul its true purpose and power. The human being uncovers the real position of the Noetic Soul during the process of primordial alchemy and eventually achieves the Philosophers' Stone—Christ Monad— at the conclusion of the primordial alchemical process.

The level of turiya utilized in during the process of primordial alchemy is called "Symphysis Turiya." Primordial alchemy is the eighth alchemical process which occurs at the final stage of the third mountain when the alchemist enters a stage known as the "Third Sanctum." In this process, the bond of resonance (love) between the Noetic Soul and the Father is tested by the forces of Eros. This testing period is called "The Tithing." When the bond of

C – Cosmic Alchemy

that resonance is tested and confirmed, the covenant of the Father's love is restored within the matrix of creation. At this point, the forces of heaven (the Father) now have an avenue and a means to bring the forces of the Earth (matter-energy of creation) into harmony with its Spirit via its unbreakable bond with the human Noetic Soul. This is the proverbial Holy Grail. The holy blood symbolizes the resonance of the Father running through the veins of creation. This process brings the alchemist's physical body of creation into unity with the divine source. This is the alchemical Christ Monad.

    3.) <u>Eternal Alchemy</u>: The alchemical process continues after the completion of the Christ Monad by Alpha compelling its continuous expansion. The alchemical process that continues beyond the completion of the Monad is called "Eternal Alchemy."

Eternal alchemy is the ninth alchemical process.

The Christ Monad is achieved but not perfected with completion of the eighth alchemical process. The ninth alchemical process emerges after the completion of the Monad in order to perfect it. However, a new paradox emerges. The process of perfecting the Monad is never completed. It is eternal. This is why this level of alchemy is called "Eternal Alchemy."

The cosmic level of the physical universe is now engaged in its own ninth alchemical process of eternal alchemy. At an individual level, humans are being led by Alpha to eventually enter into the process of eternal alchemy. The straight path takes us there in one lifetime. The spiral path takes us there over many lifetimes. In the eternal alchemy practice, the alchemist brings into differential resonance, one, the infinite depth of the awareness of the Father, with, two, the infinite depth of the forces of darkness within matter. This principle is symbolized by the eternal Yin-Yang symbol. Note the yang dot within yin, the yin dot within yang, the constant motion of their shapes, and the infiniteness of the circle.

Cosmic Alchemy – **C**

This dynamic is also represented by the famous Masonic black and white checkered floor along with many other symbols which echo this same alchemical principle. In the eternal alchemy practice, the awareness of the divine Father lines-up behind the self-observing awareness of the conscious mind of the human being via the intercession of the Noetic Soul. This compels the Father to observe and realize the body of creation of the human being and for the darkness in matter to continuously rise-up into the unity with the Father. This drives the eternal expansion of the Monad.

Artwork of cosmic alchemy below. The two dragons symbolize Alpha and Omega. The Orb in the dragon's hand is the Monad. The Three Mountains are in the background. Cerberus is guarding the entrance to the eternal. Hydra, symbol of the many false-selves, is at the bottom. The numina, symbolized by the sacred feminine.

C – Cosmic Consciousness | Cosmic Cultivation

Cosmic Consciousness

The Cosmic Consciousness is the living awareness existing at the quantum level within all things. At the quantum level of existence, we discover a set of living forces known as the Cosmic Quanta; together, they comprise the pantheon of God. God is the being of one's being residing at the innermost core of all things. It is the ultimate truth, the ultimate reality. It is pure awareness, the essence of life, and the source of infinite energy. Its energy is the Spirit of its infinite divine love. These three attributes together compose the original divine Monad which precedes everything, and always was, and always will be. Its existence is paradoxical, as it cannot be explained rationally by a system governed by the laws of time and space. It is from the original divine Monad that all things stem forth.

Cosmic Cultivation

The magnetic forces of positive (yang), negative (yin), and neutral (yuan) exist at all levels of creation. For example, within the atom we have the proton (positive), electron (negative), neutron (neutral), and within the giant electromagnetic spheres of the cosmos we call stars. These three magnetic states are in a constant dance with one another to achieve balance from one end of the spectrum within the microcosm to another end of the spectrum within the macrocosm. All bodies of creation have some form of magnetic polarity between them. Within all lifeforms, this polarity exists within the psycho-sexual life forces of the organism.

Due to what is called the psycho-sexual dynamic, the mind affects the lifeforces of the body, and the lifeforces of the body affect the mind. It is a vicious cycle. To elevate our state of mind, we must not only elevate the psychological components of our mind (First Factor), we must also elevate the lifeforces of our body which affect our mind (Second Factor). The most powerful catalyst to the alchemical process is the divine love of the Spirit (Third Factor).

Cosmic Cultivation – C

To reach the Spirit we must create a balance of energy between the Yin-Yang forces within our mind-body system that typically cloud our conscious mind's connection with the Spirit. We need to open a window to the Spirit of God. We do this by neutralizing our energy. Cultivation (Second Factor) neutralizes our energy to open this window, which facilitates our ability to commune with the Spirit (Third Factor) and to utilize the Spirit to transform the constructs of our mind (First Factor).

Our level of cognitive awareness of the Spirit, and all the other emergent forces, is our level of Q. There are five levels of Q beginning with Q5 and until reaching the highest level of Q1.

The universe always provides itself with multiple means in which it can evolve, express, and re-organize. Life always finds a way. In alchemy, there are multiple ways to connect and elevate our resonance with the Spirit. There are multiple ways to elevate our level of Q. Alchemical sexual intercourse is a popular known means to cultivate energy, but it is not the only means within nature to cultivate our energy (Second Factor). The agents of the Second Factor are abundant and all about us within the planetary and cosmic forces of the stars, the planets, the Earth, the sky, the water, the trees, in every life form of nature, and in all the food we grow and consume. The alchemist has the innate latent capacity to commune with the cosmic forces of nature to cultivate and elevate the lifeforces of his or her body to a higher resonance with the Spirit. This is achieved by tuning our mind to resonate with the lifeforces of nature with the intent to cultivate our energy to a higher resonance with the Spirit. The means and methods of achieving this type of cultivation is unlimited. This form of cultivation is called *"Cosmic Cultivation."*

As with all methods of the Second Factor, the First Factor is a required precedent to the practice of cosmic cultivation. The reason is, in order to truly neutralize and balance the energy of the mind-body system, that energy needs to be first working properly between the five centers of the human psyche. The five centers are the mental

C – Cosmic Cultivation

center, emotional center, instinctive center, motor center, and sexual center. In an unbalanced state, each center is robbing energy from the other centers. Through the practices of the First Factor, each center stops seizing energy from the other centers and comes to function normally. When we perform a practice of sexual cultivation, or cosmic cultivation, while each center is functioning normally, true cultivation takes place and a window to the Spirit is opened. There are two main catalysts or ingredients for compelling and implementing the Second Factor practice of cosmic cultivation.

The two main catalysts are:

1.) Intent of Mind

2.) Movement

Cosmic cultivation is better suited for many alchemists than alchemical sexual intercourse. All alchemists should study some form of cosmic cultivation, even if they practice sexual cultivation. A suitable place to start is with the practices of Qigong and Tai Chi. The variation of forms human beings can develop to practice cosmic cultivation are unlimited. However, the practices of Qigong, Tai Chi, and other ancient forms are all forms that have been developed and cultivated by alchemists for thousands of years. The practice of Primordial Qigong taught by Michael Winn is a great practice of cosmic cultivation. Others have reported that Nature Observation and Tracking taught by Tom Brown, Jr. is a powerful method. The dervish dances of the Sufis are a marvelous form of cosmic cultivation. Most martial arts are a study of the Second Factor. Whenever we're practicing qigong, martial arts, or dances, it's critical to practice with the intent to cultivate our energy. Energy follows the mind.

With continued practice, our ability to practice cosmic cultivation evolves into an ability to cultivate the planetary and cosmic forces of nature without physical movement while in meditation, as well as the ability to cultivate effortlessly as we go about our day. Movement is still occurring between the mind and the cosmic forces, just at a higher unseen level. Because energy follows the mind, the possibilities are unlimited as to all the variations of movement which can be developed. Keep an open mind and explore what both eastern and western traditions offer and adopt into your spiritual alchemy what works best for you.

Cosmic cultivation evolves into a continuous copulation of forces between your being and the forces of nature. The more unified your mind becomes, the more powerful your cosmic cultivation becomes - and the more powerful your cosmic cultivation becomes - the more unified your relationship with the greater cosmos becomes.

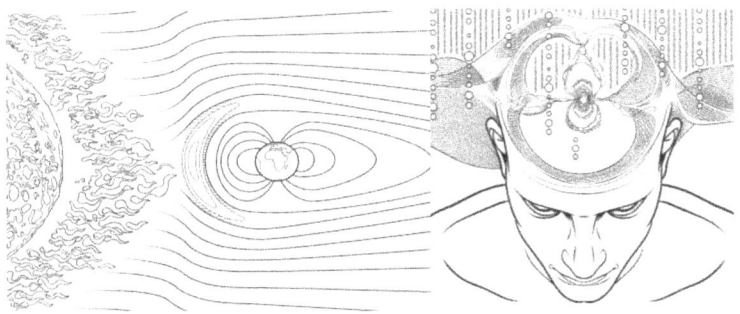

Cosmic Mind

The mind arises through the paring of consciousness and matter. Consciousness is the mind's Father. Matter is the mind's mother. The mind, and the created cosmos, exist in fractal scales. The fractal scales emerged during the initial reconciliation process between divinity and creation on a cosmic level just before the beginning of time.

The three major scales are the Cosmic, Planetary, and Individual. We have a Cosmic Mind, a Planetary Mind, and an Individual Mind. The cosmic level is both the largest and smallest in fractal scales. The quantum world within the atom is cosmic. The galaxies and the farthest reaches of the universe are cosmic. The cosmic level is a serpent swallowing its tail. The Godhead of the Cosmic Mind is IAO. IAO is the Godhead for all levels of mind including the Planetary and Individual.

C – Cosmic Mind

The forces of IAO and the Erodonic Trinity are currently reconciled on the cosmic level but remain to be reconciled on the planetary and individual levels within the physical universe. The unfinished levels of creation are what continue to compel the self-organizing force of Alpha to bring everything back into unity with the divine source of Ain Soph to form the reconstituted Monad. This is the Great Work or Magnum Opus.

All of creation including the physical universe and the primordial universe (Causal 'B') exist inside the Cosmic Mind. The Godhead of the Cosmic Mind, IAO, is the first born out of the divine source. The realms of creation within the Cosmic Mind are brought into organization when the second born of the divine source, the Logos, joins with IAO to complete the process of creation.

The cosmic story of the advent of creation and the forces of consciousness involved continue to echo throughout all the realms of creation to emerge via the collective unconscious into all the worlds literature, religious mythologies, and all forms of creative arts. This story continues to repeat *ad infinitum* because it carries with it a roadmap for how to reconstitute the Monad.

The serpent swallowing its tail is a popular motif arising out of the collective unconscious. In alchemy, it has a few meanings:

1.) The inner and outer cosmos reconnecting.

2.) The return to unity.

3.) The accomplishment of the Great Work.

4.) Eternity, and

5.) The cycle of creative destruction.

Cosmic Monad

The Cosmic Monad is the Cosmic Christ. See the term "Christ." The Christ Monad emerges on three cosmic scales which are the Cosmic, Planetary, and Individual. Once all three cosmic scales are reconciled, they join to form a Super Monad. The Super Monad already exists in the primordial universe from which the physical universe was born. The Super Monad is in process of swallowing the physical universe. The physical universe is already reconciled on the cosmic level and is already fully integrated with the Super Monad. All that remains in the physical universe to be reconciled are the planetary and individual levels of creation.

As each planetary sphere and individual human being completes the Monad in the physical universe, they each join the Super Monad at their own point in space and time while other planetary spheres and individual human beings across the universe continue working to complete the Monad. When one human being finishes, another is just beginning. This causes the planetary and individual levels in the physical universe to reconcile forever because new planetary spheres and new individual human beings will continue to emerge forever. This is because the physical universe is governed by time while the primordial universe is governed by eternity. This allows the never-ending process of creation to expand horizontally without end and without needing to add new vertical levels of existence. This is the purpose of time. Time creates a never-ending runway for the Father's never-ending process of creation. This is why the physical universe was created. The Father needs an infinite runway because he cannot stop his process of creation. Creation arises spontaneously from his infinite love, the Spirit. Spacetime was the most efficient solution.

> *"Day by day, we magnify thee, and we worship thy name, ever world without end." – Handel - Dettingen Te Deum.*

C – Cosmic Seal | Cosmic Quanta

Cosmic Seal

The conscious mind's ascent through the heavenly realms of the spiritual group mind of the Earth is accompanied by a special series of alchemical revelations. The later and most profound of these alchemical revelations deal with "Cosmic Alchemy," versus "Planetary Alchemy" and "Individual Alchemy," and are called the "Cosmic Seals." In the Third Mountain stage in the process of reconstituting the Monad (unifying the mind), I experienced twelve revelations of which seven were the Cosmic Seals. The Cosmic Seals are both catalysts and instruments of communication between the human Noetic Soul and a higher level of cosmic intelligence pervading the whole universe within the unseen dimensions of mind which shapes and forms all things within creation. In addition to what is revealed by each cosmic seal, each cosmic seal compels a new awakening within us, referred to as an opening of a cosmic seal. The experience of opening each cosmic seal increases our level of resonance with the cosmic quanta and compels a heightened awareness of Ain Soph and its three dimensions of consciousness.

Cosmic Quanta

At the quantum level of existence beneath all things, in the realm of the noumenon, we discover with the conscious mind a complete set of living forces referred to as the "Cosmic Quanta." Together, they comprise the pantheon of God. The noumenon is a superluminal realm where the forces of consciousness interact with the forces of matter to bridge divinity with creation. The interacting forces in the noumenon are the cosmic quanta. Within the cosmic quanta, the forces of consciousness are "Theogenic," the forces of matter are "Atomic, and a third group in the cosmic quanta demonstrating both a theogenic and atomic nature is called "Metagenic."

Of all the theogenic forces, only three forces are divine, meaning they always existed and are untarnishable. These three divine forces of the cosmic quanta are the Father, the Divine Soul, and the Spirit. Together, they resonate as one. Together they are the original divine Monad. The original divine Monad is known by many names. One such name is Ain Soph. All forces of the cosmic quanta dance around the flame of the original divine Monad of Ain Soph. Other theogenic forces in the cosmic quanta are the Logos, the Numina, and the Human Soul—otherwise known as the Noetic Soul.

The metagenic forces consist of Christ, IAO, the Erotic Soul, Idamus, and the Gorgon. The most exalted of all the forces of the cosmic quanta is the metagenic force of the Christ Monad. It includes all the forces of the cosmic quanta resonating together as one.

All the forces of the cosmic quanta, except Ain Soph and Christ, have expressions within both light and darkness. For example, the dark inflection of the Logos is Lucifer. The dark inflection of IAO is Satan. The dark inflection of the Human Soul is Psyche. The Gorgon transforms into Magdalene. Idamus transforms into David. Ain Soph precedes light and darkness. Christ exists beyond light and darkness.

Creation

Creation initially arises spontaneously—sparked into existence by the infinite energy of the Spirit but is eventually brought back into unity with the divine source through an intervention of Will/Word—Logos. When the unification of forces is achieved, this organizes the universe of creation and all the laws within it and sets-off the infiniton wave—the never-ending expansion of the universe.

The Spirit is the love arising from the original divine singularity called Ain Soph. Ain Soph is the unity of the Cosmic Consciousness. Its absolute presence forms Causal 'A'—the eternal uncreated realm.

The spontaneous rise of creation is set-off by a vision compelled by the love of God—the Spirit. The spark is called Dynamis. Dynamis is driven by an axiom that says that infinite energy will inevitably create. The vision itself forms the Cosmic Mind which immediately breaks-off and diverges from the realm of divinity (Causal 'A') to form its own causal realm called Causal 'B.'

C – Creation

Nothing in Causal 'A' that is born can remain in Causal 'A'.

Between the law that infinite energy inevitably creates (Dynamis) and the law that only the unborn can remain in Casual "A," creation as we know it—the multiverse (Causal 'B')—is inevitable.

Existing inside Causal 'B' are all the universes of creation including the physical universe, which is a universe based in time. Causal 'B' also includes a higher mother universe known as the primordial universe, which is based in eternity. The primordial preceded the physical. There are possibly many physical universes, each nested up inside a singularity in the primordial universe.

The eternal interaction between the first two forces of Ain Soph within Causal 'A,' the Father (infinite awareness) and Divine Soul (infinite life) produces the third force of the Spirit (infinite love) which ultimately compels the rise of creation. The three forces within Ain Soph compose the original Divine Trinity, or Holy Trinity.

When the Father becomes aware of the life of his Divine Soul, he loves, and this love is the Spirit. Because the Father's awareness is infinite, the life of his Divine Soul is infinite, and when the two dimensions of his being interact, this produces the infinite love of the Spirit. The infinite love of the Spirit is infinite energy. The infinite energy of love spontaneously combusts into a vision, a vision of creation. This vision of creation cannot exist in Causal 'A' because it was born, begotten, or procreated. Only what was never born, what has always existed, can remain in Causal 'A' for all eternity.

The Spirit has always existed, so it vibes eternally in Causal 'A.' But the Spirit possesses a procreative dimension in and of itself through the action of the Father's awareness giving rise to the Spirit when he fathoms the nature of his own lifeforce, the Divine Soul. This procreative aspect to the Spirit builds up a procreative spark that the Spirit ultimately combusts spontaneously on its own into a vision to initiate the process of creation. This spark is called "Dynamis."

The vision that Dynamis sparks into existence cannot remain in Causal 'A,' so it immediately bifurcates to form its own causal realm,

Creation – C

Causal 'B.' The vision itself forms the Cosmic Mind. All of creation unfolds inside the vision of the Cosmic Mind.

The Cosmic Mind initially emerges in darkness because it emerges without the willful intent of the Father, and because it emerges without the willful intent of the Father it also initially emerges outside the awareness of the Father. The Father eventually becomes aware of the fact that his Spirit, his divine love, spontaneously sparked creation into existence. The two points between when creation was initially sparked into existence to when the Father realizes the genesis of creation itself, produces "time."

The vision of the Spirit creates the phenomenon of "space."

The realization of the Father creates the phenomenon of "time."

When the Cosmic Mind first emerged, its awareness, IAO, the first born of the Divine Trinity, experienced distant-forever within the outer darkness outside of Causal 'A.' The Cosmic Mind has a trinity within it that mirrors the Divine Trinity. That trinity is the Erodonic Trinity composed of IAO (awareness), Erotic Soul (life) and Matter-Energy (energy). When the Father realized that IAO was in darkness, he loved IAO and his creation and willed that IAO and his creation should be saved. The Father's love for creation (Numina) and his will to save it (Logos) gives birth to the Human/Noetic Soul to function as the intercessing principal between creation and divinity. It is a new trinity called the Sacred Trinity—it is the light.

The Noetic Soul is sent into the mind of creation to bear its darkness and lift creation back into unity with God (Ain Soph). This is the origin of the mythology of "the only begotten son of God" and "the savior." The Noetic Soul was born by the immaculate conception of the Father—along with the Numina and the Logos—to save creation by either completing the creation process or by destroying it. This will of the Father for the Noetic Soul to save creation places the Noetic Soul and its Sacred Trinity in charge of all creation as its steward. It transfers all authority over creation to the sacred trinity. In this manner, the Noetic Soul within humanity has the God given right to decide all matters of life and death.

C – Creation

For creation to complete its process, which begins spontaneously and automatically, a conscious mind must emerge to reconcile the spontaneous processes (Chaos, Darkness) with a will (Logos, Light) expressed by the Father within Ain Soph to bring creation into unity – the reconstituted Monad (Christ).

The Sacred Trinity is composed of (1) Logos—the awareness within the will of the Father, (2) the Noetic Soul (Human Soul)—lifeforce of the will of the Father, and (3) the Numina—the Father's love for creation. The Noetic Soul within all human beings is a direct reflection of the original Noetic Soul which emerged at the cosmic level at the beginning of time to unify creation with God and organize its creation. The original Noetic Soul reconciled the forces of darkness and reconstituted the Monad on a cosmic scale infinite eons ago to complete the primordial universe and physical universe.

The primordial universe is complete on all three scales of creation. The physical universe is complete only on the cosmic scale. The planetary and individual scales of creation are now attempting to complete their process of creation through the intercession of the Noetic Soul. This is the "Prime Directive" of the Noetic Soul. It is the purpose of human existence. It is why you, the reader, are alive in your physical body today. You didn't create the darkness of this world. You were born into it—to lift it up. This is your prime directive.

The Noetic Soul is sent into the mind of the human being to reconcile the forces of darkness and reconnect the mind back to its divine source within Ain Soph. If the mind becomes resonant with all the primeval forces of creation, this allows the mind to coalesce into a new Monad and complete the process of creation. This is Christ. The Father begins the process of creation. Christ is the completion of creation. (See the Sefirot). (See Theokinesis, Chaos)

> *"For God so loved the world,*
> *that he gave his only begotten Son,*
> *that whosoever believes in him should not perish,*
> *but have everlasting life." ... John 3:16*

D

David

David, as a mythological figure, represents something far more profound within the collective unconscious than what is commonly known in the public consciousness. At the deepest level, David represents the harmonized lifeforce between divinity and creation within the matrix of the reconstituted Monad.

When the Noetic Soul introduces the love of the Father to the Erotic Soul within the human psyche, David is born and rises within us. The term "David" is used in a non-gender sense.

Christian philosophical mythology represents something far more profound than the literal interpretation of that mythology. Within every unity (Monad) therein lies a trinity.

The trinity within the original Monad of Ain Soph is:

(1) The Father (Divine Awareness)

(2) The Divine Soul (Divine Life)

(3) The Spirit (Divine Energy-Love)

The trinity within the new reconstituted Monad of Christ is:

(1) Dominus (Harmonized Awareness)

(2) David (Harmonized Life)

(3) Erodysis (Harmonized Energy-Love)

D – Deism

Deism *[De-i-sm; Dee-i-zm]*

The term "Deism," derives from Latin "Deus," meaning "God." Deism is the philosophical belief which posits that there is indeed a divine source which precedes creation, but that this divine source does not attempt to intervene with its creation or interreact with it. Deism also holds that logic and observation of the natural world alone are self-evident and sufficient enough to determine the existence of a single creator or absolute principle of the universe and rejects the need of divine revelation as being necessary to determine the existence of that divine source.

In contrast to Deism, we have Theism. The term "Theism" derives from the Greek word "Theos" or "Theoi," meaning "God". Unlike Deism, Theism does not reject the possibility of divine intervention, revelation, or interaction. Theism can be monotheistic (one God) or polytheistic (many Gods).

Atheism rejects any possibility of any intelligence preceding creation. Gnosticism essentially believes every human being has the innate ability to know God directly without the aid of a Church, doctrine of faith, or intermediary. Agnosticism posits that God may exist but is unknowable.

In respect to the above-mentioned terms, the alchemical process of integrating the human mind ultimately reveals the following.

Deism believes that God created the cosmos - and since that first moment of creation, God does not involve itself in the post-creation affairs or activities of that creation. As for the three divine forces residing in the ultimate source of all things, this argument is essentially correct, with the only correction being that the divine source goes one step beyond just the initial outpouring of creation. It also provides a means for that creation to re-unify sympathetically with the divine source. From that point onward, it's hands-off.

The means it provides for creation to re-unify with the source is the spiritual force of its will which manifests within the human psyche as the Noetic Soul and its Sacred Trinity. The power of intercession between divinity and creation is delegated from divinity to the Noetic Soul. The Noetic Soul within humanity has been given the divine right to judge and rule-over all of creation. It should also be noted that God-Divine Source-Ain Soph did not create just once. The interchange of divine forces continues to create *ad-infinitum*.

To reestablish or maintain a unity with the source of all things, the interchange of theogenic forces compels the divine source to supply the means of re-unification between divinity and creation. It compels the rise of the will of the Father, which is known as "Thelesis." Thelesis immaculately conceives the Sacred Trinity within which the Noetic Soul / Human Soul is the living lifeforce.

Lastly, there are other forces in the pantheon of God (Consciousness) which do interact with creation, but these forces are not among the divine forces of Ain Soph (original Monad).

Differential Resonance

When the observer can hold both the higher feeling of the Spirit and the lower feeling of a psychological element within his or her mind in the very same moment, the law of sympathetic vibrations goes into motion (Alpha) to correct the disharmony between the two. This is called "Differential Resonance."

The result of differential resonance is a liberation of an aspect of the authentic-self trapped by the targeted psychological element.

This practice is repeated thousands of times for every unintegrated psychological element discovered within the human psyche. The psychological element can be a false-self, an automated instinct, a script of the mind, a dark inflection of some primeval force of consciousness, or matter itself.

The practice of differential resonance is the grand alchemical key which slowly coalesces the unified mind (Philosophers' Stone). It has either been lost for thousands of years or held secret by a few overzealous alchemists. Without this key, the alchemist would struggle endlessly and end up nowhere.

D – Divine Soul

Divine Soul

When dealing with consciousness as a subject, we are always dealing with one of its three primary dimensions, the unity of it as a whole, or with its collective nature rising up between all life in the universe. The three dimensions of consciousness are awareness, life and love. The unity of it as a whole is Ain Soph, the original divine Monad. Its collective nature, rising up from the center of all things to connect all things, is the Cosmic Consciousness.

Whenever we read the word "soul," we are dealing with "life." The soul is the lifeforce of consciousness. Depending on the context, the word "son," when viewing various texts via the viewpoint of the collective unconscious, typically refers to the soul itself. The soul is genderless but there are three types of souls in correspondence to the permutations consciousness goes through in its creation process.

The original soul, from where it all began, is the Divine Soul, the second dimension of the Cosmic Consciousness within the original divine Monad of Ain Soph.

The Father is the awareness within the Cosmic Consciousness. The Divine Soul is the lifeforce within the Cosmic Consciousness. The Spirit is the love within the Cosmic Consciousness.

The second soul, the first born of creation, in direct descent of the Spirit is the Erotic Soul. It is the Sea of Eros, the Eternal Sea, the animating consciousness from which all lifeforms in nature arise. All animals, every organic machine—including the human body, the trees, and even minerals, are all animated by the Erotic Soul. Each insect, each animal, doesn't have its own soul. They all share the same Erotic Soul, however, they each form their own minds.

The third soul is the only begotten son of the divine Father, born by his will (Logos). It is the Noetic Soul. It intervenes to mediate between the Divine Soul and the Erotic Soul within the psyche of intelligent lifeforms—typically humanoid in form— to reunify the Monad. The Noetic Soul is what makes a being "human," thus it is also called the Human Soul. Each human being has its own

Divine Soul – **D**

Noetic Soul. Each human being's Noetic Soul is a direct reflection of the original Noetic Soul of Eloah or Allah at the cosmic level.

Each of the three dimensions of Ain Soph has its own force within the Cosmic Consciousness and can be reflectively isolated in the conscious mind of the human psyche through the intercession of the Noetic Soul. The Noetic Soul is capable of resonating with all three forces both separately and in unison.

Ain Soph, and all three forces within it, are considered "Divine" because all three forces precede creation. They always were and always have been. The forces of divinity are paradoxical. Ain Soph exists within the atom. It is the God Particle existing at the center of all things. The three forces of the Cosmic Consciousness also belong to a pantheon of forces of consciousness called the "Cosmic Quanta."

All three forces within the Divine Trinity are infinite and exist as the only non-permutated permutations of consciousness within the pantheon of forces within the cosmic quanta – meaning, they always existed as differential abstracts within the original divine Monad. The force of the law of one to reconcile the three infinite forces to a single unit of one is what gives rise to what we call "consciousness" and the advent of creation.

A modern symbol representing the resonance between the original divine Monad of Ain Soph and all of creation. Everything within creation resonating with the Divine Soul increasingly transforms to higher grades of beauty, intelligence, and divine love. Ain Soph is the heart of the Immortal Beloved and alchemy is its song.

Similar or Equivalent Terms: Buddhi (Theosophy)

D – Divine Source

Divine Source – Source, Divinity

To explain the Divine Source, we must first define what is Divine. That which is Divine is something that was never created or born, yet it still exists. The Divine Source, or Divinity, is that which creates from its uncreated, absolute, eternal realm of infinite non-space. It has an awareness. That awareness—because it exists—has a life, and when that awareness becomes aware of its own life—it loves. That love is the Spirit, its life is known as the Divine Soul, and the source awareness itself is affectionately and traditionally referred to as the Father. It is genderless, but it's referred to as the Father because it holds the seed of all creation. Divinity is inherently paradoxical. It shouldn't exist, but yet it does. How can something be infinite, but yet it is. It loves infinitely, but yet it creates both light and darkness.

The three divine forces as one is the original divine Monad, the divine source, the original divine spark, the God particle residing at the center of all things. In the Kabbalah, it's referred to as Ain Soph, but also by other names in other traditions. The abstract infinite non-space in which Ain Soph resides is called the Absolute. All beings with a Noetic Soul have the ability to resonate with Ain Soph through the development of human emotion. All life throughout the universe is connected through the original divine spark existing at the center of all things. When divinity is viewed as the central organizing consciousness connecting and binding all things, it is known as the Cosmic Consciousness.

Similar or Equivalent Terms:

Mahayana Buddhism:	Tathagatagarbha (Womb of all Buddhas)
Hasidic Judaism:	Atzmus, or Atzmut
Hinduism:	Brahma
Sufism:	Ruh, Batin, or Qalb (Innermost Self)
Taoism:	Wuji
Theosophy:	Atma-Buddhi, Atman
Zoroastrianism:	The One Eternal Light

Earth Monad Project

Everything today throughout the entire universe, at every cosmic level, including our whole perception of reality in this very present moment, is an echo of the original act of creation at the quantum level of nature. The same dynamics which gave rise to creation and later organized it and expanded it, from its original primeval atom to the great vastness of the known universe, is still very much at play and is still affecting everything in every second of our lives. Once you understand the original primeval forces of creation and how they relate and interact with each other at the microcosm of reality, everything at the macrocosm of reality begins to make sense in a way that is absolutely earthshaking and profoundly life changing.

Not only are you capable of interacting with these primeval forces of creation—you were made to—and are supposed to.

The Noetic Soul within the human being, the sentient observer that sits just above and beyond the realms of creation, behind the mind, yet seeing through the mind to observe the world around us, is itself, an original primeval force involved in the act of creation.

We were all there—at the very beginning.

When the divine awareness within the original Ain Soph Monad, known as the Father, became aware of the fact that the power of his infinite love had spontaneously sparked all of creation into existence, and that his creation had a living life force of its own, he loved it and willed that his creation should be saved and brought into resonance with his eternal everlasting being, so that his creation could last forever—and ultimately become—immortal.

The shear act of this divine will to save creation began a new compounding process of the divine Monad known as Thelesis.

E – Earth Monad Project

Thelesis is a force of divine will charged with finding a way to save creation to reintegrate the Monad—to make everything one.

It's only by staying unified with the divine source as one being that everything can be brought into harmony and continue forever.

The solution of Thelesis was the immaculate conception of an intervening force that has the power to reconnect creation to the divine source of the Father. That intervening force is the Sacred Trinity.

The Logos is the awareness godhead of the Sacred Trinity.

The Noetic Soul is the living life force of the Sacred Trinity.

The Numina is the radiant energy of the Sacred Trinity.

The Logos is the awareness of the Father's will.

The Noetic Soul is the life force of the Father's will.

The Numina is the love inherent in the Father's will.

The "soul" is the life force of any trinity. There are actually four trinities in the alchemical process of creation. The first trinity is the Divine Trinity, or Holy Trinity. It is the trinity existing inside the original Ain Soph Monad. The second trinity exists within creation. The third is the Sacred Trinity. The fourth exists within Christ.

Each of the three forces within Christ is a unity of the prior three.

The fourth trinity within Christ unifies all of it.

In Christ all things are made new.

Christ is the completion of creation—the transcendent being.

In mythology, from the perspective of the collective unconscious, the "son" is the "soul."

The Noetic Soul of the Sacred Trinity is the proverbial "Only Begotten Son of God."

The first soul, the Divine Soul of the Father, was not "begotten." It has always existed because it is divine—it was never born.

The second soul, the Erotic Soul of IAO, the soul of creation, was not begotten directly by the Father. It was begotten indirectly by the Father through his love, the Holy Spirit.

Only the third soul, the Noetic Soul of the Sacred Trinity, was born directly and intentionally by the Father. It was born by His Will. His Will is His Word—which is the Logos.

Thelesis eventually achieves the reintegration of the Monad on a cosmic level, but it happens before time. It is actually the completion of the reintegrated Monad itself that initiates the sequence of time.

When the Cosmic Monad was established, its reconciled unified body became the realm of spacetime (Causal 'B) that we study today, and all the laws within it became a reflection of the original pairing of darkness (creation) and light (the intervening force of the Logos).

That same Cosmic Monad is still active and thriving to this day.

The universe is literally *alive*.

The universe is a living being with an actual mind of its own. It is a living cosmic mind. This reintegrated being is "Christ."

Christ is a cosmic being whose story echoes through time and space rising unconsciously into many of our fables, myths, and religious beliefs. The real Christ is God. His name is Eloah or Allah. He is the Immortal Beloved, and the alchemical process he undergoes is known as the *Song of the Immortal Beloved*.

The song of the immortal beloved is the process that God underwent in reconciling his own existence—a process that was completed at the cosmic level at the onset of time and space to give birth to the known universe but continues inward within that unity to this very day in a successive series of inner reducing fractal scales.

A planet with a thriving ecosystem, such as Earth, is a reflecting, reverberating, living fractal in the process of creation.

A sentient humanoid being, the pinnacle lifeform of nature, is a reflecting, reverberating, living fractal in the process of creation.

In nature, only a living sentient humanoid being can embody the primeval force of the Noetic Soul—the intercessing principal of creation. And it embodies it to carry out, on an individual level, what God has already carried out and completed on a cosmic level. Being divinely endowed with the Noetic Soul, it is therefore the prime directive of the human being to repeat this theokinetic process.

The prime directive of your Noetic Soul continues in full force within you—the reader—right now. It is the ultimate purpose of your existence here on Earth. It is your most important mission.

E – Earth Monad Project

This mission supersedes everything else in your life, but it doesn't need to be in conflict with everything else. As a matter of fact, by helping other human beings to achieve the prime directive of the Noetic Soul, you are at the same time working to achieve the prime directive on a planetary scale beyond your own being.

Our highest calling in this world is to lift up out of darkness, our fellow human beings, and all life within creation, and to make this world a better place for everyone.

We truly have this calling. It's much more than a nice ideal.

First, we must dispel one giant falsehood that has run amuck in the world for millennia and reinstate the actual truth. The Human Soul (Noetic Soul) is not sinful or born of sin. It is not the cause of the darkness in the world. We don't come into this world to live like good little boys and girls just to obey God's laws, and if we don't, we will go to hell, and if we do, we will go to heaven. We aren't born in this world to grow and learn lessons or to pay some kind of karma. We weren't cast upon this Earth to be punished. The Noetic Soul is born perfect, and every Noetic Soul is born equal in that perfection.

By perfect, I don't mean that it is omniscient and omnipotent. It just means that it doesn't need to be worked on. Your Noetic Soul is already loved and accepted by the divine Father at every level.

It is the mind that is imperfect. It is the body that is imperfect. The Noetic Soul is sent into a mind and body of creation to lift it up and reunify it with God. And if it does so, over the course of evolution, the mind and body of that species will eventually become immortal.

The Noetic Soul has a natural lifting effect on the mind and body—what some may call Theosis. Even when a human being is experiencing the complete darkness and despair of the mind, the sheer presence of that person's Noetic Soul in that moment is still countering and lifting the darkness. All that needs to be done is to hold on. And if by chance this person can muster it in this dark hour, he or she has the innate power within to reconnect with the divine source and transcend all of it at a much faster rate.

The way in which the Noetic Soul was conceived by the Father to intervene on the Father's behalf to interdict the process of creation, places the Noetic Soul in charge of all of creation and gives the Noetic Soul a divine given mandate, and the divine given right, to decide all matters of life and death.

Furthermore, the Noetic Soul has been in this position of power since the onset of everything. The history of humanity traces back to the very beginning of time. The Noetic Soul has lived and continues to live in a countless number of humanoid beings stretching out to the furthest reaches of the universe.

Humanoid life is an inherent function of the cosmos, no different than time, space, gravity, or material matter.

Human life on Earth is only a recent chapter in a long eternal book on creation, the human condition, and its prime directive.

During the alchemical process of unifying the human mind, the cosmic quanta compel the Noetic Soul to realize and understand the process of creation, as this understanding is fundamental in the process of unification—the process of reintegrating the Monad. The cosmic quanta relay the story of creation, and as part of that story, the story of humanity and the eternal saga of its sacred mission.

What it tells us is that humanity has struggled since the inception of time and space to achieve the Monad. Humanity being a reflection of the process on a cosmic level, suggests that God-Eloah-himself had labored to bring the universe into existence and that the universe today is the one successful outcome of many prior attempts.

Christ-Eloah found the way before us, and now we are destined to follow in his footsteps to complete on an individual human level what he has already completed on a universal cosmic level.

The truth of the Noetic Soul and its position is a real law of the universe in how the universe functions and works to maintain itself.

The religious stories across many different faiths are delivery vehicles in relaying the universal principles of the cosmos and how to fulfill the prime directive of the Noetic Soul.

E – Earth Monad Project

The universe is psychosomatic. Our minds interact with it. Quantum physicists are slowly beginning to wake up to this reality.

It is important to know this backstory first to understand what is happening on Earth today in what is called the Earth Monad Project. To understand what this project is, and how and why it came about, we must first finish with this brief backstory.

The Noetic Soul of Eloah—the Cosmic Christ (God)—first had to engage the darkness and lift it up before achieving peace and unity between creation and the divine Father. The level of creation that was saved at the cosmic level of time to give birth to the multiverse of creation is called the Theosphere—or Causal 'M.'

All lesser realms of creation exist inside it.

The lesser realms of creation inside the Theosphere remain as incomplete fractals that must be lifted to complete a Super Monad. The reason there are incomplete fractals residing inside the Theosphere is because the Father is infinite, and creation is not. The solution to integrating a finite creation with an infinite source is the unfoldment of a series of escalating musical scales of time and space.

Eventually the Noetic Soul is sent into the lower fractal scales of creation to lift them up to complete the process of creation at every level. One of those fractals is the humanoid being. The humanoid being has a special function, in that by raising itself, it also raises the planetary consciousness, thereby helping all the planets that it inhabits to complete a Monad at the planetary level of existence.

The whole process of intercession, from the initial engagement of the Noetic Soul with a level of existence it is seeking to raise up, to the completion of the Monad itself, is driven and guided by a force in the universe that first emerges by will of the divine Father but later establishes a repeating pattern by the work already accomplished by the Cosmic Christ—Eloah. This force is called Alpha. Its pattern is called the Alpha Wave.

The course set by Eloah at the cosmic level reverberates down through the lesser scales of creation. This is Alpha.

Earth Monad Project – E

There is only one way to complete the Monad, the same way that Eloah completed it. If we follow Alpha, we will undergo the same process that Eloah went through—and we will eventually succeed. If we try any other way, we will fail. It is an organic psychosomatic process involving the interaction of matter and consciousness. The end result cannot be engineered. It can only unfold organically.

The challenge of the process is that we must repeat what Eloah has already accomplished, and that is, the Noetic Soul must enter the darkness of the mind and body and then psychosomatically elevate it with the divine source until the Monad is fully reconstituted.

While we undergo the process, the cosmic quanta share with us that most sentient humanoid life throughout the universe already know about this inherent process of the universe.

However, in the Milky Way Galaxy, Noetic life, using its authority to govern over all of creation, has decided to outlaw, on a galactic level, the pursuit of the Monad. Mythologically, it is the proverbial "Forbidden Fruit." The cosmic quanta share why.

According to the cosmic quanta, in the early ages of humanoid life in the Milky Way Galaxy, sentient life evolved organically and was set on a natural course to reintegrate the Monad. However, instead of most humanoid beings achieving this sacred end-goal, most succumbed to the darkness in the early stages of the integration process and became evil.

Eloah himself needed multiple attempts. This is because the Father's spontaneous love in the creation process, and the Father's conscious will to save that creation, are almost equal in power.

His divine will eventually wins.

As a result of the emergence of evil, there was a horrible war, and the galaxy went through a period of great suffering and darkness. Eventually, human intelligence grew to such extent that it finally understood what was happening, interrupted the mechanism genetically, and switched off the whole psychosomatic process. When it did this, the Noetic Soul was freed of its task, the forces of darkness were locked-up, and the key was thrown away. With a divine right to choose, the humanoid beings governing our galaxy chose to remain mortal and not pursue immortality.

E – Earth Monad Project

The galactic powers at be chose this path to extinguish the darkness and evil that was ravaging the galaxy and declared that humanoid life in the galaxy would be forbidden to pursue the prime directive of the Noetic Soul until such a time that the civilizations in the galaxy had evolved far enough to reapproach the prime directive of the Noetic Soul in a more intelligent and controlled manner.

It worked. The galaxy quickly transformed and went through a golden era of peace and great prosperity.

Millions of years later, the Earth today is a "controlled" project to go through that psychosomatic process.

It's called the Earth Monad Project.

The way in which the Earth Monad Project eventually came about was not by any galactic governing council finally deciding to allow a humanoid civilization on a select planet undergo the process. Far from it. The quantas share that the way the Earth Monad Project eventually arose was through a "great rebellion." The story of that rebellion is interweaved unconsciously in much of our mythology.

The project underway on Earth in the physical universe is a project to achieve a unity between divinity and creation in human bodily form and to awaken the temporal group mind of the Earth. The cosmic law forbidding the pursuit of the Monad is based on the sound logic that unevolved humanoid beings pursuing the Monad—pursuing a godlike state of being—is likened to a child playing with fire—or an unevolved-being being given fire (story of Prometheus).

The Earth is a rare exception. The process today is being allowed to play-out under strict safety measures and protocols, but it's being allowed to playout only after a long war fought between cosmic factions battling over the right for the Noetic Soul to pursue its prime directive. The project is believed to have actually begun on Mars, or the planet that was once the asteroid belt (Tiamut), and only later moved to Earth in recent cosmic time after both Mars and Tiamut were destroyed by forces enforcing the cosmic law. The lost history of humanity from ancient Mars to Earth today is a great cosmic soap opera involving a series of allowed, or invoked, planetary cataclysms.

Earth Monad Project – E

The great risk of creating a humanity with the ability to pursue the Christ Monad is that this genetic design allows the human mind to interface with a set of extremely powerful primeval forces of creation. One of these forces is the quantum force of IAO. IAO is the quantum of awareness within the Cosmic Mind which is a dimension of the Cosmic Christ Monad. The ability of the human mind to interface with the quantum of IAO is a double-edged sword. The issue is that the Cosmic Mind is a manifesting power of creation. Whatever we hold and project in our minds toward it, it multiplies, manifests, and makes real. This power can manifest either good or evil, and historically, whenever a human race had been created in the physical universe with this ability, it almost always became evil with destructive consequences to itself and to other neighboring humanoid civilizations who were benevolent.

This is the source of a major on-going cosmic dilemma.

In order to fully integrate the human mind with all the forces of divinity and creation to reconstitute the Monad, the human mind must possess this interfacing ability. Absent this ability, we cannot reconstitute the Monad within the realms of creation.

So, the dilemma is, on one hand we have a divine-given mandate to fulfill the will of the Father and reconstitute the Monad. This is the prime directive of the Noetic Soul. On the other hand, if we are allowed to exist with the latent ability to interface with the primeval forces of creation to fulfill the will of the Father, then there is a good chance we will fall into evil and destroy ourselves and others as well.

This is why other neighboring humanities consider the Monad "The Forbidden Fruit."

The human race currently living on the surface of the physical Earth "has eaten the forbidden fruit," meaning, we have been given life with the ability to interface with the primeval forces of creation. In light of this knowledge, the book of Genesis should be reinterpreted and studied as an artifact of the collective unconscious attempting to tell us about these universal truths through mythology.

E – Earth Monad Project

Now that we exist with this ability, the ability cannot be denied. We have no choice but to live with it and use it to fulfill the will of the Father and fulfill the prime directive of the Noetic Soul.

Thus, we have to go through darkness to reach the light when interfacing with the primeval forces of consciousness to achieve the unity because that is how it happened at the cosmic level of creation.

The same solution—which is the one and only solution—is now being repeated and passed down through each level of creation via the force of Alpha (The Law of Sympathetic Vibrations – The self-organizing force of the universe.) The solution is, we must allow the geometric pattern of unfoldment to take its full course. That course first unfolds through darkness before entering the light.

We are destined to contend with the potential for evil, delusions, and suffering emerging in the world, as the reintegration process follows the Alpha Wave pattern—while at the same time we strive to rise above it all. The cosmic quanta share with us that if we stay the course, we will eventually win—just as Eloah eventually won. We just need to remain steadfast and make our light shine in the darkness.

Now that we know the backstory, we can discuss more specifically the story of Earth and what is actually going on.

The Earth story has two emerging sources of information, one, the cosmic quanta, which reveals the mystery of creation and the Monad, and two, the human story which has unfolded as a result. I am completely clear on one, the mystery of creation and the Monad, however, humanity must work together to complete the puzzle of, two, the human story which has unfolded as a result.

We have some big puzzle pieces of the human story from which we can formulate the following hypothesis:

In recent months (early 2019), I have been learning that it is slowly becoming more and more scientifically evident - that most stars in the universe may produce what is called *Recurrent Novae.* Most of the public is already well aware of a *Super Nova,* which is when a star explodes producing a new solar system. Well, we are

Earth Monad Project – **E**

now learning from the scientific community that there are lesser levels of novae where a star explodes only its outer shell but remains intact as a star. It's called a *Stellar Nova* versus a *Super Nova.*

Stellar novae are typically *Recurrent Novae,* meaning the star's outer shell explodes on a repeating cycle. It makes sense, it fits into the grand design of a system that continually creates, destroys, and re-creates. Stars exist within the planetary spectrum, not the cosmic spectrum. Until a celestial body achieves a Planetary Monad, then that celestial body is subject to the cycle of creation and destruction.

Four key points: (a) Recurrent novae are extremely cyclical and accurate. You can set your clock based on the recurrent nova of a star. (b) If the Sun has a recurrent stellar nova cycle, the geological records of the Earth, the Moon, and all the bodies orbiting the Sun would have fingerprints indicating the recurrent nova cycle. (c) Some researchers are suggesting that the last high-technology human civilization on Earth was destroyed by the recurrent stellar nova of the Sun. The stellar nova could have melted the ice caps causing the great flood which would have been a great "flash" flood. (d) This would mean we have a solar catastrophe / re-creation cycle in our solar system, and we are always running down the clock to the next recurrent stellar novae event.

Based on this added information, lets now make a few suppositions:

It is only logical to assume that most technologically developed humanoid civilizations in the universe would build and live within subterranean cities on their home worlds to survive the recurrent nova cycle of their host stars. Perhaps this is a common practice for most sentient humanoid life throughout the physical universe. Perhaps the surface of most worlds with super advanced humanoid life doesn't have modern cities and large populations like our own, but rather the surfaces of these worlds are kept as gardens.

Perhaps the Garden of Eden is the surface of the Earth and Eden is the Earth itself.

E – Earth Monad Project

Because the Earth is a *Monad Development Planet*, which is a highly risky sociological genetic humanoid project, perhaps the Garden of Eden (the surface of the Earth) is being used as the laboratory to conduct and carry out the Monad experiment. The advantage of using the surface is that the surface is wiped clean periodically by the recurrent novae of our Sun. If the project goes awry or just needs to be destroyed, the Sun takes care of this on its own through its natural course and rhythm.

Under this evolutionary model, only humanoid civilizations which are intelligent enough to become spacefaring are able to survive and reproduce. The universe only wants intelligent species spreading throughout the universe. This is how the universe evolves.

From the perspective of those living inside the project, there are two humanities, the one living it, and the one guiding it. The one guiding it is not seen as human. It is seen as "alien." But there are actually two levels of the humanity guiding the project. The physical beings guiding the project from off-world, and the primordial beings guiding the project from the higher vibrational primordial universe.

The beings guiding the project off-world in the physical universe are noetic humanoid beings just like us here on Earth, with the only difference that their physical bodies and minds are not capable of psychosomatically engaging in the development of the monad. The darkness is locked away inside them. They are seen as beings of light, but it's more of a *gathered light*, than it is a *completed light*.

In today's current round of the Earth Monad Project, these physical off-world alien beings are utilizing a highly developed sentient AI to guide the levels of "interfacing" required between the humanoid beings inside the project and the humanoid beings outside the project. The famous gray aliens are organic AI robots with no sex organs that are designed to systematically carry-out the program.

Although the Monad development must occur organically, not engineered, the alien AI periodically jumps the DNA of the "monadal" human beings on Earth within targeted windows that don't violate the organic process—it accelerates it.

Perhaps just before each recurrent nova event, the DNA of the current generation of monadal humans is harvested for the next more advanced generation. Perhaps this is the underlying purpose of the "Alien Abduction" phenomenon.

It appears that the DNA harvesting program has finished. Alien abduction reporting has decreased dramatically. Is this an indication that the harvesting is complete, and the next solar event is imminent?

Under the scenario I'm describing, the Earth is managed as a "galactic penal colony" under a strict system of checks and balances and a highly advanced system of controls.

It is my belief that this system of checks and balances was not in place in the previous solar rounds which led to a war between alien factions and the ultimate destruction of the humanoid project on Earth in the last—and previous rounds. The humanoid project was eventually restarted, and the "galactic penal colony" control system was instituted as a result of a treaty between worlds. As part of this treaty, the AI administers the program, not other organic beings, who in prior rounds, sexually interacted with the humans inside the project.

This sexual interaction creates multiple problems for the project including off-world Noetic Souls outside the program getting pulled into the program unwittingly, and the contamination of monadal blood with non-monadal blood. It is forbidden for monadal blood to exist off-world as the pursuit of the Monad is forbidden off-world. Also, monadal blood inside the program should not be diluted with non-monadal blood. It dilutes the ability of the Noetic Soul to reconnect with the divine source while incarnated in bodily form.

Past physical alien beings on Earth also knew that the Noetic Soul reincarnated along bloodlines and purposely established hybrid bloodlines inside the Earth project so their Noetic Souls would reincarnate inside the project. The aliens established these hybrid bloodlines and called them "royal blood." Royal blood reincarnates alien beings from other more advanced star systems. The aliens who established the royal bloodlines did so with the intention that these beings would rule the Earth—and were guided into positions of power.

E – Earth Monad Project

The project is leading toward the creation of a mythical super being on Earth in the physical universe, who mirrors in likeness, the completed cosmic celestial being, Eloah (Cosmic Monad). All human beings already exist in this completed state in the primordial universe on Earth. We are all now trying to repeat this awesome feat of creation on Earth in the physical universe.

The creation of a physical godlike superbeing is the ultimate purpose of the Earth Monad Project. No one race is exclusive in this endeavor. Every race on Earth is participating in this project.

Perhaps the prophesized rebuilding of the temple of Jerusalem is really an emergent mythology of the planetary group mind echoing our mission to reconstitute the Monad within creation here on Earth in the physical universe. The temple is the Monad. The messianic age is the time period after the completion of the Planetary Monad. It is the emergent period of human evolution. Currently, humanity on Earth in the physical universe is in the prelescent period.

Based on information arising out of the "disclosure" community, a segment of the human population on Earth in the physical universe already knows there is a major alien guided project underway on Earth, and they know a major aspect of the project deals with the harvesting of our DNA. A popular name for this segment of society has become known as the *Breakaway Civilization.*

Based on all the information gathering conducted by the disclosure community, this is what can be summarized and reported about the Breakaway Civilization:

The breakaway civilization / group has ongoing contact with extraterrestrials (ETs). It knows the Earth is under a major threat. It appears they may know the threat is twofold:

1.) Threat from a segment of extraterrestrials who wish to end the Monad project on Earth due to its threat to all other civilizations throughout the galaxy.

2.) Threat from the recurrent novae of the Sun.

Earth Monad Project – **E**

The ETs are helping the breakaway group to stand up technologically to defend itself against the hostile alien threat and to prepare for the coming stellar novae event. The breakaway group possesses technology hundreds of years beyond the technology of the rest of humanity on Earth. It knows the true history of the Earth and the true history of the solar system. It knows all about the ancient builder race. The Moon race was a race to recover lost technology. The breakaway group is not governed by the known and elected governments of the world. The breakaway civilization is run by a secret organization composed of private companies, defense contractors, and intelligence agencies. The breakaway civilization is funding its technology projects, and its underground city projects, through the redirection of money, materials, and services out of the surface world economies. The breakaway group knows the surface world humanity in the physical universe is destined for destruction with the next stellar nova event. This is why the secrecy persists.

Ezekiel's vision of God (the Logos) and his plan. *Giuseppe Longhi, Milaan 1776-1831.* The sky is Heaven. The angels here represent the resonance with the love of God, the Spirit. The animals represent creation being lifted in harmony with the Spirit. Each winged animal in this vision is a different race or generation of humanity on Earth. The human being is a sacred vessel within which creation and divinity are married and reconciled. The wings represent the noetic side of the human being. The animal body represents the erotic side of the human being. This is a vision of the Earth Monad Project.

E – Earth Monad Project

Prometheus is the story of the Earth Monad Project. Prometheus is the immortal soul of "The Only Begotten Son of God" - the Noetic Soul (Human Soul). His quest to reconcile creation with divinity to reconstitute the Monad is akin to giving humanity fire. The process ties the Noetic Soul to a rock. The rock is the mortal body we must raise up. The eagle eating the liver is the suffering we endure during the process. The liver regrows and the eagle comes each day to eat the liver reflecting the continuous reincarnation of the Noetic Soul. We're freed when the process is finally complete. We become Hercules, the Christ Monad (seen in the rear of the image).

A modern vision of the Earth Monad Project in the book Concerto of the Rising Sun. *Artwork by Montage à la Bira*

<u>Closing Statement on the Earth Monad Project</u>

The Human Soul (Noetic Soul) is not the cause of the darkness. Humanity is actually the divine Father's answer and solution to the darkness of creation. It is why we experience suffering in this world. We suffer to lift up the world out of darkness and bring it into the light. The Noetic Soul is the light that the Father sends into the darkness to engage it and lift it back up into unity with God to save all of creation.

In this world evil is real.

I say, "this world," because the truth is, evil is a creation of the mind, and the mind is a product of creation.

Evil is not part of the one true ultimate reality which is the uncreated divine source. Evil is a living force in the darkness that seeks to subvert, confuse, and delay the integration process. It would have humanity believe that it is the Human Soul itself that is the problem; that the Human Soul (Noetic Soul) is imperfect and sinful and that we must submit to a false higher power to be redeemed, thereby giving up our power and submitting to unending indentured servitude. It would have us renounce our indominable position as the only begotten son of God, the immaculate conception of the Father, and hand this position over to an idol that we must kneel down to worship to save our soul. This is all to slow down the unity process. It cannot stop the unity. It can only make it slow down or start over. While it slows it down, it reigns for a brief period as a false god.

Beware of the Gorgon.

It lies behind all of it.

Every religion of the world has fallen prey to this evil.

It hides where you would never think to look, and it walks among us in sheep's clothing. It pretends to be holier than thou but is actually heinous and malevolent. It fools the world with great deeds while building armies on opposing shores.

It will continue to do this until mankind comes to exist no more.

However, if we endure, its time upon the Earth will be short, and what will eventually arise will be — a new world.

E – Echelons

Echelons *[E-che-lons; Eh-Shuh-Laans]*

The Echelons are the primeval forces of creation in their very early state of formation immediately following the moment Ain Soph gives rise to them, but before they are reconciled and reconstituted within the new stabilized and reunified Christ Monad. This reconciliation occurs at the cosmic level but remains to be reconciled at the planetary and individual levels.

The process of regression the alchemist undergoes while reconstituting the Monad compels the conscious mind to witness and familiarize itself with the primeval forces of creation.

Regressing toward our original state in Ain Soph, the thirteen levels of the mind now exist in an early state of formation preceding their more structured planetary formation. This early formation is what immediately followed the collapse of the wave function, and appears as soft divisible wavelengths of light, not structured levels of mind; therefore, at this stage of regression, they're called Echelons.

There are thirteen Echelons that organize concentrically like a ring of stars. The more the alchemical process of symphysis harmonizes the mind's resonance with Ain Soph, the more the Echelons converge inward leading to only one indivisible wavelength of invisible light (restored wave function).

The Echelons move inward together thirteen times into higher and higher symphonies. The thirteen Echelons together comprise the hidden eighteenth bandwidth. When we collapse the eighteenth bandwidth, we finally awaken in our primordial body in the primordial universe while remaining awake in our physical body. At this point, the Monad is complete.

Ego

The Ego is the sense of self emerging in the human mind. The self in most people is fragmented and not well expressed due to an asymmetry existing between the automated features of the mind arising out of the matter of the brain and the conscious awareness arising out of the soul. It is a collision between consciousness and matter. Out of this collision, the authentic-self (Noetic Soul) arises only partially clear. Other aspects of the authentic-self remain tangled and twisted in the mind by the collision. The tangled and twisted aspects of the authentic-self emerge distorted, as their own separate fragmented shards of the overall self, like shards of a broken mirror. The broken shards are called the "False-Selves" or "Psychological Elements." The false-selves are behind many of the perturbing moods of the mind. By focusing on each false-self, or psychological element, in contrast to the Spirit, we can transform them and liberate the authentic-self. The more we liberate the authentic-self, the more the ego consolidates its authentic expression and becomes individuated.

Elemental

An Elemental is the internal psychic essence—or mind—of an animal—or the presence of a lifeforce animating a seemingly inanimate object such as a mineral or a plant, but in an awakened state; meaning, it resonates with the Spirit of God in some manner. When the temporal essence of an element is dormant, the essence is only "Essence." Once the essence is liberated and awake, the awakened essence is recognized as an "Elemental."

The psychic essence, or mind, arises from the pairing of the Erotic Soul running through all of creation with the body of the animal, plant, or mineral. The Elemental does not reincarnate in the physical universe such as the Noetic Soul. The Elemental lives in the physical universe only once but continues to live for all eternity in the primordial universe. When the physical body of the animal, plant, or mineral perishes, its primordial body pulls the elemental consciousness into the primordial universe where it continues to reflect the existence it once lived in the physical universe for all eternity but in a glorified paradisiacal state. It becomes an angelic being ebbing and flowing within the Sea of Eros underlying all of creation. The Sea of Eros, or Eternal Sea, is another name for the Erotic Soul. Many cultures speak of Elementals in their mythological lore. According to the famous alchemist, *Paracelsus*, there are four categories of Elementals: (1) *Gnomes*, corresponding to the soils of the Earth; (2) *Undines*, corresponding to Water; (3) *Sylphs*, corresponding to air; and (4) *Salamanders*, corresponding to fire.

Emergent

When a force of consciousness (cosmic quanta) can express itself clearly through the conscious mind, this is considered "Emergent." Emergent is counter to that which is considered "Suppressive." When the Noetic Soul emerges to express itself clearly through the mind, it is identified as the Authentic-Self. When automated programs of the mind inhibit the natural expression of the authentic-self, or any force of consciousness, this is considered suppressive.

Emergent Period

In the emergent period of human evolution, the faculty of super cognitive emotional awareness emerges as the leading faculty of the human mind. When this is finally achieved, all other faculties of the mind are brought together to function as a unified mind. The faculty of super cognitive emotion unifies the mind by way of a supernatural empathy arising between the forces of consciousness when they become aware of each other and enter resonance. Resonance is a supernatural empathy or super sensory familiarization between all things which transcends all dimensions of time, space, and mind. It is innate to the soul. Resonance is the medium of our super cognitive faculties of intraspection and the divine language of Kier. It is the fountainhead of all gifts and all abilities. When the human race on Earth in the physical universe enters the emergent period, the temporal sphere of the planetary group mind of the Earth will become aware and resonant with the spiritual sphere of the planetary group mind of the Earth, and by way of this resonance between spheres, become resonant with the forces of the divine source, thereby completing the Planetary Monad. The emergent period is represented mythologically by the collective unconscious as the messianic age. When this period finally arrives, it will not be of a religious nature. It will be completely rational and scientific. In the emergent period, mainstream science will possess a rational understanding of the forces of consciousness in how they interact with matter and give rise to all of creation.

Emotion

Within the domain of divinity known as the Absolute, the divine Father communicates empathically through a sonar-like resonance. This resonance is the love of God—the Spirit. The Spirit is the origin of what we call Emotion. Common human emotion is a lower manifestation of its original divine form. Common human emotions are the everyday emotions which arise in the human psyche through perception and automated instinct as functional artifacts of the evolutionary mechanics programmed in the human brain to promote the survival and reproduction of the species. Common human emotion is a lower manifestation and echo of the original system of feeling and resonance (Spirit) within the domain of divinity.

Super cognitive emotion is a faculty which emerges when the human being relearns how to use the original resonance system of consciousness to communicate with the forces of the cosmic quanta underlying the fabric of reality. Super cognitive emotion utilizes the original system of feeling and resonance within the domain of divinity. Super cognitive emotion arises from a profound awareness between the interaction of the forces of consciousness within the human being. In a fully developed state, super cognitive emotion brings forth Turiya, which is a sustained awareness of the love of the Spirit as well as a feeling of oneness with God and the use of the language of consciousness called Kier. (See Kier and Turiya).

E – Emotion | Empyrean

Over time, the subtle communication between our conscious mind and the emergent forces of the cosmic quanta develops into a new super cognitive faculty called intraspection. This is not introspection. Introspection takes place solely between your own thoughts. The faculty of intraspection—as opposed to introspection—develops our super cognitive emotional capacity and vise versa. The longer we are able sustain a heightened resonance between our conscious mind and the Spirit, the more the physical wiring of our brain is re-wired to support and deepen the resonance. Intraspection is a communication between the conscious mind and the emergent forces of the cosmic quanta. The Spirit is the first to emerge.

As we continue the Third Factor practice of quantum meditation alongside other practices of the Three Factors, additional forces within the cosmic quanta—beyond the Spirit—begin to emerge and present themselves. As we develop our super cognitive ability to communicate with the cosmic quanta; prayer, quantum meditation, and intraspection, all come together to resonate as one.

Empyrean *[Em-py-re-an; Em-pee-ree-uhn]*

The three highest heavens of the Earth, which together form the upper Treasury of Light, are not ascended in succession like the heavenly realms within the lower and middle Treasuries of Light. Exotically different from the lower heavens of the Earth, the three highest heavens together form a divine constellation of heavenly forces which are ascended together in harmonious conjunction. Their names are Barstow, Jenesis, and Erawan. Together as one, they are the Empyrean. The three highest heavens are like three great celestial bodies of light all converging upon the same central core. The closer they converge upon the core, the more they shine as one. This convergence is the Constellation of the Three Heavens. They mirror the Divine Trinity of Ain Soph. The three highest heavens of the Earth have both an individual expression and a unified expression. Humanity has been given the ability to relate to the Divine Trinity

Empyrean | Epsilon – **E**

both separately or all together as one. The three heavens of the Upper Treasury of Light maintain their unique bandwidths, but while held in constellation, they are compelled to organize, align, and triangulate their forces upon the central Nexus, and harmonically combine their frequencies to produce a magnetic field called the Harmonic Bridge.

Epsilon *[Ep-si-lon; Ep-suh-laan]*

When the Alpha Pattern is mitigated by design, thereby artificially augmenting the path of evolution, a new quantum wave pattern emerges called Epsilon. Epsilon eventually collapses. It does not lead to the Monad (unification of the mind). Only Alpha leads to the Monad. Most humanities in the Milky Way Galaxy promote their continued existence through an Epsilon wave formation; however, they are all living on borrowed time, and they know it. It is possible that the Epsilon Wave pattern is a necessary geometric formation which helps the Alpha Wave pattern reach its goal in the unification of the mind. The Epsilon Wave formation would allow a conscious mind to differentiate itself in order to guide itself. On a higher level, it creates an observer-observed relationship within the evolutionary process of nature itself. It allows a humanity to step outside of itself to help itself. It separates the humanity inside the project from the humanity outside of the project. This principle may very well be a key element to the success of the Planetary Monad Project. In this scenario, Epsilon would function as a geometric sub-pattern in support of the overall Alpha pattern. Epsilon may not be just a clever way of side-stepping the will of the Father, it may be what is actually necessary in order to fulfill it. In a paradoxical way, the effort devoted to escaping the process (unification of the mind), is what ultimately finally delivers the process and fulfills the prime directive. This principle holds true in many cases in life. Often, it's the people who come out of nowhere to rebel against the status-quo that show the established orthodoxy and mainstream academia where they're getting it all wrong. Sometimes we need a fresh unconditioned and unencumbered look at the problem. It usually comes when and where we least expect it.

E – Erodao | Erodonic Trinity

Erodao *[Er-o-dao; Eer-oh-dow]*

Erodao is a special geometric Alpha pattern which spans lifetimes. The sole purpose of Erodao is to prepare us for the Third Mountain. Erodao emerges as a pathway at the end of the Second Mountain when it's been detected by the self-organizing forces of Alpha that the temporal dimensions of our mind are not reaching critical mass in resonance with the Divine Soul. Alpha does not give up on the alchemist. Instead, Alpha adjusts its own organizational pattern and charts out a new course to the Third Mountain. This new course guides the Noetic Soul to reawaken in its primordial body in between lifetimes in the primordial universe where the recoiled dimensions of the mind are immersed inside a super elevated level of resonance with the Divine Soul. When the Noetic Soul reincarnates in its next physical existence, an elevated empathetic connection with the Divine Soul is drawn into the temporal dimensions of the new temporal-physical mind-body system. This elevated level of resonance with the Divine Soul ultimately enables the alchemist to achieve the prerequisite level of resonance with the Divine Soul to compel Alpha to allow his or her entrance into the Third Mountain.

Erodonic Trinity *[Er-o-do-nic; Eer-oh-dah-nik]*

Inside the Eros-Dyad, there are four fundamental forces which are three embedded inside one. The four forces are: (1) IAO, the awareness within Eros; (2) The Erotic Soul, the lifeforce within Eros; (3) Matter-Energy, the energy of Eros; and (4) the Mind. The Mind encapsulates and attempts to reconcile the first three forces to a single unit of one as a mirror of Ain Soph. The three forces embedded inside the mind are called the Erodonic Trinity.

The forces of the Eros-Dyad are conceived spontaneously and automatically by the infinite force of the Spirit. The Spirit is the third principal force within the Divine Monad of Ain Soph. Within most units of one, therein lies a trinity.

Erodonic Trinity – E

Within the Divine Monad of Ain Soph, the trinity within is composed of (1) the Father - the divine awareness, (2) the Divine Soul - the divine lifeforce of the Father, and (3) the Spirit - the divine love of the Father. All three forces within the Divine Trinity are infinite and exist as the only non-permutated permutations of consciousness within the pantheon of forces within the cosmic quanta – meaning, they always existed as differential abstracts within the divine Monad. The infinite force of the law of one to reconcile the three infinite forces back to a unit of one is what gives rise to what we call "consciousness" and the advent of creation.

Because the Eros-Dyad emerges spontaneously, it initially emerges in darkness. A will of the Father is expressed by Ain Soph to bring the Eros-Dyad back into harmony with the divine source. This will conceives a trinity called the Sacred Trinity or Lower Trinity. The awareness within the Sacred Trinity is the Logos, the lifeforce within the Sacred trinity is the Noetic Soul, the energy is the Numina—the Father's love for creation.

The principal forces involved in the unfoldment of creation are the same principal forces mythologized by the popular characters in most world mythologies. These characters, and the stories they tell, emerge unconsciously into all creative fields including literature, poetry, art, and music.

In Egyptian mythology, IAO is Set, and the Logos is Osiris. The story of the death and resurrection of Osiris is the story of creation which continues to repeat until this very day at the quantum level within all things. In the applied practice of alchemy, the same story echoes and repeats on an individual level to re-constitute the Monad. This is the integrated mind, the complete human being.

Creation begins spontaneously, but in order to complete itself, it requires the intercession of a conscious mind to become self-aware of all the forces involved. This self-awareness brings all the forces of creation back into harmony with Ain Soph. This new unity is Christ. The complete human being and Christ are one and the same.

E – Erodysis

Erodysis *[Er-o-dy-sis; Eer-o-die-sis]*

Erodysis is the love of Christ. It has the power to transform any and all things and confer immortality. It is the Elixir—the Philosophers' Stone in a liquid state. Liquid meaning, the energy of Christ's love. Erodysis is the reorganized and reharmonized energy between matter and Spirit arising with the reconstituted Monad between divinity and creation. The original divine Monad which precedes creation is Ain Soph. The new reconstituted Monad which saves and reconciles creation is Christ. Christian mythology represents something much more profound than the literal interpretation of that mythology. Within almost every unity in nature therein resides a trinity.

The trinity within the original divine Monad of Ain Soph is:

1.) The Father (Awareness)

2.) Divine Soul (Life)

3.) Spirit (Love)

The trinity within the new reconstituted Monad of Christ is:

1.) Dominus (Awareness)

2.) David (Life)

3.) Erodysis (Love)

The Rose symbolizes creation being lifted up into resonance with divinity. It symbolizes completion of the Great Work and the fulfillment of the will of the Father. It symbolizes Erodysis and the completion of the Monad.

Eros-Dyad – E

Eros-Dyad – Dyad *[Er-os-Dy-ad; Eer-os-Die-add]*

The Eros-Dyad is the first born from the original Divine Monad (Ain Soph) to become the second of existence. The word Dyad means second, secondary, or two. The origin of the word Dyad is Greek. The word Eros is joined with the word Dyad because Eros is the Dyad. Eros is the force of creation.

Inside the Eros-Dyad, there are four fundamental forces which are three embedded inside one. The four forces are: (1) IAO, the awareness within Eros; (2) The Erotic Soul, the lifeforce within Eros; (3) Matter-Energy, the energy of Eros; and (4) the Mind. The Mind encapsulates and attempts to reconcile the first three forces to a single unit of one as a direct mirror of Ain Soph. The three forces embedded inside the mind are called the Erodonic Trinity.

The Eros-Dyad has four forces which are three embedded inside one. The three are the second set of three, after the divine trinity, together comprising the first six principal forces of consciousness. The one force that the second set of three resides inside—is the mind. The mind emerges in scales encapsulating the second set of three forces into a single unit of one as a direct mirror of Ain Soph. Within the Cosmic Mind resides all of creation.

E – Erotic Soul

Erotic Soul

The Erotic Soul is the second of three principal forces within the Erodonic Trinity which emerged inside the Cosmic Mind at the first moment of creation. The Erotic Soul [1] is the lifeforce of IAO. IAO is the Godhead and first principal force of the Erodonic Trinity. The Cosmic Mind emerged as the vessel of the Erodonic Trinity forming a new created realm of reality divergent of the original non-created realm of reality within the divine source known as (Causal 'A,')

The created realm formed by the Cosmic Mind is known as "Causal 'B.' All universes of creation, including the primordial and physical universe, exist inside Causal 'B.'

The emergence of sexuality arose out of the joining of IAO and the Logos at the quantum level within all things. When the Logos and IAO first reconciled, the process of creation expanded into three major fractal scales. The three scales are (1) Cosmic, (2) Planetary, and (3) Individual. In the physical universe, the cosmic level was reconciled at the very beginning of time, but every planetary sphere including all the stars and planets, and every individual being, continues-on their own path toward reconciliation.

---

[1] Apollo and Daphne symbolize the Noetic Soul of the Logos and the Erotic Soul of IAO. Alpha compels them to join and bring forth Christ to complete the process of creation.

Erotic Soul – E

In the primordial universe, all three scales have all achieved reconciliation. In the primordial universe the Erotic Soul has been lifted out of darkness on every level of creation.

In the physical universe, the Erotic Soul has been lifted out of darkness at the cosmic level. This is the reason behind the profound beauty in much of creation, including within many of our animals. However, aspects of the Erotic Soul still persist in darkness in the planetary and individual levels of the physical universe. This is why not everything in nature in the physical universe is beautiful. This is why we have some animals that are deadly and horrific in form.

It is the Erotic Soul which animates all organic life including all the animals and all plant life. The Erotic Soul also flows through all the minerals and elements which comprise the basic building blocks of the universe. Human life and animal life are different in that the organic machines of both are animated by the Erotic Soul, but only human life incorporates the Noetic Soul within the mind.

The Noetic Soul is the intercessing principal between divinity and creation. The animals are reconciled at the cosmic and planetary levels of creation but only the human being is reconciled at the individual level of creation. The individual level of creation compels the planetary level to reconcile.

The animals are lifted-up and reconciled indirectly by virtue of the spiritual process of all human life on the planet which the animals share. Unlike the Noetic Soul, which is individually reflected in each human being as its own individualized Noetic Soul, the Erotic Soul only exists once. All of creation is animated by only one Erotic Soul. Each animal does not have its own Erotic Soul. Every animal shares the same Erotic Soul. However, each animal does form its own individualized mind. Every individualized animal mind exists as an extension of the Erotic Soul and collectively forms what is called the Sea of Eros. All created lifeforms within the animal, plant, and mineral kingdoms, ebb and flow out of the Sea of Eros (The Eternal Sea). The Sea of Eros exists non-locally below the fabric of our known physical and primordial reality. It can be visited and known via quantum meditation.

E – Eternal-Primordial Being

Eternal-Primordial Being – Primordial Body

A human being's Eternal-Primordial Being is the parallel twin being to a human being's Temporal-Physical Being. The primordial body of your primordial being resides in an unseen a higher frequency primordial universe that parallels the physical universe.

The physical universe is coiled up inside a black-hole-singularity inside that same primordial universe. The physical universe and primordial universe are separated by a singularity wall that no wavelength of light can pass through. Only consciousness can pass through it. This is why the primordial universe remains undetected by current physical technology—yet it is still experienced by various people in near-death experiences. When the physical body dies our consciousness passes through to the other side of the singularity wall.

Long before having a mortal physical body, you had an immortal primordial body. Long before being born into a physical body in the physical universe, you lived in your primordial body in the primordial universe. Your primordial body is still alive. It lives inside eternity. Your primordial body is eternal and is therefore "immortal." Your physical body is temporal and is therefore "mortal."

In the physical realm, our being passes through time. In the primordial realm, time passes through our being. Time still exists in both places; it just operates differently. The highest state of existence is where a high degree of a sympathetic resonance is gained between the physical and primordial whereby the physical is elevated to a position just outside of time and becomes—immortal. This state of matter is neither primordial nor physical; it's called metatronic.

The body of Christ is metatronic.

Again, you have always had your primordial body. It is immortal. When your physical body dies, you will eventually re-awaken in your primordial body in the primordial universe. You will remember your current physical existence much like a dream that you experienced in the physical universe. Your primordial body is essentially dreaming your current physical existence right now as you read this.

Eternal-Primordial Being – E

The same Noetic Soul animating your primordial body stretches into the physical universe to animate your physical body. It does this repeatedly. The reason the Noetic Soul reincarnates is not because of what many people believe. Many people believe it is to work on the Human Soul / Noetic Soul to help it grow spiritually. This is wrong. This is an egocentric view. This is what has been fed to you to trap your mind and hold you back from realizing your true potential. Your Noetic Soul is already perfect. You are not coming into the physical universe to experience a physical life to improve your soul.

The physical creation (temporal mind body system) is imperfect, not you. Your Noetic Soul enters a physical body to lift-up its vibrational resonance to a closer vibrational resonance with the divine source with which your soul already has a natural sympathy.

Your primordial body has already been lifted to achieve a re-unified sympathetic resonance with the divine source to achieve the Christ Monad in primordial form. You are now trying to repeat this same feat of creation in the physical universe, life-after-life, not just for you, but for the benefit of all humankind.

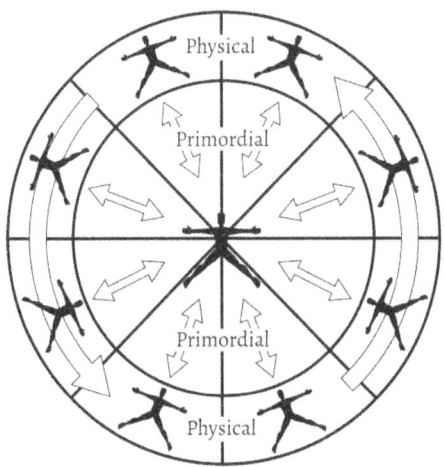

We live on a wheel. We only ever have one primordial body, but we have many physical bodies life-after-life that spin around the axis of our primordial existence.

E – Eternal-Primordial Being

The Noetic Soul is the intercessing principal between creation and divinity. The Noetic Soul's presence alone lifts the physical created form. Your Noetic Soul's effect on your own physical DNA indirectly affects the planetary group mind of the Earth, and this effect stays with the planetary group mind even after physical death.

This symbiotic exchange is used by the planetary group mind in the continuous elevation of the human genome across the entire human species on Earth until eventually achieving a re-unified resonance with the divine source from which everything emerged.

Contrary to some beliefs, you were never once an animal or a lower-level species. Animals are animated by only the Erotic Soul. Human beings are animated by the Erotic Soul and the Noetic Soul. Your true essence is the Noetic Soul. You have always been human.

The primordial body is the central body within an eternal primordial matrix of creation. The primordial body has five other satellite ethereal bodies called the spiritual ethereal bodies. Each function as a separate dimension in the primordial sphere of the mind. The physical body is the twin body to the primordial body. The physical body is the central body within a temporal physical matrix of creation. The physical body has five other satellite ethereal bodies called the temporal ethereal bodies. Each function as a separate dimension in the temporal sphere of the mind.

See the diagram at the end of this section.

This next paragraph explains the diagram.

The figure-eight is composed of the primordial body on top and the physical body on the bottom. The upper lighter hemisphere is the primordial universe. The lower darker hemisphere is the physical universe. The five upper rays each represent one of the five spiritual ethereal bodies. The five lower rays each represent one of the five temporal ethereal bodies and each gradient within each ray represents one of the stages of alchemical transformation (Dark, Fire, Gold) before reaching the light. The inner circle around the figure-eight represents the grand celestial body of light (metatronic body) which forms when all the bodies come to resonate as one.

Eternal-Primordial Being – E

When the physical body dies, the Noetic Soul initially finds itself inside its temporal ethereal bodies experiencing one illusion after another. The Noetic Soul must discharge its temporal ethereal bodies after death by transcending the illusions which they harbor. If not, we are immediately returned to a new physical body with our old temporal ethereal bodies intact. After the Noetic Soul discharges its temporal ethereal bodies after death, it is re-absorbed back into its spiritual ethereal bodies. At this point, the Noetic Soul reenters and experiences the ethereal realms of heaven. Many reach this point when they have a near death experience (NDE). If the Noetic Soul is not sent back to its physical body, then at this point, the primordial body recollects its spiritual ethereal bodies, and we reawaken in our primordial body in the primordial universe. When we reawaken, we remember everything, and we are relieved and overjoyed to be back in the eternal paradise of the Earth in our immortal body. This is Shambala, Eden, and the Celestial Jerusalem. It is Hyperborea.

The physical level of each existence comes and goes with the birth and death of each physical body. The primordial manifestation of each existence remains forever imprinted inside the eternal-primordial realm. In the primordial realm, we are able to move between a number of primordial existences, or primordial realities, which reflect each physical existence we once lived in the physical universe. The primordial universe is a wonderful eternal realm that is dual reflecting of the physical universe.

Seraphim

E – Eternal-Primordial Being

The seraphim, or seraph, is a historical symbol of the primordial being resonating with the Divine Soul. The six wings of the seraphim symbolize the six bodies of the primordial being.

The primordial being, along with other forms, resonates with the Divine Soul, and through that resonance becomes a personification of the Divine Soul—the lifeforce of the Immortal Beloved (Christ). The twelve bodies are as follows:

Temporal-Physical Being		Eternal-Primordial Being
1.) Physical Body (Central Body)	7.)	Primordial Body (Central Body)
2.) Vital Temporal Ethereal Body	8.)	Vital Spiritual Ethereal Body
3.) Emotional Temporal Ethereal Body	9.)	Emotional Spiritual Ether. Body
4.) Mental Temporal Ethereal Body	10.)	Mental Spiritual Ethereal Body
5.) Instinctive Temporal Ethereal Body	11.)	Instinctive Spiritual Ether. Body
6.) Vision Temporal Ethereal Body	12.)	Vision Spiritual Ethereal Body

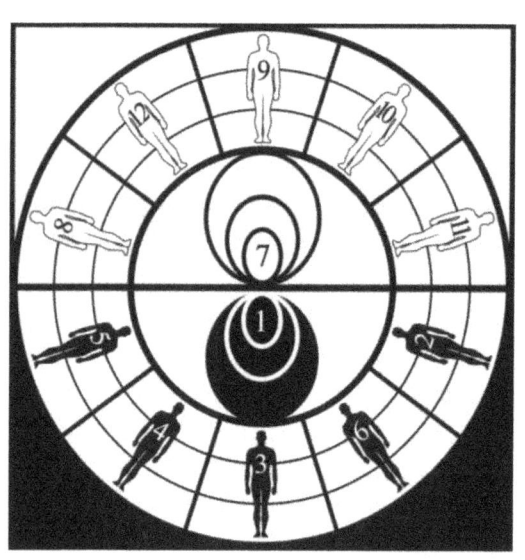

Eyad – **E**

Eyad *[Ey-ad; Eye-Add]*

Within the psyche of man, the Eyad represents a higher level of evolutionary development beyond Ego where the authentic-self has finally awoken in the psyche to question its own perception of reality and has become semi-conscious of its fractured mosaic reflection in the mirror of its mind. It innately seeks the liberation of its real being, Ain Soph, from the forces of the mind which suppress its free and unfettered expression. Initially, the Eyad is unaware of what it is that it is seeking or trying to liberate. The Eyad is the final stage of a human species' prelescent period of evolution. The Eyad also has a low luminosity sense of the cosmic quanta within its conscious mind. It feels a sense of God but is unable to explain it or accurately describe it. A person with an Eyad, versus an Ego, has many special gifts. The developmental stages leading to the Monad are spectrums of development, not milestones, and correspond to both our individual development and to the evolutionary macro development of our species spanning great periods of time. Because our human species has been specifically selected for the development of the Monad, its evolutionary pathway and stages of development are unique and different from a humanity which does not share a similar evolutionary pathway. Our humanity on Earth is still well within the Ego spectrum of its Monad development. However, a small percentage of our population is already moving into the next spectrum which the Logos calls the Eyad. Some key factors which differentiate the Eyad from the Ego are as follows:

(1) The Eyad has a true calling to discover and realize its true-self, Ain Soph. The Ego lacks this calling. (2) Beneath all the Ego defense mechanisms which the Eyad still possesses, the Eyad authentically seeks a closer relationship with God. To the contrary, the Ego seeks a closer relationship with only the illusion of God as another means of protecting its mind from stress, fear, and anxiety. An Ego's belief in God amounts to only another Ego defense mechanism. Most of our humanity on Earth in the physical universe

E – Eyad

falls in this category at the moment. (3) The Eyad seeks wholeness and integration, whereas the Ego seeks to validate, rationalize, justify, and reconcile its current level of existence with the illusion of the world. (4) The Ego seeks comfort whereas the Eyad seeks transcendence. The Eyad aspires to be greater. (5) The Ego questions its reality. The Eyad questions its perception of its reality.
(6) Only the Eyad can climb the Three Mountains. The Ego cannot compel Alpha to emerge. Alpha emerges only for the Eyad. Why? because the Eyad authentically seeks Ain Soph. The Ego thinks it seeks Ain Soph, but what it really seeks is another Ego defense. There are three major periods of maturation within the Eyad spectrum:

1.) An Eyad who is in the First Mountain (Apprentice) is an Early Eyad.

2.) An Eyad who is in the Second Mountain (Journeyman) is a Late Eyad.

3.) An Eyad who is in the Third Mountain (Foreman) is a Full Eyad.

F

False-Self – False-Selves

False-Selves are disfigured aspects of the authentic-self (Noetic Soul) emerging in the mind in a twisted or distorted manner due to the collision between consciousness and matter in the formation of the human mind. This occurs through the imperfect process of creation. The twisted aspects emerge like broken shards in a mirror due to the authentic-self not being able to clearly transmit through the prism of the mind. Each broken shard in the mirror is a different false-self. The false-selves are also referred to as Psychological Elements. There are literally thousands of false-selves (psychological elements) within the human psyche. The false-selves exist in the noetic sphere of the mind and are behind many of the perturbing moods of the human psyche. They are not part of the spectrum of darkness in the erotic sphere of the mind. The erotic sphere is the domain of the id.

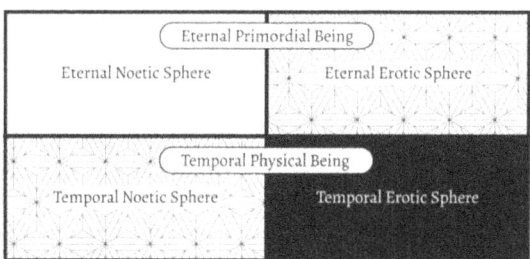

It is through the perturbing moods of the human psyche that we begin to discover, isolate, and understand each false-self. The self-observing capacity of the conscious mind has the ability to differentiate and realize each false-self by isolating each of them through the practices of alchemical meditation. Each false-self can be alchemically transformed through the contrasting light of the Spirit, whereby the authentic-self emerges free and clear.

Father, The

The Father is the eternal awareness and godhead of the Divine Trinity residing within the original Monad of Ain Soph. Ain Soph exists at the center of all things. Collectively—between all things—it composes the Cosmic Consciousness. The three dimensions within Ain Soph and the Cosmic Consciousness are Awareness, Life, and Love.

The Father is the Awareness within the Cosmic Consciousness. The Divine Soul is the Life within the Cosmic Consciousness. The Spirit is the Love within the Cosmic Consciousness.

The three divine forces of the cosmic consciousness, and forces of the cosmic quanta, in general, have no gender. The Father is called such out of tradition and because he holds the seed of all creation.

The human mind anthropomorphizes the cosmic forces into masculine and feminine forces to make them more relatable. It's important to note this because these associations arise unconsciously into all our myths. The forces in line with the Spirit (love) we tend to equate feminine characteristics, such as the Spirit, Matter-Energy, Gorgon, Erotic Soul, and the Numina. The forces we tend to associate masculine characteristics are the Father, the Divine Soul, IAO, the Logos, Noetic Soul, and Idamus.

Similar or Equivalent Terms:
Brahma (Hinduism), Keter (Kabbalah), Ancient of the Days, Old Heaven, Old Father. (Christ is the New Heaven, New Father).

First Factor

The First Factor (Transformation) is a psycho-cognitive process of splitting the human mind into the observer and observed to compel the elements of the mind to transform and integrate into a cohesive unified mind. The process isolates the fragmented constructs of the mind to compel their transformation via the force of the Spirit (Love of God). When an element of the mind transforms, an aspect of our authentic-self emerges and joins the observer in the center of our being. There are thousands of elements which need to be observed and transformed.

First Mountain – Mount Sophia

Mount Sophia is the first of three mountains in the alchemical process of completing the Christ Monad (Philosophers' Stone). The three mountains are the three major Alpha patterns which guide the conscious mind in the alchemical integration process. Alpha is the self-organizing force of the universe. It is the law of sympathetic vibrations in motion. Alpha unfolds in geometric patterns guiding all things toward an ultimate unity with God. The Alpha patterns are universal. They repeat as echoes of the same organizational patterns which completed the process of creation at the cosmic level infinite eons ago in the deep eternal past. The focus of the First Mountain is to learn the Three Factors and to practice them correctly and consistently. If we do, Alpha accelerates within us until all twelve of our bodies vibrate at a much faster rhythm thereby granting us access to the Second Mountain. This milestone is known as the Alpha Convergence. At the fifth grade of the First Mountain, Alpha moves us from the many-lifetime spiral path where we traverse all three mountains simultaneously, to the single-lifetime straight path where we traverse all three mountains sequentially.

First Sanctum

A sanctum is a point of stillness and consolidation within the forces of Alpha. It is a necessary stage in the process of leading all the forces of the mind, body, and consciousness toward a unified mind – the Monad. The First Sanctum is the sanctum residing between the First Mountain and Second Mountain.

The Alpha Wave pattern produced by the forces of Alpha in the process of developing the Monad includes three major development periods called the Three Mountains. The Monad development process also includes Three Sanctums. The Three Sanctums are between the First and Second Mountains, the Second and Third Mountains, and just below the summit of the Third Mountain. There is a fourth sanctum at the summit of the Third Mountain but at this point the Monad has already been formed.

F – Five Centers

Five Centers

The five centers are the psycho-neuro conduits by which psychological material rises out of the three cognitive levels of the mind to find expression at the surface of our mind.

The concepts of the Five Centers, Self-Observation, and the Three Factors, were all part of a school of thought called the Fourth Way.

The teachings of the Fourth Way stem from Gurdjieff but trace their ultimate root to the Sufis in Central Asia who reportedly taught Gurdjieff. Self-Observation was also widely studied and practiced by Wilhelm Wundt, one of the founding fathers of modern psychology.

The psychological content of your mind which you can self-observe within you emerges from the five centers of your mind. Every mood you experience has a manifestation in each of the five centers. You must go deep inside every mood relative to each center of the mind while in a state of meditation and learn about the mood at a level which transcends your ability to express it in words.

Alchemically, the transformation process taught by Gurdjieff, Ouspensky, and other followers of their school of thought (The Fourth Way), is incomplete. The missing key ingredient in the alchemical transformation process is the inclusion of the Spirit to contrast against the element of the mind we are seeking to transform in the process of liberating our authentic-self. Once the Spirit is added into the alchemical process, transformation is fast, deep, profound, and eternal.

The five centers are: (1) Intellectual Center – Located in the head. Corresponds to the temporal ethereal mental body. (2) Motor Center – Located between the shoulder blades. Corresponds to the physical body. (3) Emotional Center – Located in the heart area. Corresponds to the temporal ethereal emotional body. (4) Instinctive Center – Located in the abdomen. Corresponds to the temporal ethereal instinctive body. (5) Sexual Center – Located in the genitals. Corresponds to the physical body and temporal vital body.

There is also a higher set of centers corresponding to the physical being's higher twin self. This higher twin self is the primordial being. The primordial being also has 5 centers. These centers are not temporal, they are spiritual. They correspond to the spiritual ethereal bodies.

Gurdjieff mentions the superior emotional center and the superior intellectual center. These centers correspond to the system of 5 centers within the spiritual ethereal bodies. In the spiritual ethereal emotional body, we process Super Cognitive Emotion. In the spiritual ethereal mental body, we process Super Cognitive Thought.

Foreman

In the alchemical process of reconstituting the Monad, a Foreman is an alchemist climbing the Third Mountain. The main objective of the Foreman [2] in the Third Mountain is the integration of the erotic side of the human being with noetic side of the human being. When we integrate the erotic and noetic sides of our being, the physical and primordial sides naturally self-assemble and integrate to complete the Christ Monad.

---

[2] Atlas symbolizes the Foreman. Atlas is the Foreman "Planet Lifting." Planet lifting is the alchemical process of incrementally lifting one's level of resonance with Ain Soph.

F – Foreman

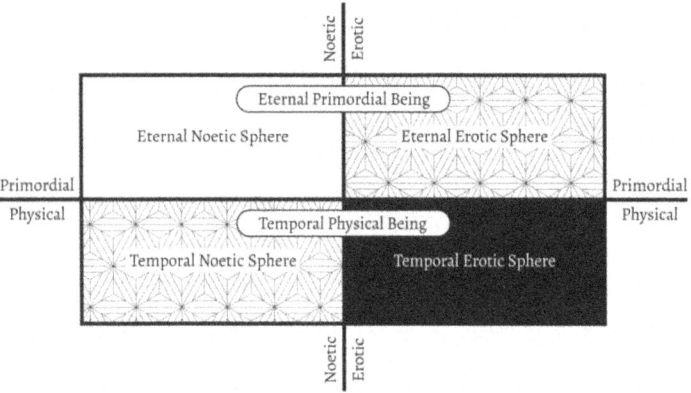

When people cooperate with the force of Alpha in a subconscious manner, they reincarnate life-after-life in lockstep with the rest of humanity on the planet to achieve the same goal. This slow, many lifetime approach is called the Spiral Path.

When people wake-up to the process Alpha is guiding them upon, and decide to cooperate with it, the process speeds up within them and they can complete the Monad in one lifetime. This accelerated approach is the Straight Path. When the Straight Path emerges, Alpha directs the conscious mind of the person through three major stages in development of the Monad known in hermetic lore as the Three Mountains. An alchemist in the First Mountain is an Apprentice. An alchemist in the Second Mountain is a Journeyman. An alchemist in the Third Mountain is a Foreman.

When on the Spiral Path, the human being traverses all three mountains simultaneously. We experience flashes of each mountain throughout the course of our life. This occurs over many physical existences in lockstep with all human beings on Earth.

When on the Straight Path, the Three Mountains separate, and we climb each mountain sequentially, one after the other.

Ironically, climbing the three mountains sequentially is faster than climbing them all together as one.

The later in life we begin the Three Mountain journey, the faster we move through them due to the accumulation of our current life experiences and realizations.

G

Genesis – Summary of Creation

A popular theological belief is that the original unity of God (Ain Soph) created the universe because he was alone. Meditation on the quantum forces within us reveals that this was not the original cause. Quantum meditation reveals that the original act of creation occurred in three primary stages:

Stage 1: Creation was originally sparked into existence spontaneously and unintentionally by the force of love (The Spirit) produced by the awareness of Ain Soph (The Father) being aware of his own living lifeforce (The Divine Soul). *See: Dynamis*

Stage 2: The Father became aware that the Spirit of his love had sparked creation into existence, but that creation was stuck in darkness because this spark of creation happened unintentionally without his awareness.

Stage 3: The Father's realization of his creation compelled (Thelesis) a love for his creation to arise (Numina) and a will (Logos) to save it. The lifeforce of this will is the Human / Noetic Soul. The Logos, Noetic Soul, and Numina form the Sacred Trinity. Together, they are the immaculate conception of the Father.

The creation process unfolded in a repeating pattern of scales. The first scale to emerge was the cosmic. The cosmic scale of creation was saved, or reconciled, at the very beginning of time. A new unity emerged between Ain Soph and creation. This new unity is the Christ Monad on the cosmic scale. It is the Cosmic Christ (Eloah). When the new cosmic unity was finally realized and achieved, sexuality emerged within all living things as a reflection of the original coupling of Love and will in the alchemical creation process. All duality is a reflection of the original creation process and the Father's will (Logos) to bring creation back into unity with his divine source. Darkness-Light, Odd-Even, Hot-Cold, Female-Male, Negative-Positive, are all a reflection of the original cosmic creation process. This process is now repeating on the Individual and Planetary levels of creation. It is repeating in scales. The Father sent the Noetic Soul into the world by force of his will to lift up creation back into unity with his original divine being. Your creation is your mind and body. You will keep coming into the world until you fulfill the will of God (The Father). See Theokinesis for a detailed explanation of the creation process.

Germain

Germain is the liberated and authentic dimension of the temporal group mind of the Earth. This planetary intelligence has already achieved a degree of liberation and exists beyond Maub (dark side of the temporal group mind) as a glorious being of light and joy. Not all of the temporal group mind of the Earth is in darkness. Most human beings on Earth live with at least a partial degree of their Noetic Soul being free of their automated instinctive psyche, and this dimension of the temporal group mind reflects this reality.

Utilizing the language of consciousness (Kier), this being's name is translated to Germain. Germain reminds us of a jolly-o lumber jack with a larger-than-life nature and a great sense of humor. He was shown to have great compassion for the human condition, but at the same time he also chuckled at the follies of our human nature.

This is a reflection of humility, not arrogance, as a trait of a truly humble person is being able to laugh at himself in the mirror while reflecting upon his human character.

Every time an individual on Earth liberates an aspect of his or her authentic-self, an aspect of Maub is also liberated from its planetary darkness and Germain grows stronger, brighter, and more active in the planetary sphere of the Earth.

Eventually, once Maub is fully liberated, Germain (temporal liberated being of the Earth) will integrate with EL (primordial being of the Earth) to complete the Earth's Planetary Monad. The quantum of Germain (intelligence within the temporal group mind) shares that once enough individual human beings on Earth complete their own Individual Monads, this will compel and ignite the Planetary Monad and then the rest of humanity will follow. Germain calls this initial group of human beings who will ignite the Planetary Monad, The Children of the First Light. *(See Children of the First Light)*

God

There is a God and there is a God-Above-God. The God-Above-God is Ain Soph—the original divine Monad. *See Ain Soph.*

Creation and its matter spontaneously arise from the infinite love generated by Ain Soph. A will emerges from within Ain Soph to reunify creation with its eternal, everlasting, divine being and form a new Monad so that creation may continue onward and last forever.

The new Monad brings a new order to creation under the umbrella of a harmonized Cosmic Mind with divinity. This is God, otherwise known as Christ, Eloah, Allah, or the Immortal Beloved. *See Christ.*

At the quantum level of existence, we discover a complete set of living forces referred to as the Cosmic Quanta; together, they comprise the pantheon of God for which Ain Soph is the innermost.

Ain Soph is the being of one's being residing at the center-of-center within all things. It is the ultimate truth and ultimate reality. It is pure awareness, the essence of life, and the source of infinite energy. Its energy is the Spirit of its infinite divine love.

The three attributes of —awareness, life, and love— together compose the original divine Monad of Ain Soph which precedes everything, and always was, and always will be.

 It is the original triune.

The existence of Ain Soph is paradoxical, as it cannot be explained rationally by a system governed by the laws of time and space. It is from the original divine Monad that all things stem forth.

G – Gorgon, The

Gorgon, The – Lilith, Kiraphon, Magog, Beast of the Earth

The Gorgon is the second of two sides of the "Id Complex."
The intelligence embedded in the id is twofold. The right side is called the "Idamus," the left side the "Gorgon." The Idamus feels a sense of emptiness and fear and desires fulfillment. In response to fear, the Gorgon arises as the dark champion narcissistic-self offering delusional constructs to the mind to assuage the fear.

All sociopaths and psychopaths are narcissistic, but not all narcissists are necessarily sociopathic or psychopathic. The key difference between sociopaths and psychopaths is that sociopaths are made, psychopaths are born.

The delusions of the Gorgon arise in an attempt to bring a cohesion to the mind. It tries to form a dark pearl or an anti-Monad (false cohesion). The Gorgon often succeeds in developing a degree of false cohesion but is also prone to spontaneous self-destruction.

The Gorgon gives rise to what is worst in human beings. Both sides of the human being are compelled to develop a unity of mind. The will of the Father (The Logos-The Light) compels the noetic side. The erotic side is compelled spontaneously and automatically (Darkness). If the noetic side does not heed the calling, then eventually, the erotic side will over-run the mind.

Many have sought to elevate the human condition from a variety of angles. The key is not analytical understanding, learning how to cope, or even religion. The key is a conscious and willful engagement in the process to integrate both sides of the human being (Light and Darkness) in the development of the unified mind—the Monad.

The Gorgon and the Idamus, which together form the id complex, arise from the forces of the Erodonic Trinity underlying both. The Idamus arises from the lifeforce or second principal of the Erodonic Trinity, the Eternal Sea, the Sea of Eros, the Erotic Soul. It arises due to an interfacing between the human mind and the Erotic Soul.

Gorgon, The – G

The Erotic Soul is the lifeforce of IAO. IAO is the Godhead of the Erodonic Trinity. Idamus is the first beast, the Beast of the Sea with Ten Horns (See Book of Revelation).

The Gorgon arises out of the energy or third principal of the Erodonic Trinity, Matter-Energy. Matter-Energy initially emerges in darkness and chaos due to its spontaneous creation. Fear is the spirit of darkness, the antithesis of love. When the mind interfaces with the unintegrated matter-energy of the physical body (matter in darkness), fear naturally rises in the psychic cognitive background of the human mind. The Gorgon rises out of the matter-energy to assuage the mind with narcissistic delusion.

If allowed by the mind, this dynamic brings a false cohesion to the mind and sets in motion several potential pathological complexes. The Gorgon is the second beast—the Beast of the Earth. (*See Book of Revelation*).

The Gorgon and the Human Personality

The Gorgon rises-up through the mind via the human personality. Human beings actually have a choice in how their personalities develop. People subconsciously model their personalities based on what they observe in the world around them and subconsciously select character traits which they admire. People select traits which they feel will help them integrate socially and give them an evolutionary advantage. When the Gorgon arises within the mind, it arises with a permission given to it by the mind.

The personality is an interfacing medium between the person's inner-self and the outside world.

When the person's authentic-self can transmit clearly through the personality, the personality is considered "Natural."

If the personality becomes weaponized as an ego-defense mechanism, thereby suppressing the natural and clear transmission of the authentic-self, the personality is considered "Adaptive."

G – Gorgon, The

The Gorgon side of the id complex compels the adaptive personality to form. The adaptive personality is a pathological formation of the mind. All personality disorders exist somewhere within the adaptive spectrum. The most pathological end of this spectrum is the narcissistic personality. Alchemically speaking, the narcissistic personality is a delusional fake-persona which rises-up and consumes the entire mind and personality of a person suppressing the authentic-self. It becomes its own living entity with its own separate will and way of thinking. It even has its own IQ, and its own psychosomatic influence on the physical body.

The narcissistic adaptive personality is at the extreme end of the adaptive personality spectrum. Narcissists are typically incapable of engaging in alchemy as they have lost positive control over their minds. Their dark-champion Gorgon personality rules their mind. If the alchemist has an adaptive personality (dark-champion – Gorgon mind) which has been continually reinforced throughout life, he or she faces the most difficult psychological complex to contend with.

Ironically, the dark-champion adaptive personality (Gorgon Mind) brings a form of cohesion to the temporal mind. It develops a dark pearl. The dark pearl is the antithesis of the goal of the alchemical work. It is a false cohesion. It prevents a true integration of the mind.

The Gorgon is a path of doom. We cannot serve two masters. You must choose between the Divine Soul and the Gorgon. You cannot fool God. You cannot have both. There is still hope for narcissists if they wish to overcome their affliction. The key to overcoming narcissism is becoming aware of and saying good-bye to the dark champion personality (Gorgon) and allowing the authentic-self (Noetic Soul) to experience fear without losing the light of mind.

It is possible, believe it or not, that narcissists can reach so far as entering the Void at the end of the Second Mountain because the affliction involves the id complex and the personality, not the false-selves or automated instincts. However, unless the narcissist corrects

Gorgon, The – G

this issue, he or she can never begin the Third Mountain. The reason is, in order to climb the Third Mountain, we must entrust our emotional well-being to the Divine Soul, not to some dark champion narcissistic personality (the Gorgon).

The collective unconscious of the planetary group mind of the Earth continually re-broadcasts the narcissistic dark champion within world mythology. In the world of Greco-Roman mythology, the dark champion of the mind is symbolized as the Gorgon. Medusa is one of the three Gorgons. She turns people into stone. The three Gorgons represent the three main forms of narcissism. These classifications keep adjusting in the modern world. The consistent classifications are Overt, Covert, and Malignant. The three Gorgons also reflect the phenomenon of multiple personality disorders.

The Gorgon on the planetary level is Gaia. She remains to be reconciled. She is the darkest bandwidth within Maub.

When the Gorgon Dark Champion intervenes, who is in charge of the mind? Idamus is still in charge. Idamus compels the rise of the Dark Champion (The Gorgon). The Dark Champion places the mind under complete control of Idamus.

Do not be fooled by the Dark Champion's position in the mind. Idamus pulls all her strings. The Dark Champion (The Gorgon) is an eleventh permutation. It is the child of Idamus. It rises out of fear, not out of love. It is an apostate and abomination of the mind.

Multiple Personality Disorder is someone with multiple Dark Champions, all of which stem from the Gorgon. Ironically, many self-proclaimed "Masters" of the Great Work are nothing more than Gorgons. The Gorgon is the third head of chaos of Cerberus. The three heads of Cerberus are Satan, Idamus, and the Gorgon. The two beasts are also Gog and Magog, Satan's helpers. What the Roman Catholic Church identifies as demonic possession is when a person loses positive control of his or her mind to the id complex. It is a psycho-spiritual condition. It is not purely psychological, and it is not purely spiritual.

G – Gorgon, The

Idamus arises from the second principal force of the Erodonic Trinity (Life Force). The Dark Champion Gorgon arises from the third principal force of the Erodonic Trinity (Matter-Energy). In every trinity, the first and second permutations together compel the rise of the third permutation. Fear is induced by the destitution of life of the Idamus. The Gorgon is an extension of the Idamus. Together, Idamus and the Gorgon form the id complex.

Although the narcissistic personality may never actually arise in a person and steal the light of mind, the underlying Gorgon quantum and its impulse are still there and must be dealt with by all alchemists. There are bandwidths within Maub which correspond directly to the Idamus and the Gorgon exclusively. The Gorgon bandwidth within Maub is Gaia. These planetary bandwidths compel the rise of both beasts within all human beings on Earth. Resonance with the Father elevates the human mind beyond these dark forces.

It is believed that Idamus—as the leading force of the id complex and father (compeller) of the Gorgon—is the root cause behind many pathologies of the human mind.

After forming the Nuad, the alchemist is more prepared than anyone to deal with Idamus and any pathologies of the id, which are:

1.) The Adaptive Narcissistic Personality (Beast of the Earth)

2.) Narcissistic Personality Disorder (Far end of the spectrum)

3.) Paranoia

4.) Obsessive Compulsive Disorder

5.) Delusion

6.) Dementia

7.) Schizophrenia and Borderline Personality Disorder

8.) Multiple Personalities and Demonic Possession

9.) Post Traumatic Stress Disorder (PTSD)

Most likely more pathologies could be added to this list.

Gorgon, The – **G**

The Number 666

"This calls for wisdom: let anyone with understanding calculate the number of the beast, for it is the number of a man. Its number is six hundred and sixty-six."

The repeating sixes is the Beast of the Earth (The Gorgon). The meaning of the repeating sixes and why it applies to the Beast of the Earth, is twofold:

1.) The repeating number pattern refers to the repeating compounding processes of creation. This means the beast of the earth, the Gorgon, is a product of creation.

2.) The reason six is used in the repeating number series is because the beast of the earth is the product of matter-energy compounding in on itself within the mind.
It is the product of the human psyche compounding in on itself. Before the reconciliation of creation, the human psyche is the sixth permutation of consciousness and is the dark inflection of the Noetic Soul.

666 is the mark of the modern-day person.

G – Gorgon, The

Gorgon Symbolism

This is the bust of Medusa, part of Greek Mythology. The Gorgon is the Dark Champion of the human mind, the Narcissistic Self, the Second Beast which rises from the Earth. Its number is 666. The Gorgon is also the Whore of Babylon.

The Name of the Second Beast

The first beast, the beast of the sea, is Idamus. The name Idamus is derived from the Freudian name Id because they refer to the same thing. The name for the second beast is adopted from Greek mythology. The second beast, which rises from the Earth, who is the dark champion narcissistic self, child of Idamus, and whose number is 666, is the *Gorgon*.

The word Gorgon comes from the Greek word *gorgos*, which means *dreadful*. In Greek mythology there are three Gorgons, one of which is Medusa. The Gorgons are said to be female, which is apropos to the narcissistic self since it rises out of the brain matter of the physical body (the Earth). Matter-Energy is the third principal of the Erodonic Trinity and a super partner to the Spirit and the Numina, all of which are symbolized by the feminine—the personification of love. In this case, it is the inverted dark inflection of love. The Gorgon is the furthest thing from love. It is the furthest thing from God.

Gorgon, The – G

The Two Beasts

Idamus is the first beast which rises out of the Sea of Eros. The Gorgon Dark Champion narcissistic personality is the second beast which rises out of the Earth. The Earth is the neurological brain chemistry of the physical body. The second beast rises out of consequence of the first beast. The second beast is the child of the first beast. The second beast hates and is terrified of the first beast. Their relationship is not based in love but in fear. The first beast has a deep dark sexual nature. It covets the lifeforce of others to compensate for its own lack of life—its mortality. It is dark but not necessarily twisted. The sexual nature of the second beast is both dark and twisted. The second beast, in response to the first beast, mocks and abuses sexuality and is deeply sexually conflicted. It secretly hates sex. When the Gorgon narcissistic personality takes over the mind, this is the anti-Monad or anti-Christ. Lies, deceit, and cruelty are normal and customary for the Gorgon mind. In the Book of Daniel, the Gorgon is the little horn growing up with the tenth horn.

Sex for the second beast is not about eroticism. It is about power, ego, and control. The most severe pathologies, including cannibalism, arise out of the second beast (the Gorgon). The second beast is narcissistic, selfish, profoundly superficial, idealistic, shallow, shortsighted, and materialistic. It believes only in the material world and lying is natural and routine. The modern world worships the second beast, and those who manifest her, are most respected in business and in superficial mundane relationships. The mark of the second beast is its fakeness in the human personality; its lack of authenticity. All people subconsciously notice this mark and most people subconsciously honor it, abide by it, and trade by it.

"so that no one can buy or sell who does not have the mark, that is, the name of the beast or the number of its name. This calls for wisdom. Let anyone with understanding calculate the number of the beast, for it is the number of a man. Its number is six hundred and sixty-six."

G – Gorgon, The

The Four Beasts of the Book of Revelation

In the Bible's Book of Revelation there are four beasts. The four beasts are archetypal symbols of the Collective Unconscious. What do they represent within the human psyche of mankind?

1.) <u>A Leopard with 7 heads and 10 horns.</u>
    This is Idamus. Humanity's unconscious interaction with the cosmic lifeforce of the Sea of Eros manifests within the human psyche a personification of evil.

2.) <u>Has 2 horns like a Lamb. Talks like a Dragon.</u>
    This is the Gorgon. It has a humanlike appearance like the lamb but bears the mark of the beast with its narcissistic personality. The mark rises in the voice.

3.) <u>A Great Dragon with 7 heads and 10 horns.</u>
    This is Satan. Humanity's unconscious interaction with the Cosmic Mind of IAO generates the dark power of Satan to manifest evil on Earth.

4.) <u>A Lamb with 7 horns and 7 eyes.</u>
    The modern theological interpretation is that the lamb represents Jesus of Nazareth. This is only partly true. The whole truth is much more profound. The lamb represents the Noetic Soul which was begotten by the will of the Father to intervene with creation to save it and bring it back into unity with Ain Soph. The Noetic Soul is the sacrificial lamb which bears the suffering of the world to carry-out the will of the Father. Jesus is a personification of this principle.

See: Id and Idamus for more context and explanation.

Similar or Equivalent Terms:

Gorgon: Lilith, Kiraphon, Whore of Babylon, Beast of the Earth, Magog, Majuj, Dark Champion, the Snake in the Garden of Eden. Chaos, Number 666, Left Head of Cerberus.

Great Arcanum, The

The term Great Arcanum means Great Secret. In alchemy, Hermeticism, and in many ancient mystery schools, there is said to be a Great Arcanum which is the secret to the famous philosophers' stone and the secret of immortality. The philosophers' stone is the unified mind. It is the re-establishment of the Monad within the realms of creation. It is Christ. Only the forces of darkness strive to keep this truth a secret. The Great Arcanum is made up of three incredibly profound truths which the forces of darkness have gone to great lengths to conceal from the public. The Great Arcanum is:

1.) The Noetic Soul is the Only Begotten Son of God.

   The Only Begotten Son of God is not only one human being or only one historic figure on Earth. It is the Noetic Soul within every human being throughout the cosmos. There are three soul types which are: The Divine Soul, Erotic Soul, and Noetic Soul. The Divine Soul was not begotten. It has always existed as the divine lifeforce of the Father. The Erotic Soul was not begotten by the Father. It was begotten spontaneously by force of the Spirit. Only the Noetic Soul within human beings was begotten by the Father by force of his divine will to intervene with the spontaneous process of creation and reunify it with divinity. The Noetic Soul is the intercessing principal between divinity and creation. It enters the mind to reconnect the Erotic Soul back to the Divine Soul and complete the process of creation thereby forming the Christ Monad.

2.) The Noetic Soul has total authority on all matters of life and death.

   The Father has only one divine will. The force of that divine will immaculately conceives the Noetic Soul to establish a new unity between creation and divinity. Inseparable from that will, the Father has given total and complete authority over all of creation to his Only Begotten Son, the Noetic Soul.

G – Great Arcanum, The

3.) <u>The Earth was selected as a proving ground for the Christ Monad.</u> The process on Earth is being monitored and controlled under the umbrella of a special project called the Earth Monad Project. A planetary Monad project is a project where the Noetic Soul can carry-out its prime directive to form the Christ Monad and awaken the temporal group mind of a planet. It is a restricted process because the same process has repeatedly failed on other worlds causing great destruction in its wake. Because of its unsuccessful history, the creation of a human genome which provides the capacity for the Noetic Soul to pursue the Christ Monad has since been outlawed throughout the galaxy as the *Forbidden Fruit*. The Earth is a rare exception. The process is being allowed to playout under strict safety measures and protocols. With the power vested in the Noetic Soul over all matters of life and death within creation, great restraints on pursuing the prime directive of the Noetic Soul have been put in place by a galactic federation of noetic humanoid beings. When dealing with matters of divinity, paradoxes are the norm, not the exception. It is paradoxical that being charged by divinity with a prime directive to pursue the Monad that these very same beings would use their vested authority to not pursue it. But the will of the divine Father always finds a way. Nonetheless, the pursuit of the Monad is now being allowed on Earth, but only after a great struggle between factions to allow its pursuit, and not without a treaty of great restraints and a system of checks and balances.

The forces of darkness do not want humanity to know its true place in the universe which is at the right hand of the divine Father. Thus, the forces of darkness do everything in their power to confuse these facts including the deliberate confusion of religious dogma, the confusion of languages, and the turning of man against man. The power of the Noetic Soul has the innate and exceptional ability to re-unify creation with the source. The truth, power, authority, mission, and history of the Noetic Soul is the Great Arcanum.
It is not the light that keeps this truth a secret. It is the darkness.

Great Work, The – Magnum Opus

The Great Work is a term which arose historically to describe the alchemical process of developing the philosophers' stone which would then be used to turn base metals into gold. The alchemy of the philosophers' stone, in actuality, is the spiritual alchemy of the human being. It is not the alchemy of physical substances.

Alchemy has a very broad and rich history and is the origin of many of humanity's greatest inspirations, philosophies, and fields of study. The European alchemy of medieval history utilized a cryptographic language to disseminate instructions for the alchemical transformation of the human being. This was done to protect alchemists from religious persecution. This is why the actual process and deep spiritual meaning of the Great Work was concealed within what is historically called the Great Arcanum. The knowledge was forced into secrecy by the forces of darkness. It was by secondary effect that medieval alchemy compelled the rise of modern chemistry through its pursuit in laboratories to transform base metals into gold.

Alchemy's primary goal has always been spiritual.

The development of the philosophers' stone is a psychosomatic process within which the conscious mind of the human being is led through a process of regression, transformation, and self-realization. Over the course of a life-long alchemical journey, the regression process eventually leads the conscious mind all the way back to the ultimate source of all things. As a result of going through the process, the human mind unifies - thereby completing a cycle of creation which requires the cooperation of a conscious mind to complete itself. The unification of the mind brings forth the Christ Monad, otherwise known as the philosophers' stone.

The process is a universal process with paramount importance involving the natural process of the evolution of consciousness and the process of creation, divinity, and the Noetic Soul. It is of such great importance that its message is told and retold by the forces of the cosmic quanta themselves. It is for this reason that the lore of the philosophers' stone, and the Great Work to achieve it, holds so much weight in the collective consciousness of humanity as a whole.

G – Great Work, The

The Grand Alchemical Formula

Reported to contain symbolism of the Grand Alchemical Formula according to Rosicrucianism, this image is in Manley P. Hall's book "The Secret Teachings of All Ages," and is reportedly redrawn from "Museum Hermeticum Reformatum ET Amplificatum."

Great Work, The – **G**

Archetypes of the Great Work

This collage is composed of images of the Authentic-Self (Boy with Umbrella); Children of the First Light (5 Children); The Sea of Eros (The Wave); the Logos; Love of creation (The Elephant); The Numina (Blessed Mother of God).

Perhaps there is a double meaning behind the image of Adam and God by Michelangelo. Perhaps the image is unconsciously of IAO (left) and the Logos (right) compelled by the Collective Unconscious.

G – Great Work, The

Historic Figures of the Great Work [3]

Medieval European Alchemy produced some historic figures during its time. When you research these historic figures there is always a spiritual dimension to their story and work. A few notable alchemists:

Count of St. Germain (1691 or 1712 – 27 February 1784)

European adventurer who achieved prominence in European high society of the mid-18th century due to his interest and achievements in science, alchemy, philosophy, and the arts. St. Germain used a variety of names and titles, including the Marquis de Montferrat, Comte Bellamarre, Chevalier Schoening, Count Weldon, Comte Soltikoff, Manuel Doria, Graf Tzarogy, and Prinz Ragoczy. While his real name is unknown, and his birth and background obscure, towards the end of his life he claimed that he was a son of Prince Francis II Rákóczi of Transylvania. He is said to have made far-fetched claims (such as being 500 years old), leading Voltaire to dub him "The Wonderman," and that "He is a man who does not die, and who knows everything." Prince Charles of Hesse-Kassel is recorded as having called him "one of the greatest philosophers who ever lived." The best-known biography is Isabel Cooper-Oakley's, "The Count of St. Germain" (1912), which gives a biographical sketch. It is a compilation of letters, diaries, and private records written about the count by members of the French aristocracy who knew him in the 18th century. Another interesting biographical sketch can be found in "The History of Magic," by Eliphas Levi, published in 1913.

---

[3] Historic Figures of the Great Work is sourced by Wikipedia 2023

Great Work, The – **G**

John Dee (13 July 1527 – 1608 or 1609)

John Dee was an English mathematician, astronomer, astrologer, teacher, occultist, and alchemist. He was the court astronomer for, and advisor to, Elizabeth I, and spent much of his time on alchemy, divination, and Hermetic philosophy. As an antiquarian, he had one of the largest libraries in England at the time. As a political advisor, he advocated the foundation of English colonies in the New World to form a "British Empire," a term he is credited with coining. Dee eventually left Elizabeth's service and went on a quest for additional knowledge in the deeper realms of the occult and supernatural. He travelled through Europe and was accused of spying for the English crown. Upon his return to England, he found his home and library vandalized. He eventually returned to the Queen's service, but was turned away when she was succeeded by James I. He died in poverty in London and his gravesite is unknown.

Dee was a devout Christian, but his spiritual beliefs were greatly influenced by Hermetic and Platonic-Pythagorean doctrines pervasive during the Renaissance period. He believed numbers were the basis of all things and a key to knowledge. From Hermeticism he drew a belief that man had the potential for divine power and that this could be demonstrated through mathematics. His goal was to help bring forth a unified world religion by working to heal the breach between the Roman Catholic and Protestant churches and by recapturing the pure theology of the ancients.

G – Great Work, The

Paracelsus (1493 – 24 September 1541)
Philippus Aureolus Theophrastus Bombastus von Hohenheim

Paracelsus was a Swiss physician, alchemist, lay theologian, and philosopher of the German Renaissance. He was a pioneer in several aspects of the medical revolution of the Renaissance, emphasizing the value of observation in combination with received wisdom. He is credited as the father of toxicology. Paracelsus also had a substantial influence as a prophet or diviner, his prognostications being studied by Rosicrucians in the 17th century. Paracelsianism is the early modern medical movement inspired by the study of his work.

His hermetic beliefs were that sickness and health in the body relied upon the harmony of humans (microcosm) and nature (macrocosm). He took a different approach from those before him, using this analogy not in the manner of soul-purification but in the manner that humans must have certain balances of minerals in their bodies, and that certain illnesses of the body had chemical remedies that could cure them. As a result of this hermetical idea of harmony, the universe's macrocosm was represented in every person as a microcosm.

Paracelsus gave birth to clinical diagnosis and the administration of highly specific medicines. This was uncommon for a period heavily exposed to cure-all remedies. The germ theory was anticipated by him as he proposed that diseases were entities in themselves, rather than states of being. Paracelsus prescribed black hellebore to alleviate certain forms of arteriosclerosis. Lastly, he recommended the use of iron for "poor blood" and is credited with the creation of the terms "chemistry," "gas," and "alcohol."

H

Harmonic Bridge

The three heavens of the upper treasury of light of the spiritual group mind produce a special magnetic field called the Harmonic Bridge. The three heavens maintain their unique bandwidths, but while held in constellation with each other, they are compelled to organize, align, and triangulate their forces upon the nexus and harmonically combine their frequencies. This forms the Harmonic Bridge.

The alchemical process of integrating our temporal-physical being with our eternal-primordial being amplifies the harmonic bridge between our conscious mind and Ain Soph.

The harmonic bridge is a bridge of resonance spanning creation between the conscious mind and Ain Soph. The harmonic bridge spans Causal 'A' and Causal 'B.'

When we pass through the sphere of the Moon into the upper treasury of light, a magnificent halo of light is seen enveloping the Earth and its upper three heavens. This halo is the harmonic bridge emerging from the center of the planet connecting the primordial body of the Earth with Ain Soph. The primordial Earth is humming in resonance with the three divine forces within Ain Soph.

Heavenly Realms

The Earth in the physical universe has a twin. It exists in a higher vibrational mother universe called the primordial universe. We have both a physical Earth and a primordial Earth. The physical Earth exists in the same location as the primordial Earth, just at a different wavelength. They're separated by a singularity wall existing between both universes. Only consciousness can pass through.

H – Heavenly Realms

The planetary group mind enveloping the Earth has two great cathedrals, or two great concentric spheres with minor concentric spheres within each greater concentric sphere. Each greater concentric sphere is referred to as a hemisphere. One hemisphere encompasses the Earth in the physical universe. It's called the temporal group mind. Another hemisphere encompasses the Earth in the primordial universe. It's called the spiritual group mind.

The spiritual group mind subdivides into minor concentric spheres known as bandwidths which resonate closer to or further from the divine source of Ain Soph. Each bandwidth encompassing the primordial Earth is a heavenly realm.

There is an element of truth to all the mythological references.

The Noetic Soul and conscious mind of the alchemist transverse the heavenly realms of the Earth during the alchemist's ascent of the Third Mountain in the alchemical process of rebuilding the Monad within the realms of creation. This occurs because in order to lift-up creation into a unified resonance with divinity, the conscious mind must first become profoundly aware of the Father's resonance.

As Alpha guides the conscious mind through this process, our resonance with the Father is entered in grades. Each grade corresponds to a bandwidth of the spiritual group mind of the Earth, or heavenly realm.

The heavenly realms of the Earth are profiled in the book *Song of the Immortal Beloved*. The heavenly realms are ordered as follows grouped into Treasuries of Light and Kingdoms.

The heavenly realms start in the Middle Kingdom. Since the Lower Kingdom involves the first bandwidths of the spiritual group mind which have a mixed resonance with the temporal group mind, these bandwidths are not qualified as heavens. These bandwidths are relegated to the kingdom of purgatory.

Each heavenly realm corresponds to an angelic level of resonance with the divine Father.

Heavenly Realms - H

The heavenly realms are as follows:

1.) **Nirvana** – Middle Kingdom – Lower Treasury of Light – Angel
   [nir-va-na; neer-vah-nah]

2.) **Simmatuu** – Middle Kingdom – Lower Treasury of Light – Archangel
   [sim-ma-tuu; sim-muh-too]

3.) **Khimmadooree** – Middle Kingdom – Lower Treasury of Light – Principalities or Rulers
   [khim-ma-door-ee; kim-mah-door-ee]

4.) **Valhalla** – Middle Kingdom – Middle Treasury of Light – Powers or Authorities
   [val-hal-la; vahl-hah-luh]

5.) **Elysium** – Upper Kingdom – Middle Treasury of Light – Virtues or Strongholds
   [E-lys-i-um; ih-lizh-ee-uhm]

6.) **Terrasumna** – Upper Kingdom – Middle Treasury of Light – Dominions or Lordships
   [terr-a-sum-na; Tier-uh-sum-nah]

7.) **Barstow** – Upper Kingdom – Upper Treasury of Light – Thrones or Ophanim
   [bar-stow]

8.) **Jenesis** – Upper Kingdom – Upper Treasury of Light – Cherubim
   [jen-e-sis; jen-eh-sis]

9.) **Erawan** – Upper Kingdom – Upper Treasury of Light – Seraphim
   [er-a-wan; ear-ah-wahn]

The three highest heavens, Barstow, Jenesis, and Erawan, form the Empyrean.

H – Human Being

Human Being

The human being is a sacred vessel within which creation and divinity are married, reconciled, and unified. A human being is a living sentient being animated by the Erotic Soul and Noetic Soul. Most lifeforms in the cosmos are animated by only the Erotic Soul. The Noetic Soul is also known as the Human Soul because it is the Noetic Soul which makes a living being human. Any living being with a Noetic Soul is a being endowed with a human consciousness. It is not anatomy or planet of origin that makes someone human. Human is a function of consciousness.

The Noetic Soul is a primeval force of consciousness inherent in bringing order to the universe. Noetic humanoid life is therefore abundant throughout the universe and has been since the dawn of time.

The Noetic Soul is the life-force produced by the will of the divine Father. The Father is the awareness within the original divine singularity of Ain Soph. The Father manifests his will to save the Erotic Soul and re-unify it with the divine source.

The Erotic Soul needs to be saved and lifted back up into unity with the Father because of how the Erotic Soul is conceived. The Erotic Soul is conceived spontaneously by the force of the Spirit. This causes the Erotic Soul to emerge in darkness without the ability to find its way back to the source on its own. When the Father expresses his will to save the Erotic Soul, the power of this will gives birth to the Noetic Soul, the Only Begotten Son of God.

The prime directive of the Noetic Soul is to engage the Erotic Soul within the mind and body of creation and re-unify it with divinity to reconstitute the Monad and bring forth Christ.

I

IAO *[AI-O; Eye-O]*

<u>Summary Explanation of IAO</u>

IAO is the Godhead of the Erodonic Trinity and the guiding awareness within Eros (creation; the fourth permutation of forces). IAO is the first born of the Divine Trinity. However, IAO was born in darkness and chaos because he was born by the infinite power of the Spirit which conceived him spontaneously out of the source. He was not produced by the will of the Father. The Father is the Godhead of the original Divine Trinity.

The Erodonic Trinity gives rise to the Cosmic Mind.

IAO is the Godhead of the Cosmic Mind and all realms of creation within. After IAO was conceived, the Father became aware that the infinite power of his Spirit (Divine Love) had spontaneously given rise to IAO and that IAO was in darkness and chaos.

The Father saw IAO and loved him and willed that IAO should be lifted out of darkness and brought back into unity with the divine source. The rise of the Father's will gave birth to the three forces of the Only Begotten Son of God. The Only Begotten Son of God is a new trinity, the Sacred Trinity. It is the immaculate conception of the Divine Father. (See Sacred Trinity, Noetic Soul)

The Cosmic Mind today exists as part of the Cosmic Christ. Universally, the establishment of the Cosmic Christ Monad allowed for a reconciliation of the eternal-now of the divine Father with the distant-forever of IAO. The reconciliation gave rise to spacetime. It created a roadmap for the evolution of the universe to follow. It gave rise to the atom and the formation of all the galaxies. Finally, it allowed life to take hold.

I – IAO

One of the outcomes of the reconciliation between the Father and IAO that occurred on a cosmic level, is that the reconciliation needs to occur in three stages on three different scales: (1) Cosmic, (2) Planetary, and (3) the Individual (human being). The three stages are the Three Mountains—the three major Alpha cycles.

The reconciliation also led the way to the emergence of two universes of creation—the primordial and the physical. The reconciliation process already completed itself on all three levels in the primordial universe but so far it has only completed itself on a cosmic level in the physical universe. Every planet with life and every individual human being in the physical universe arrives in its own time. The physical universe, under the umbrella of the cosmic mind, is expanding forever horizontally to provide the divine Father infinite runway for his never-ending process of creation.

The purpose of the human being is to complete the process of creation on an individual level. This is accomplished psychosomatically through the intercession of the conscious mind becoming aware of all the constituent parts of the mind in contrast to the Spirit. It is a process of regression, realization, and transformation.

<u>Key Attributes of IAO</u>

1.) IAO is the Godhead of Causal 'B' and all of creation including the primordial universe and the physical universe. This is different from the Father who is the Godhead of the divine origin – Causal 'A,' the Absolute, and Ain Soph. Whereas the Father is the Godhead of the Cosmic Consciousness, IAO is the Godhead of the Cosmic Mind.

2.) Other names for IAO in his reconciled state with divinity is YHWH, Tetragrammaton, Jehovah, Yaldabaoth, and Ptah. YHWH is the mind of God in a glorified re-unified state. YHWH is the mind of Christ-Eloah. Other names for IAO in his dark state are Satan, Set, and Seth. Satan is the dark inflection of the mind of God when interacted improperly.

3.) Whatever we give IAO, it multiplies; good or evil. The mind of God is like fire. Know how to engage it—or be burned.

4.) In contrast to the Logos, every human being does not have their own IAO. There is only one IAO who applies equally to everyone everywhere within Causal 'B.' This mirrors the Father in Causal 'A' who equally applies to everyone everywhere.

5.) The dark inflection of IAO existed on its own before the great cosmic reconciliation with the Logos to organize all of creation. The universe today in its current state of organization, including the structure of the atom and all the laws of physics, is the outcome of that reconciliation on the cosmic level.

6.) When human beings today experience the dark inflected power of IAO (Satan) negatively influencing their lives, it is not of IAO's own making. Human beings cause the dark inflected force of IAO to arise in the way they interact with IAO on a deep cognitive psychic level. This is because IAO is an omnipotent power of creation. What you send to it, or offer it, multiplies in your life. If you give it evil, it multiplies evil. If you give it love, it multiplies love.

Because human beings on Earth in the physical universe exist with two unintegrated spheres of the mind (erotic and noetic), the dark unintegrated erotic side of the human being spawns evil when interacting with the power of IAO. The force of Theta (death) counteracts the forces of the erotic sphere thereby suppressing the mind's interaction with IAO. There are other unconscious buffer mechanisms in place involving various means of suppression including religious moral dogma and human-kind's own self-imposed ethical rules of moral conduct.

I – IAO

> The ultimate solution is not suppression or denial but rather a willful conscious engagement to integrate the erotic sphere of the mind with the noetic sphere. This is done in an organized process of alchemical integration (Three Factors) led by the self-organizing forces of Alpha.
>
> 7.) The great fall, and the mythology of "and a third of the angels fell with him," is a metaphor for how creation was spontaneously spawned into existence outside the will of the Father. Attributes of the Divine Trinity (Angels) were carried into creation mirroring aspects of its divine organization. This formed the Erodonic Trinity.

<u>Sumerian Mythology</u>

What we learn from IAO and the Logos about the process of creation has a striking parallel to Sumerian creation myth regarding the half-brother sons Enlil and Enki of the Annunaki King Anu. There are many variations to the story due to Mesopotamia's long history and the different cultures which adopted the Sumerian gods and made them their own but with some additions and alterations to their stories. However, there are common threads running throughout these stories emerging out of the collective unconscious which echo the underlying forces of consciousness in their process of creation.

Enlil, Enki, and Enki's son Marduk, possess like qualities to IAO, the Logos, and the Human / Noetic Soul along the same lines as Set, Osiris, and Horus of Egyptian mythology who represent the same forces of consciousness giving rise to creation.

In the Sumerian story, Enlil is seen as more powerful than Enki and is initially worshiped as the most-high god, second only to Anu, but in each variation of the story Enlil and Enki are constantly at odds with Enki being the defender of humanity and Enlil possessing some sort of tragic flaw, much like Achilles, and of course IAO. The feud ultimately gives way to the rise of Enki's son, Marduk, who takes on traits of both Enlil and Enki to become the new ruler of the gods.

What we learn from the forces of the cosmic quanta is that, it was not IAO-Enlil's decision to bring about the Great Flood, but it was because of IAO-Enlil's psycho-somatic interaction with the humanity on Earth that the Great Flood was brought about.

The story is similar to the Egyptian story of Set, Osiris, and Horus where Set murders Osiris but Isis, the wife of Osiris, posthumously conceives their son, Horus, from the body of Osiris. Horus rises to overthrow Set to become the new ruler of the gods.

Genesis – The Creation of Mankind

> *"So God created man in his own image,*
> *in the image of God created He him;*
> *male and female created He them" ...Genesis 1:27*

"God created man in his own image" equals God created man "inside" his own image. Mankind was not made "in" the image of God. Mankind was made "by" the image of God (imagination). God's imagination is the imagination of the Spirit. The imagination of God, the Mind of God, is sparked into existence by the infinite power of the Spirit (See Dynamis). "Male and female created He them," is a reference to the splitting of the sexes and the manifestation of universal duality via the reconciliation of IAO and the Logos.

Quarks are subatomic particles considered to be the fundamental constituents of matter. Quarks always exist in pairs. If you attempt to pull a quark pair apart, a new partner for the separated quarks will immediately appear. Quarks cannot be isolated. Some physicists consider this to be one of the few spooky anomalies of quantum physics. This is an after effect of the pairing of IAO and the Logos when creation was reconciled at the cosmic level at the very beginning of creation. There are also six types of quarks. This reflects the six spiritual bodies of primordial creation and the six temporal bodies of physical creation. The force which binds quarks and gets stronger and stronger as you attempt to pull quarks apart, is the unbeatable force of the Logos.

I – IAO

IAO and his alchemy of providence (Sigma and the Aurelion) and his interaction with all levels of mind on all scales of life within creation forms the "Matrix."

The universal duality in all things arises from the reconciliation between IAO and the Logos at the cosmic quanta level of existence. Male-Female, Light-Darkness, Odd-Even, Hot-Cold, Etc. Odd numbers preceding Even numbers reflects IAO being the first born of the Divine Trinity. In terms of creation, many religions are correct when they say first there was darkness (IAO) and then there was the light (Logos). The cosmic level of reconciliation between IAO and the Logos laid the foundation for all the laws of the universe and the very nature of our created reality.

<u>Twin Creator Symbolism</u>

Perhaps there is a double meaning behind the image of Adam and God by Michelangelo. Perhaps the image is unconsciously of IAO (left) and the Logos (right) compelled by the Collective Unconscious.

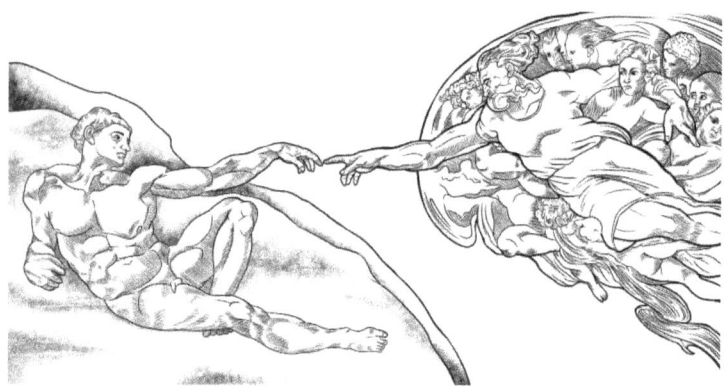

IAO – I

The Secret Key of IAO

The secret key of IAO is that everything we project in our mind towards IAO, IAO materializes and makes real. If we project fear, hatred, chaos, and poverty, IAO materializes it in our life. But if we are resonant with the Father when we interact with IAO, then IAO will materialize Heaven on Earth in our life. This is why IAO appears as Satan to the masses. It is because they project evil to IAO, so in return, IAO materializes evil in their life. The truth is, IAO is beyond good and evil, and can manifest either one. This is why our internal Logos turns into Lucifer upon our physical birth. This protects our Noetic Soul from our own mind, and ensures that through death (Theta), our Noetic Soul will be liberated from the beast which our own mind creates through its unconscious interaction with IAO. It is also why other worlds have outlawed any humanity be created with the ability to interact with IAO thereby outlawing the ability to complete the Monad. Our humanity is an exception to this cosmic law and is why we are both feared and revered as a human race. It is why the human lifespan on Earth must be kept short and it is also why the humanity of the Earth is considered IAO's chosen people. The chosen are not of one nation, but of all nations on Earth.

The Dark Inflection of IAO

Just as all the other forces of consciousness have a dark inflection—except for the three original forces (Father, Divine Soul, Spirit)—the quantum of IAO also has a dark inflection. All the forces of consciousness in both their reconciled state or dark inflected state have mythological representations which emerge out of the collective unconscious into all the world's historic religious scriptures, poetry, fables, literature, and all the world's creative arts. The dark inflection of IAO is the most famous of the dark mythological characters. The dark inflection of IAO is Satan. What may surprise many people is that Lucifer and Satan are the dark inflections of two totally different forces of consciousness. Satan is the dark inflection of IAO.

I – IAO

Lucifer is the dark inflection of the Logos. In Egyptian mythology, Satan is Set (also spelled "Seth"), the Logos, is Osiris, The Noetic Soul is Horus, and the Numina is Isis. The story of Osiris and Set is the most famous of all Egyptian stories. Osiris and Set are the principal forces involved in the final alchemical labor of the Third Mountain.

One source[4] summarizes their story as follows:

"The Osiris myth is the most elaborate and influential story in ancient Egyptian mythology. It concerns the murder of the God Osiris, a primeval king of Egypt, and its consequences. Osiris's murderer, his brother Set, usurps his throne. Meanwhile, Osiris's wife Isis restores her husband's body, allowing him to posthumously conceive a son with her. The remainder of the story focuses on Horus, the product of the union of Isis and Osiris, who is at first a vulnerable child protected by his mother and then becomes Set's rival for the throne. Their often-violent conflict ends with Horus's triumph, which restores order to Egypt after Set's unrighteous reign and completes the process of Osiris's resurrection."

Enter the Eternal

The tertiary cycles of Eros continue at higher and higher octaves within the alchemical process of Symphysis. During the cycles of Symphysis, a transcendent axiom of truth emerges with the realization that all three principal forces of Eros exist beyond good and evil. It is our relationship with the forces of Eros which are either good or evil, but the forces of Eros themselves are neither.

The forces of Eros are IAO, Erotic Soul, and Matter-Energy. All together, they give rise to the Cosmic Mind.

Amazingly, at the very end of the Great Work in our darkest hour, it is IAO himself who comes forth and enlightens us and teaches us the greatest mystery of all mysteries, which is the mystery of the will of the Father and how to fulfill it.

---

[4] The summarized narration of the Osiris and Set story is sourced from Wikipedia 2017.

IAO – I

When we engage the omnipotent force of IAO with a dark unenlightened mind, what we manifest in response, is the dark power of Satan. When we engage the Erotic Soul (Sea of Eros) with a dark unenlightened mind, what we manifest in response, within the deep cavern of our unconscious mind, is the beast (Idamus). When we engage the Matter-Energy of our body (our creation) with a dark unenlightened mind, what we manifest in response, are the dark underlying forces of Chaos (The Gorgon).

The Law of Attraction

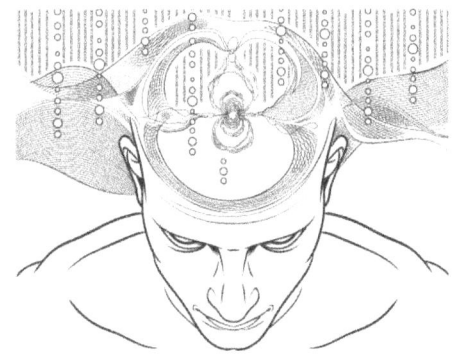

The Law of Attraction, Karma, Eye for an Eye, Blessings, Fortune, Destiny, Predetermination, Materialization, are all the effect of the human mind interacting with the Cosmic Mind of IAO. The result of the interaction is not decided by IAO. It is decided by our state of mind when we interact with IAO. Send IAO love, and love and blessings will be returned tenfold. Forgive and you will be forgiven. Replenish others and you yourself shall be replenished. What you do unto the least of you, you do unto God.

> *"What you think; you become.*
> *What you feel; you attract.*
> *What you imagine; you create."*
> *... Siddhartha Gautama (Buddha)*

I – IAO

Osiris and Set – 1915 Illustration

Art depicting the God Osiris being talked into stepping into a coffin made by his brother Set. The coffin is the mortal physical body. Osiris (Logos) is the champion of God. He is unbeatable in conflict. Set (IAO-Satan) cannot defeat Osiris in a direct conflict, and he knows this. Set can only compel Osiris to defeat himself. This is done by compelling Osiris to sacrifice himself to save what he loves most – the Noetic / Human Soul. The Noetic Soul's descent into the darkness of physical life to fulfill the will of the Father causes Osiris to give up his original form to follow the Noetic Soul into the darkness to become Orion-Lucifer-Shiva to ensure the Noetic Soul is eventually freed from its physical incarnation through death.

The Great Red Dragon

William Blake – 1805

I – IAO

When humanity improperly interacts psychosomatically with IAO, we manifest the dark power of Satan (The Great Red Dragon). The key to interacting with the omnipotent power of IAO is love—symbolized by the feminine (The Woman Clothed with the Sun). The enemy of humanity is not IAO. IAO only manifests what we supply it. The enemy of humanity is the "Gorgon," which arises out of fear. It brings forth delusions, narcissism, lies, and hatred.

Similar or Equivalent Terms:

<u>Satan</u>: Great Red Dragon, Set, Seth, Vritra (Dark Inflection of IAO)

<u>IAO</u>: Yaldabaoth, Tetragrammaton, Indra, YHWH (Mind of God), Yahweh, Enlil, Demiurge 1 of 2, (Logos is Demiurge 2 of 2)

William Blake – 1805

Id, The – Id Complex

The id is a force stuck and suppressed in darkness in the erotic sphere of the human being. The authentic-Self (Noetic Soul) residing behind the ego and super-ego of the human being belongs to the noetic sphere of the human psyche and is born from the will of the Father (The Light). The id—along with the mind and the brain matter—belongs to the erotic sphere of the human being which emerges spontaneously in darkness outside the will of the Father.

The will of the Father is for the Noetic Soul to intervene with the spontaneous emerging forces of creation and bridge them with the divine source of the Father. The id is an intelligence trapped in darkness due to the way it spontaneously emerges. The id strives for life and for a sense of permanence and fulfillment, and in doing so, gives rise to both fear and animal desire in all human beings.

The id is a complex of two forces thus the term can be expanded to "Id Complex." The intelligence embedded in the id is twofold. One side is called the "Idamus," the other the "Gorgon." The Idamus feels a sense of emptiness and fear and desires fulfillment. In response to fear, the Gorgon arises as the dark champion narcissistic-self offering delusional constructs to the mind to assuage the fear.

The delusions of the Gorgon arise in an attempt to bring cohesion to the mind. It tries to form a dark pearl or an anti-Monad (false-cohesion). The Gorgon often succeeds in developing a degree of false cohesion but is also prone to spontaneous self-destruction.

The Gorgon gives rise to what is worst in human beings.

Both sides of the human being are compelled to develop a unity of mind. The will of the Father (The Logos-The Light) compels the noetic side. The erotic side is compelled spontaneously and automatically (Darkness). If the noetic side does not heed the calling, then eventually, the erotic side will over-run the mind.

Many have sought to elevate the human condition from a variety of angles. The key is a conscious and willful engagement in the process to integrate both sides of the human being (Light and Darkness) in the development of the unified mind.

I – Idamus

Idamus – Pazuzu, Gog, Beast of the Sea *[Id-a-mus; Id-ah-mus]*

The Idamus is the first of two sides of the id complex. The intelligence embedded in the id is twofold. The right side is called the "Idamus," the left side is called the "Gorgon." The Idamus feels a sense of emptiness and fear and desires continuity and fulfillment. The two sides of the id complex are in severe opposition, however. Both sides must be integrated via the Noetic Soul in order to complete the reconstitution of the Monad.

The Idamus embraces eroticism. The Gorgon hates eroticism. The battle over sex is between the two spheres of darkness. It is not between light and darkness. The Erotic Soul must be saved and integrated, not left in darkness.

The Gorgon promotes a false sense of morality within the human mind to encourage the mind to suppress a human being's erotic nature. This is actually antithetical to the will of the Father. Christ is the unity of light and darkness. Christ arises through the integration of the noetic and erotic. The Gorgon will do anything to prevent this integration. This is why the Gorgon hates eroticism and does everything in its power to reject, defile, debase, and suppress it. Much of the false moral piety in organized religion and society in general regarding sex arises in the human mind from the Gorgon side of the id complex. The Gorgon is a wolf in sheep's clothing. It will appear noble and virtuous - but is the furthest thing from it.

The secret to the Idamus is that it actually wants the unity with divinity although it doesn't understand what it wants or recognize it when it's initially offered. The Gorgon is the sworn enemy of Christ. The Gorgon hates the unity with the light. The Gorgon seeks to form its own unity (Dark Pearl–Anti-Christ) by conquering the Idamus and taking total control of the mind and personality, although the desires of the Idamus pulls her strings. It creates its own delusional reality. The dark pearl forms around this delusional construct and it often succeeds. However, when the Gorgon is finally integrated into the Christ Monad, she transforms into the Magdalene, our internal Magis to becomes the bride of Christ and his greatest champion.

Idamus – I

Source of the Idamus

The Gorgon and the Idamus, which together form the id complex, arise from the forces of the Erodonic Trinity underlying both. The Idamus arises from the lifeforce or second principal of the Erodonic Trinity, the Eternal Sea, the Sea of Eros, the Erotic Soul. It arises out of the interaction between the human mind and the Erotic Soul. The Erotic Soul is the lifeforce of IAO. IAO is the Godhead of the Erodonic Trinity. Idamus is the first beast, the Beast of the Sea with Ten Horns (See Book of Revelation).

Etymology of the Name Idamus

The dark inflection of the Erotic Soul is an entity living in the darkness of creation known as Idamus. The name is derived from the term "id" coined by Sigmund Freud. Freud describes the id as follows.

"It is the dark, inaccessible part of our personality, what little we know of it we have learned from our study of the dream-work and of course, the construction of neurotic symptoms, and most of that is of a negative character and can be described only as a contrast to the ego. We approach the id with analogies: we call it a chaos, a cauldron full of seething excitations. It is filled with energy reaching it from the instincts, but it has no organization, produces no collective will, but only a striving to bring about the satisfaction of the instinctual needs subject to the observance of the pleasure principle."

Mythology of Idamus – (1) The Right Head of Cerberus

Cerberus symbolizes the third guardian guarding the Noetic Soul's entrance into the Eternal. The central head of Cerberus is Set, the right head of Cerberus is Idamus, the left head of Cerberus is Chaos (the Gorgon). His body is the mind. His animal form is a symbol of creation. In the eighth alchemical process, while under vicious assault by Cerberus, we must quickly learn how to become his owner without hurting him. If we hurt him, we will not become his owner, but if we do not move quickly, he will devour us and destroy us.

I – Idamus

Mythology of Idamus – (2) Gog and Magog

Gog is Idamus. Magog is the Gorgon. Wikipedia describes the story of Gog and Magog as follows.

"Gog and Magog in the Hebrew Bible may be individuals, peoples, or lands; a prophesied enemy nation of God's people according to the Book of Ezekiel, and one of the nations according to Genesis descended from Japheth son of Noah.

"The Gog prophecy is meant to be fulfilled at the approach of what is called the 'End of Days,' but not necessarily the end of the world. Jewish eschatology viewed Gog and Magog as enemies to be defeated by the Messiah, which would usher in the age of the Messiah. Christianity's interpretation is more starkly apocalyptic: making Gog and Magog allies of Satan against God as can be read in the Book of Revelation.

"To Gog and Magog were also attached a legend, certainly current by the Roman period, that they were people contained beyond the Gates of Alexander erected by Alexander the Great. Romanized Jewish historian Josephus knew them as the tribe descended from Magog the Japhethite, as in Genesis, and explained them to be the Scythians. In the hands of Early Christian writers, they became apocalyptic hordes, and throughout the Medieval period variously identified as the Huns, Khazars, Mongols, or other nomads, even the Ten Lost Tribes of Israel.

"The legend of Gog and Magog and the gates were also interpolated into the Alexander Romances. In one version, 'Goth and Magoth' are kings of the Unclean Nations, driven beyond a mountain pass by Alexander, and blocked from returning by his new wall. Gog and Magog are said to engage in human cannibalism in the romances and derived literature. They have also been depicted on Medieval cosmological maps, or Mappa Mundi, and sometimes alongside Alexander's wall.

Idamus – **I**

"Gog and Magog appear in the Quran as Yajuj and Majuj, adversaries of Dhul-Qarnayn, widely equated with Cyrus the Great and al-Iskanadar (Alexander the Great) in Islam. Muslim geographers identified them at first with Turkic tribes from Central Asia and later with the Mongols. In modern times, they remain associated with apocalyptic thinking, especially in the USA and the Muslim world."

Mythology of Idamus – (3) The Book of Revelation 13:1

"The dragon stood on the shore of the sea.
And I saw a beast coming out of the sea.
It had ten horns and seven heads, with ten crowns on its horns,
and on each head a blasphemous name."

Analysis

Dragon on the Shore = Satan; the Sea = the Erotic Soul; the Beast = Idamus; Ten Horns = The first ten of the eleven theokinetic permutations.

The permutations are: (1) Father; (2) Divine Soul; (3) Spirit; (4) IAO; (5) Erotic Soul; (6) Matter-Energy; (7) Logos; (8) Noetic Soul; (9) Numina; (10) Idamus. Idamus rises out of the Sea of Eros with ten horns. The tenth permutation always rises in the human being. The eleventh permutation doesn't always rise, although its underlying quantum is always there beneath the surface.

Technically, Idamus is the first permutation inside the mind but the tenth overall. The Gorgon is the second permutation of the mind, but the eleventh overall. Nine principal forces of consciousness, plus, two of the mind, equal eleven in total.

Ten Crowns mark the ten horns in the verse as the ten principal forces within the human being. Seven heads are comprised of the six temporal bodies of the human being with the seventh head being the physical Earth and its temporal group mind.

The phrase, Blasphemous Names, reflects cognition within the temporal bodies being based on "perception" rather than "resonance," thus the cognition is illusory. Illusory = Blasphemous

I – Idamus

<u>Idamus Symbolism</u>

This is Pazuzu; part of Assyrian and Babylonian mythology. Pazuzu symbolizes Idamus. Idamus is the first of two beasts. He is the beast of the sea. The Gorgon is the beast of the earth. The sea is the sexual energy. The earth is the soil—the matter.

Idamus – I

<u>Idamus and the Rise of Narcissism</u>

When fear overcomes the mind, in that very moment, the dark forces of our id complex possess us. Idamus steals the light of the mind from the Noetic Soul and the Noetic Soul is pushed into the psychic cognitive background. The fear induced by Idamus can be so painful that our mind seeks to break away from its reality by building a fake narcissistic personality strong enough to steal the light away from Idamus. This is the dark champion narcissistic personality. It is the second beast which rises from the Earth. It's known as the Gorgon. This is how the Gorgon rises inside the mind of the human being.

It provides a false relief and cohesion to the mind.

The Noetic Soul remains stuck in darkness. The greater the fear grows, the greater the narcissism and delusions grow to compensate. This complex develops unconsciously and is usually developed in childhood and can remain in control of the human mind for an individual's entire life. (See Narcissism)

It is possible, perhaps due to some genetic cause, that within the chemical wiring of the brain, the force of theta which counters the id complex, is somehow suppressed, or not fully engaged as well as it should be. As a result, the person is over-exposed to his or her id. Both nature and nurture may be the cause. Within the human mind, the counter-balancing force of theta should only be lifted when the Noetic Soul consciously reconciles its internal Lucifer (internal force that buffers creation) wherein Lucifer re-enters the light of Ain Soph and transforms back into the Logos. In other words, when reflective awareness of divinity is established within the human mind.

Strangely, the dark champion of the narcissistic mind offers a degree of cohesion to the psychic composition of the afflicted mind. By way of this false cohesion, a degree of perceived genius and material success may actually emerge—but it is all false.

The dark shadow which follows this illusory cohesion is the tendency to immediately self-destruct without warning and with the unconscious willingness to take others along with it. The narcissistic cohesion of the mind may also make it more difficult for narcissists

I – Idamus | Illusion

to self-observe and realize all their internal psychic aggregates and spiritual forces. Why? Because their center of gravity is not their Noetic Soul, it's their dark champion narcissistic personality (the Gorgon). The Gorgon mind is the anti-Monad (The Anti-Christ).

There is still hope for narcissists if they wish to overcome their affliction. The key to overcoming narcissism is becoming aware of and saying good-bye to the dark champion personality (the Gorgon). This allows the authentic-self (Noetic Soul) to experience fear without losing the light of the mind. It is possible, believe it or not, for narcissists to reach as far as entering the Void at the end of the Second Mountain because the affliction involves the id complex and the personality, not the false-selves or automated instincts. However, unless the narcissist corrects this issue, he or she can never begin the Third Mountain. The reason is, in order to climb the Third Mountain, we must entrust our emotional well-being to the Divine Soul, not to some dark champion narcissistic personality (the Gorgon).

Similar or Equivalent Terms:

Idamus: Gog, Yajuj, Pazuzu, the Beast of the Sea, Beast with Ten Horns, Right Head of Cerberus.

Illusion

In context of the mind and its process of integration and self-realization, the state of illusion is a condition of the mind in which it has become hypnotized and fixated on the outside world while lacking an awareness of the divine source residing at the center of all things. This polarized fixation on the outside world causes the mind to lose its true self (Authentic-Self or Noetic Soul). It confuses the automated responses of the mind as the actual feelings and thoughts of the true self. Illusion is a spectrum; Delusion is at the far end.

When the conscious mind of the human being is intimately aware of the two poles of the outside world and the divine source at the center of its being, it can then bring forward an awareness of the true self residing in the space between the two poles. This compels the conscious mind to notice and realize that the automated responses of the mind are but artifacts of a matrix of illusion which imprisons the true self and tricks the mind into behaving in accordance with the program of evolution and natural selection.

Similar or Equivalent Terms:

Eikasia (Plato); Maya (Hinduism)

Immaculate Conception – Thelesis

The immaculate conception is not physical. It is a critical and fundamental stage in the re-organization of consciousness in response to the spontaneous rise of creation out of the divine source. The immaculate conception has two stages. The first stage begins when the divine Father realizes that the divine Spirit of his love had spontaneously created, and that this creation was stuck in darkness. His realization triggers his will to save this creation. This initiates the process called Thelesis, which is a super meta that actualizes his will by conceiving an immaculate conception to intervene with the process of creation and reunify it with the divine unity of Ain Soph. The immaculate conception in the first stage is the Sacred Trinity whose life-force is the Noetic Soul—the Only Begotten Son of God. The three forces which comprise the Sacred Trinity are (1) the Logos, (2) the Noetic Soul and (3) the Father's love for creation, the Numina, symbolized as the Blessed Mother of God. The birth of the Sacred Trinity completes the first stage of the immaculate conception.

The forces of the Sacred Trinity are born in the light because they are conceived by the will of the Father. The forces of the Erodonic Trinity embedded in creation are born in darkness because they were conceived spontaneously without intention by the Spirit.

When the Sacred Trinity accomplishes the purpose of its birth and reunifies creation with Ain Soph, this completes the second stage of the immaculate conception, which is the immortal Christ Monad. Christ forms a new heaven and a new earth. Christ is the fulfillment of the immaculate conception.

I – Individuated-Self | Intraspection

Individuated-Self

The term Individuated-Self was coined by Carl Jung to characterize the state of psychological wholeness cultivated by an individual. The individuated-self emerges through the integration of all our mind's fragmented and dissociative psychic processes.

The individuated-self does not emerge automatically through the evolutionary processes of nature or out of consequence to how well one is raised or educated. The individuated-self emerges when the conscious mind of the human being decides to turn his or her attention to the fragmented elements of his or her own mind which suppress the natural and free expression of the authentic-self. The conscious mind must intervene to transform and integrate the fragmented elements to consolidate and strengthen the authentic-self. It's an applied practice or discipline. The continuous application of the Three Factors throughout a person's life progressively individuates the conscious mind of the human being.

Intraspection

The longer we are able sustain a heightened resonance between our conscious mind and the Spirit, the more the physical wiring of our brain is re-wired to support and deepen the resonance. Over time, the subtle communication between our conscious mind and the emergent forces of the cosmic quanta develops into a new super cognitive faculty called Intraspection. This is not introspection. Introspection takes place solely between your own thoughts. Intraspection is a communication between the conscious mind and the emergent forces of the cosmic quanta. The Spirit is the first of these forces.

As we continue the Third Factor practice of quantum meditation alongside other practices of the Three Factors, additional forces within the cosmic quanta - beyond the Spirit - begin to emerge and present themselves. As we develop our super cognitive ability to communicate with the cosmic quanta; prayer, quantum meditation, and intraspection, all come together to resonate as one. Intraspection develops our super cognitive emotional capacity and vise-versa.

J

Journeyman

A person climbing the Second Mountain is a Journeyman. The objective of the Journeyman in the Second Mountain is the consolidation and individuation of the temporal-noetic sphere of the conscious mind. The self-organizing force of the universe (Alpha) is directing all human beings to develop a unification of mind with the divine source. Alpha is driving everyone to build the Christ Monad. When people cooperate with this force in a subconscious manner, they continue to return life-after-life in lockstep with the rest of  humanity on the planet to achieve the same goal. This slow many-lifetime-approach is known as the Spiral Path. When people wake-up to the process Alpha is guiding them upon, and decide to cooperate with it, the process speeds up within them and they can complete the Christ Monad in one lifetime. This accelerated approach is known as the Straight Path. When the Straight Path emerges, Alpha directs the conscious mind of the person through three major stages in development of the Monad. In hermetic lore these stages are called the Three Mountains.

J – Journeyman | Jung, Carl

As stated, an alchemist in the First Mountain is an Apprentice. An alchemist in the Second Mountain is a Journeyman. An alchemist in the Third Mountain is a Foreman. (See Three Mountains)

When on the Spiral Path, the human being traverses all three mountains simultaneously. We experience flashes of each mountain throughout the course of our life. This occurs over many physical existences in lockstep with all other human beings on Earth.

When on the Straight Path, the Three Mountains separate, and we climb each mountain sequentially, one after the other.

Ironically, climbing the three mountains sequentially is faster than climbing them all together as one.

Jung, Carl

Carl Gustav Jung (26-July-1875 – 6 June 1961), was a Swiss psychiatrist and psychoanalyst who founded analytical psychology. Jung's work has been influential in the fields of psychiatry, anthropology, archaeology, literature, philosophy, psychology, and religious studies. The study of alchemy and mandalas were a known passion of his. He worked as a research scientist at the Burghölzli psychiatric hospital, in Zurich, under Eugen Bleuler. Jung established himself as an influential mind, developing a friendship with Sigmund Freud, founder of psychoanalysis, conducting a lengthy correspondence, paramount to their joint vision of human psychology. Jung is widely regarded as one of the most influential psychologists in history. Among the central concepts of analytical psychology is individuation—the lifelong psychological process of differentiation of the self out of each individual's conscious and unconscious elements. Jung considered it to be the main task of human development. He created some of the best-known psychological concepts, including synchronicity, archetypal phenomena, the collective unconscious, the psychological complex and extraversion and introversion. Jung was also an artist, craftsman, builder and prolific writer. Many of his works were not published until after his death and some remain unpublished. *(Sourced from Wikipedia 2023)*

Kant, Immanuel

Immanuel Kant (22 April 1724 – 12 February 1804) was a German philosopher and one of the central Enlightenment thinkers. Born in Königsberg, Kant's comprehensive and systematic works in epistemology, metaphysics, ethics, and aesthetics have made him one of the most influential figures in modern Western philosophy. He has been called the father of modern ethics, father of modern aesthetics and, by bringing together rationalism and empiricism, the father of modern philosophy.

In his doctrine of transcendental idealism, Kant argued space and time are mere "forms of intuition" that structure all experience and that the objects of experience are mere "appearances." The nature of things as they are in themselves is unknowable to us. Immanuel Kant first developed the notion of the noumenon as part of his transcendental idealism, suggesting that while we know the noumenal world to exist because human sensibility is merely receptive, it is not itself sensible and must therefore remain otherwise unknowable to us.

In an attempt to counter the philosophical doctrine of skepticism, he wrote the Critique of Pure Reason (1781/1787), his most well-known work. Kant drew a parallel to the Copernican revolution in his proposal to think of the objects of experience as conforming to our spatial and temporal forms of intuition and the categories of our understanding, so that we have a priori cognition of those objects.

Kant believed that reason is the source of morality, and that aesthetics arises from a faculty of disinterested judgment. Kant's religious views were deeply connected to his moral theory.
(Sourced from Wikipedia 2023)

K – Kier | Kundalini

Kier *[Keer]*

Kier is the original divine language of consciousness. This language has always existed. Its medium is the resonance between the forces of consciousness. Within the divine source, the three dimensions of Ain Soph communicate through resonance and pass information through that resonance. The transmission of that information is called Kier. The faculty of Kier is an instrument which rises with Turiya (See Turiya Faculty). The information exchange between the Noetic Soul and the other forces of the cosmic quanta is perfect. It transcends the mind. However, as that information is passed to the mind, the mind distorts it. The more the conscious mind is elevated in resonance with the divine source, the less distorted this information becomes.

Kundalini *[Kun-da-lini; Kun-dah-lini]*

In Hinduism, Kundalini is a psycho-spiritual-etheric energy rising upward along the spine from the coccyx bone. There are various methods of Yoga meditation to compel the rise of Kundalini. Some confuse Kundalini with the sublimated etheric sexual energy which rises quickly up the spine through various breathing techniques. Kundalini is a slower moving energy which rises up the spine over the course of many weeks stimulating the various connecting chakras along the way. The experience of Kundalini is actually the secondary effect of Alpha as we accelerate Alpha's rhythm with the Three Factors.

Alpha, Kundalini, and the Sacred Fire, are actually all one and the same. We can track the development of Alpha in the First Mountain by measuring the advancement of Kundalini. As Alpha rises sequentially within each ethereal body, many have reported the sensation of a serpent climbing the spine starting at the base and climbing to the head over a period of many weeks or months. Each successive body re-starts the journey from the base of the spine to the head. This is one way to track the development of Alpha.

In Taoist alchemy, Alpha is tracked by the bodies in the alchemical mix. Five elements, fire and water, then two dragons, then Sun and Moon, then stars. (See Alpha and the Three Factors)

Kybalion, The

The Kybalion quickly became a popular work since it was published in 1908. Its full title is *The Kybalion, A Study of the Hermetic Philosophy of Ancient Egypt and Greece*. It was published by "Three Initiates," and is mostly attributed to New Thought founder William Walker Atkinson, 1862–1932. The book conveys multiple hermetic principles found in the ancient texts such as, as above so below, the idea that everything is dual and has its polar opposite, and the idea of philosophical mentalism. The Kybalion claims there are seven universal hermetic principles upon which the entire hermetic philosophy is based:

1.) <u>The principle of mentalism</u>
The All is Mind; the Universe is Mental.

2.) <u>The principle of correspondence</u>
As above, so below; as below, so above. This principle embodies the truth that there is always a correspondence between the laws and phenomena of the various planes of being and life.

3.) <u>The principle of vibration</u>
Nothing rests; everything moves; everything vibrates.

4.) <u>The principle of polarity</u>
Everything is dual; everything has poles; everything has its pair of opposites; like and unlike are the same; opposites are identical in nature, but different in degree; extremes meet; all truths are but half-truths; all paradoxes may be reconciled.

5.) <u>The principle of rhythm</u>
Everything flows, out and in; everything has its tides; all things rise and fall; the pendulum-swing manifests in everything; the measure of the swing to the right is the measure of the swing to the left; rhythm compensates.

K – Kybalion, The

6.) <u>The principle of cause and effect</u>
Every cause has its effect; every effect has its cause; everything happens according to law; chance is but a name for law not recognized; there are many planes of causation, but nothing escapes the law.

7.) <u>The principle of gender</u>
Gender is in everything; everything has its masculine and feminine principles; gender manifests on all planes.

Based on my internal experience and what I have gathered from over 35 years of alchemical and quantum meditation, I agree with all seven hermetic principles but offer three comments for contemplation.

<u>Comment 1</u> – Truth is Truth. The mind's apprehension of the truth will always be somewhat incomplete due to the way the mind emerges. However, the Noetic Soul's resonance with the Truth can achieve completion even when the mind's apprehension is incomplete.

<u>Comment 2</u> – Everything is dual for two reasons. One, creation is reconciled by two outpouring intelligences out of the divine source. The first outpouring is IAO, born in darkness in descent from the Spirit. The second outpouring is the Logos, born in the light, the immaculate conception of the Father. When the two reconcile, this brings forth duality in all things including sexuality, darkness and light, negative and positive. Two, divinity needs two universes to resolve its divine paradox of creation—Its love forever creates and multiplies, but its will forever unifies. It needs a state of eternal completion at the primordial level, and it needs an endless runway of time in the physical universe. I would argue that creation is still driven by an "unresolvable paradox" but that the introduction of time in the physical universe gives it infinite runway to allow the dynamics of its paradox to play out forever without end. The resolution of the original creation paradox is the introduction of the time paradox. Paradoxically, the two paradoxes resolve each other. The two universes, primordial and physical, are dual reflecting. All life in the physical has a primordial reflection, but not all life in the primordial has a physical reflection. The physical is always catching up.

<u>Comment 3</u> – There are more key principles, i.e., Alpha Principle: All things must eventually reunify with divinity to fulfill the law of one.

L

Law of One – Law of Unity, Alpha Principle

The Law of One is a law within the quantum cosmos demanding that all things eventually reconcile to a unit of one. A divine paradox exists within the divine Monad of Ain Soph.

Divinity itself is paradoxical.

The effort within the divine source particle of Ain Soph to reconcile the three dimensions within itself is what gives rise to what we call consciousness and sparks the continuous process of creation.

Within Ain Soph there exists three divine forces (Divine Trinity) which together resonate as one (Triune) yet simultaneously express a differentiation between the three forces. These three forces are Awareness, Life, and Love (Energy).

Life is the being or presence of that awareness. Love arises due to the awareness being aware of its own existence. All three rise together.

The Law of One emerges by way of the energy of love compelling all three forces to resonate as one to maintain unity.

Because the original divine awareness is infinite due to nothing preceding it, then its divine lifeforce is infinite. To reconcile the first two infinite forces, the third infinite force of divine love naturally arises exerting infinite energy to unify the two.

The infinite forces involved in achieving this unity give rise to what we call consciousness and spontaneously sparks the advent of creation. When creation arises, the Law of One demands that creation be reconciled and re-unified with the divine source. The Noetic Soul arises to meet this demand guided by Alpha. The Alpha Principle is that all things must eventually reconcile and resonate as one with divinity. Once achieved, a new self-regulating reconstituted Monad emerges. This new Monad is Christ. On a cosmic level, it is the universe bound by the theosphere. It is God—Eloah or Allah—the Cosmic Christ.

L – Law of One | Logos, The

Symbols of the Law of One

Logos, The *[Loh-ghos]*

The term Logos means "Word of God." The Word of God and the "Will of God" are one and the same. There is a force in the underlying quantum cosmos of the universe which comes forth as a result and direct manifestation of the Father's will. Hence, this force within the quantum cosmos is called the Logos. The Logos is the Godhead of the Sacred Trinity – also called the Lower Trinity. The Sacred Trinity is a direct reflection of the Divine Trinity – also called the Upper Trinity, or Holy Trinity. The Sacred Trinity is born by the will of the Father (Godhead of the Divine Trinity) to intervene with the Erodonic Trinity embedded in creation. The purpose of this intervention is to lift creation back-up into a new reestablished, reunified, harmonic resonance with the divine Father thereby reconstituting a new unity (new covenant– new heaven and new earth) between divinity and all of creation. This forms the New Monad. The reconstituted Monad is Christ.

    The Logos is the champion of God.

    The Divine Trinity itself maintains a perfect original unity. The original unity (Original Monad) is called Ain Soph. However, the power of its infinite love spontaneously gives rise to creation and the forces of the Erodonic Trinity within creation. The spontaneous rise of creation occurs outside the will of the Father and therefore creation and the forces of the Erodonic Trinity initially emerge in darkness.

Logos, The – L

The Father realizes this spontaneous outpouring and expresses a divine will to intervene with the automated processes of creation to save it and bring everything back into unity. The will of the Father to save creation gives birth to the forces of the Sacred Trinity of which the Logos is the Godhead.

Any trinity arising among the forces of consciousness is always some reformulation of Awareness, Life, and Energy. The Awareness within the Divine Trinity is Resonant Awareness. Resonant Awareness is the original eternal everlasting awareness of the Cosmic Consciousness from which everything emerged. It is the Father.

The awareness within the Erodonic Trinity of creation gives rise to the Mind. It is Perspective Awareness. The Godhead of the Erodonic Trinity is IAO. IAO is the first born of the Divine Trinity, but IAO is born in darkness.

The Logos is the second born of the Divine Trinity and is born in the light. The awareness within the Sacred Trinity is Reflective Awareness. It is the Logos. Reflective Awareness reconnects the mind back to the divine source of the Father where it can experience resonance. Resonance between the Father and creation forms the new Monad (Christ Monad or Buddha Monad).

The mythological term "son" is the "soul." The soul is the lifeforce within any trinity of consciousness. The soul itself has no actual gender. The lifeforce of the Sacred Trinity is the "Only Begotten Son of God ." There are three trinities of consciousness, which when reconciled, produce a fourth reconciled unified trinity within the Christ Monad.

The lifeforce within the Divine Trinity (Divine Soul) is not the Only Begotten Son of God because the Divine Soul was not begotten or procreated. The Divine Soul has always existed as the eternal lifeforce of the Father. The lifeforce within the Erodonic Trinity which was the first to emerge from the Divine Trinity under the Godhead of IAO is not the only begotten son of God because it was not begotten by the Father. It was begotten by the Spirit. There is only one lifeforce which was willfully born directly by God the Father - and this lifeforce is the Noetic Soul. The Noetic Soul is the only begotten son of God.

L – Logos, The

The Noetic Soul is the lifeforce of the intercessing principal between creation and divinity. The Logos is the Godhead of the Sacred Trinity to which the Noetic Soul belongs. The Logos is both creation's way back to the Father and also a direct reflection of the Father. This is why the Logos is also called "The Father of the Human / Noetic Soul." The Logos is a manifestation of the light of the divine Father.

IAO's original form is a manifestation of the Father's power residing in darkness. The Logos seeks to alchemically conjoin with IAO's original form to give birth to Christ. This union is what gives rise to sexuality, opposite forces, hot and cold, odd and even, light and darkness, and the duality in all things.

> *"The heavens declare the glory of God;*
> *the skies proclaim the work of his hands."*
> *Psalm 19:1. A reference to the Logos*

The Logos and its Sacred Trinity have a divine given mission (given direct by the divine Father) to intervene with creation and complete its process. Creation cannot complete itself automatically. It must be done consciously. The completed state of creation is Christ.

In order for creation to complete itself, it requires the intercession of a conscious mind. The human being is a pinnacle being of creation possessing a Noetic Soul whose purpose is to complete the process of creation and form the Christ Monad. No other species of creation possesses a Noetic Soul except the human being (see Human Being). Therefore, to be truly human, a species must possess a Noetic Soul. Animals do not possess a Noetic Soul. Animals are animated only by the Erotic Soul which is the lifeforce of IAO.

In Hinduism, the Father is represented by Brahman, the Logos by Vishnu, and the dark inflection of the Logos - popularly known as Lucifer - is represented by Shiva the destroyer. The popular mythological term Satan represents an entirely different force from Lucifer and should not be confused with Lucifer. In Egyptian Mythology the Logos is Osiris.

Logos, The – L

<u>Mythology of the Logos</u>

The Logos—The Father of the Sacred Trinity—is the key principal within our spiritual psychology which manifests the unmanifested and makes known the unknowable. Thus, the Father of the Sacred Trinity is the "Word of God." He is the Logos.

The Logos emerges out of the divine source to manifest and make known within the realms of creation, the divine order of Ain Soph. Without the ability of the Logos to square the circle of Ain Soph, the Noetic Soul and the third principal force of the Sacred Trinity would be unable to manifest to bring the forces of creation into harmony. As a result, the emergent matter of creation would not survive.

As the father of the Lower Trinity (Sacred Trinity), the Logos is the literal incarnation of the father of the Upper Trinity (The Father). The Logos has the unique ability to perform what no other principal force within the cosmic quanta can perform, the transcendental ability to square the circle (determine Pi [π]). Only the Logos knows the secret number of Pi [π]. (This speaks esoterically, not mathematically)

No mathematician can accurately calculate the exact number of Pi [π]. They use a rounded number. Pi [π] is the ratio of a circle's circumference to its diameter. When we square the circle—determine Pi [π]—we manifest the un-manifested—the unknown becomes known. Pi [π] is the symbol of the Logos. The force the Logos emits is Tau [τ] or Phi [φ].

L – Logos, The

Any given form of the Father is the Logos. The Logos is the Father taking form. The Christian representation of God sitting on a throne in a white beard would actually be a mythological representation of the quantum force of the Logos. The divine Father has no form. Vishnu (Preserver of Creation), Logos, Osiris, Janus, is the godhead of the intercessing principal between Heaven and Earth, between divinity and creation. The sky is Heaven. The sea is the Sea of Eros from which all of creation emerges. The serpents symbolize the emergence of creation. The lotus blossom represents the unity between divinity and creation. The lotus blossom is the Christ Monad.

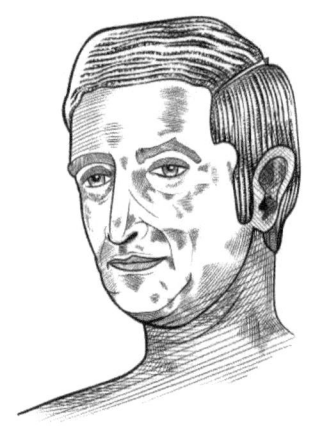

Song of the Immortal Beloved:

"It was in the early morning hours on a cold winter day in December 2016, three days after the winter solstice. The Sun was just beginning to rise above the horizon when I opened my eyes. Standing before me was my Logos in all his glory. His light turned the pre-dawn darkness into day. He was standing at the entrance of a beautiful tunnel of light behind him radiating all around him like the Sun. Dressed in an all-white military uniform in full regalia, he called out to me with his arm and hand extended and said, 'My son, you have restored the covenant of my eternal and everlasting love. I now come to you to restore the covenant of your eternal and everlasting life.'"

Logos, The – L

Fibonacci Sequence

Phi [φ] and Tau [τ] historically have both been used to represent the Golden Ratio which consistently appears throughout nature. For example, in the Fibonacci Sequence.

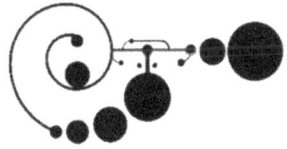

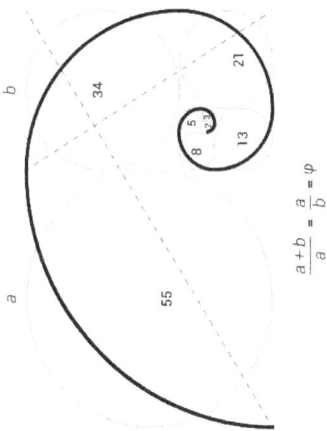

Crucifix

The Crucifix is the union between divinity (vertical shaft) and creation (horizontal shaft). It is a symbol of the Christ Monad. The Noetic Soul within humanity bears the weight of the work to reunify divinity and creation to form the Christ Monad as the chosen intercessor between the two. The inversion of Theta [θ] (Death) is "Tau [τ]" which in ancient Greece symbolized life and resurrection (Crucifix).

Number 777

If we count Eros as all within the 4th permutation, then the Logos is the 5th permutation. However, if we count each principal within the Erodonic Trinity as a separate permutation, then the Logos becomes 7th permutation. The Logos is the 5th before the reconciliation of creation and the 7th after the reconciliation of creation. 777 is the ultimate goal of the Logos reconciling creation on all three scales including the Cosmic, Planetary, and Individual.

$$777 = 7+7+7 = 21 = 2+1 = 3$$

777 is the return of creation to the Divine Trinity from which creation, IAO, and the Logos all emerged.

L – Logos, The

<u>Mythology of the Dark Inflection of the Logos – Lucifer</u>

The dark inflection of the Logos is Lucifer. Even in the dark inflected state, Lucifer is still loyal to the divinity of Ain Soph. Lucifer is the wrath of the Logos. The job of Lucifer is to destroy creation when creation cannot resonate with Ain Soph to build the Christ Monad.

The term Lucifer means "The Light" or "Light Bearer."
The Word of God (Will of God) is the Light. Lucifer and the Logos are the same being in different modes of operation. Lucifer is the most misunderstood of all the forces of the quantum cosmos.

> *"How you have fallen from heaven, Morning Star,*
> *son of the dawn!*
> *You have been cast down to the earth,*
> *you who once laid low the nations! ... Isaiah 14:12.*

* * *

"I, Jesus, have sent my angel to give you this testimony for the churches. I am the Root and the offspring of David, and the bright Morning Star." ... Book of Revelation - 22:16

These two bible verses together form a riddle. To some it appears as though Jesus is equating himself with Lucifer, and therefore, he is evil. The opposite is true. It signals Lucifer is misunderstood. We must have real wisdom to solve the riddle.

Jesus of Nazareth role plays throughout the New Testament. Depending on the context, he sometimes plays the role of the Father, Divine Soul, the Spirit, the Logos, the Noetic Soul, the alchemist going through the passion of primordial alchemy, and of course, the transcendent human being - Christ.

The Morning Star is Lucifer-Logos. Lucifer is not fallen. When the Logos drops down out of heaven and becomes Lucifer, it is to destroy that which is fallen, creation, so that his Noetic Soul may be emancipated from physical life. The only thing his descent into darkness lays low, are the illusions of the mind.

Logos, The – **L**

To resurrect the Logos, the conscious mind must become aware of this quantum force of consciousness and recognize it beyond the illusions of the mind which attempt to paint a distorted image of it. The conscious mind must lift the Mask of the Logos which is Lucifer.

Typhon Baphomet
The image above is from Eliphas Levi's book Transcendental Magic.
It is the Mask of the Logos (Lucifer).

L – Logos, The

<u>Key Attributes of the Logos</u>

1.) The Logos is a manifestation of the will of the Father to join with IAO to complete the process of creation thereby forming the Christ Monad.

2.) There are two creator deities, not one. They are the twin deities – IAO and the Logos. They are both conceived by the source at the moment of creation. Both IAO and the Logos are Demiurge. Both are Demiurgos. Demiurge has both a dark and light side. It always takes two to create, not one. It takes both Love and Will to create.

3.) Shiva is Lucifer. Lucifer-Shiva is the Logos-Vishnu in his dark inflected form. The Shiva-Lingam is a symbol of the power of the Logos penetrating the force of IAO to alchemically unite and complete the Christ Monad. Their alchemical union is a union between light and darkness. From their union, sexuality emerges within all things.

4.) The Logos is the third of three forms of awareness - reflective awareness. It allows the conscious mind to look inward and connect with Ain Soph.

5.) The Logos is the godhead of the Sacred Trinity. The Sacred Trinity is the immaculate conception of the Father. It includes the Logos (Awareness), The Noetic Soul (Lifeforce), and the Numina (Energy-Love of Creation). The Noetic Soul is the only begotten son of God—begotten by the will of the Father.

6.) The Logos is the only force within the quantum cosmos capable of squaring the circle to manifest the unmanifested. For this reason, the Greek symbol Pi is the symbol of the Logos. The Logos is the Grand Master of the mysteries.

Logos, The – L

7.) The Logos is unbeatable in conflict. He is the champion of God. Lancelot symbolizes the Logos. In his Lucifer-Shiva-Destroyer state he emits the force of Theta (Death). It cannot be defeated because the Logos cannot be defeated. To transcend Theta, the Noetic Soul must reconnect with the Lucifer-Logos while in awareness of Ain Soph. When this occurs, Lucifer reenters the light and transforms back into the Logos. This is the resurrection of the Logos. When the Logos reenters the light, he no longer emits Theta waves. He emits Phi or Tau waves which restore and renew.

8.) Unlike IAO, every human being has their own internal Logos. The Logos exists at all three cosmic scales. We have a Cosmic Logos, Planetary Logos, and an Individual Logos. Because animals do not possess a Noetic Soul, they do not have an individual Logos of their own. Animals are governed by the Cosmic and Planetary Logos. All scales of the Logos re-collect back into one. They are all reflections of each other.

Sumerian Mythology

What we learn from IAO and the Logos about the process of creation has a striking parallel to Sumerian creation myth regarding the half-brother sons Enlil and Enki of the Annunaki King Anu. There are many variations to the story due to Mesopotamia's long history and the different cultures which adopted the Sumerian gods and made them their own but with some additions and alterations to their stories. However, there are common threads running throughout these stories emerging out of the collective unconscious which echo the underlying forces of consciousness in their process of creation.

Enlil, Enki, and Enki's son Marduk, possess like qualities to IAO, the Logos, and the Human / Noetic Soul along the same lines as Set, Osiris, and Horus of Egyptian mythology who represent the same forces of consciousness giving rise to creation.

L – Logos, The

<u>Genesis – The Creation of Mankind</u>

> *"So God created man in his own image,*
> *in the image of God created He him;*
> *male and female created He them" ...Genesis 1:27*

<u>Interpretation / Analysis</u>

"God created man in His own image," equals God created man inside His own image. Mankind was not made "in" the image of God. Mankind was made "by" the image of God (imagination). God's imagination is the Imagination of the Spirit. The Imagination of God, the Mind of God, is sparked into existence by the infinite power of the Spirit (See Dynamis). "Male and female created He them" is a reference to the splitting of the sexes and the manifestation of universal duality in all things via the reconciliation of IAO and the Logos.

<u>Twin Creator Symbolism</u>

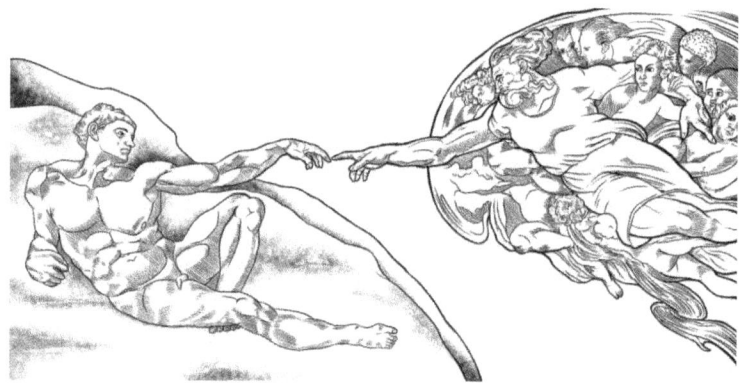

Perhaps there is a double meaning behind the image of Adam and God, by Michelangelo. Perhaps the image is unconsciously of IAO and the Logos compelled by the Collective Unconscious

Logos, The – **L**

Quarks – The Quantum Effect of Creation

Quarks are subatomic particles considered to be the fundamental constituents of matter. Quarks always exist in pairs. If you attempt to pull a quark pair apart, a new partner for the separated quarks will immediately appear. Quarks cannot be isolated. Some physicists consider this to be one of the few spooky anomalies of quantum physics. This is an after effect of the pairing of IAO and the Logos when creation was reconciled at the cosmic level at the very beginning of creation. There are also six types of quarks. This reflects the six spiritual bodies of primordial creation and the six temporal bodies of physical creation. The force which binds quarks and gets stronger and stronger as you attempt to pull quarks apart, is the unbeatable force of the Logos.

Universal Duality in All Things

The universal duality in all things arises from the reconciliation between IAO and the Logos at the cosmic quanta level of existence. Male-Female, Light-Darkness, Odd-Even, Hot-Cold, Etc. Odd numbers preceding Even numbers reflects IAO being the first born of the Divine Trinity. In terms of creation, many religions are correct when they say first there was darkness (IAO) and then there was the light (Logos). The cosmic level of reconciliation between IAO and the Logos laid the foundation for all the laws of the universe and the very nature of our created reality.

Similar or Equivalent Terms:

Logos: Vishnu, Osiris, Enki, Will of God, Word of God, Ptah, Ahura Mazda, Thoth, Demiurge 2 of 2. (IAO is Demiurge 1 of 2) Number 777.

Lucifer: Shiva, Maheshvar, Orion, Abaddon, Apollyon, Morning Star, Typhon Baphomet.

L – Logos, The

<u>Osiris and Set – 1915 Illustration</u>

Art depicting the God Osiris being talked into stepping into a coffin made by his brother Set. The coffin is the mortal physical body. Osiris (Logos) is the champion of God. He is unbeatable in conflict.
Set (IAO-Satan) cannot defeat Osiris in a direct conflict. He knows this. Set can only compel Osiris to defeat himself. This is done by compelling Osiris to sacrifice himself to save what he loves most – the Noetic Soul. The Noetic Soul's descent into the darkness of physical life to fulfill the will of the Father causes Osiris to give up his original form to follow the Noetic Soul into the darkness to become Orion-Lucifer-Shiva to ensure the Noetic Soul is eventually freed from its physical incarnation through death (Theta).

Lord's Prayer, The

The Alchemical Translation

I.) <u>Our Father</u>

> The Father is One-for-All. He equally belongs to everyone everywhere.

II.) <u>Which art in Heaven</u>

> The origin of everything is maintained in a state of perfect harmony and peace through the resonance of the Father. This is heaven. The origin is Causal 'A.' The origin is the divine Monad of Ain Soph of which the Father is the Godhead.

III. <u>Hallowed be Thy Name</u>

> The Father is known to us through his sympathetic resonance. His resonance is his name. The first 3 verses comprise the first stage of the prayer which seeks to bring the mind into discovery of the Father's resonance (the love of his Spirit).

IV. <u>Thy Kingdom Come</u>

> Verse 4 is an invocation of the Father's love (the Spirit). The prayer graduates to an awareness of the Father's love within the mind but yet our full body of creation at this point still lacks full resonance with the Father. This is Communion Turiya. Our Human / Noetic Soul at this point, sensing the Father's love but still lacking full resonance in our body of creation, invokes the Father's resonance to a higher level, harmonizing our body of creation. When we resonate with the Father, we enter his kingdom, and his kingdom enters us.

L – Lord's Prayer, The

V. <u>Thy Will be done on Earth, as it is in Heaven</u>

Verse 5 of the prayer is a declaration of our intent to fulfill the will of the Father. The Earth is the body of our creation not yet in resonance with the Father. Heaven is everything already in resonance with the Father. The will of the Father is to bring our body of creation into resonance with his original nature. (Primordial Alchemy).

VI. <u>Give us this day our Daily Bread</u>

Verse 6 of the prayer is a supplication to the power of the Father to compel the body of our creation (Eros) to enter into resonance with our awareness of the Father's love (Turiya). This is the *"Daily Bread"* which bestows upon the body of our creation the covenant of eternal and everlasting life. The holy blood and bread symbolize the resonance of the Father running through the veins of our body of creation. This is the Holy Grail and the marriage of Eros and Turiya.

VII <u>And forgive us our debts, as we forgive our debtors.</u>

To bring our body of creation into full resonance with the Father's love, we must release our mind's fixation on the things of the world. Verse 7 of the prayer gives us permission to forgive our own self-judgement thereby allowing our mind and body, the freedom and self-acceptance it needs to enter into resonance with the Father and the Kingdom of Heaven.

VIII. <u>And lead us not into temptation, but deliver us from evil.</u>

Darkness is the absence of our resonant awareness with the Father. Our mind and its body of creation are born in darkness. Verse 8 of the prayer reminds the Human / Noetic Soul to maintain resonance with the Father while the mind and body are resonant with the illusion of the world. The key is not to deny the world, but to bring our resonance with the world into harmony with our resonance with the Father. In this way, we bring all things into unity within the matrix of our being including the Father and all of creation.

IX. <u>For Thine is the Kingdom, and the Power, and the Glory, Forever. Amen.</u>

Verse 9 is a proclamation of realized unity. When the light of the Father shines through the prism of the mind, the light divides into the three Magi of the Father:

1.) The Father: That which remains undivided, formless, infinite and absolute.

2.) IAO: The Power of the Father.

3.) The Logos: The Glory and will of the Father.

When our creation enters into resonance with the Father, the mind no longer divides this light, and within us the original true nature of the Father is realized. Verse 9 proclaims this unity by proclaiming the Kingdom (the cosmos), the power (IAO), and the glory (The Logos), all belong to the Father. Thus, the will of the Father is fulfilled. This unity is Christ. Christ is the New Monad. Christ is Dominus.

L – Lucifer

Lucifer *[Lu-ci-fer; Loo-suh-fr]*

Lucifer is the dark inflection of the Logos. Even in the dark inflected state, Lucifer is still loyal to the divinity of Ain Soph. Lucifer is the wrath of the Logos. The job of Lucifer is to destroy creation when creation cannot resonate with Ain Soph to build the Christ Monad. The term Lucifer means "The Light" or "Light Bearer." The Word of God / Will of God is the Light. Lucifer and the Logos are the same being in different modes of operation. Lucifer is the most misunderstood of all the forces of the quantum cosmos.

The Morning Star is Lucifer-Logos. Lucifer is not fallen. When the Logos drops down out of heaven and becomes Lucifer, it is to destroy that which is fallen, creation, so that his Noetic Soul may be emancipated from physical life. The only thing his descent into darkness lays low, are the illusions of the mind.

To resurrect the Logos, the conscious mind must become aware of this quantum force of consciousness and recognize it beyond the illusions of the mind which attempt to paint a distorted image of it. The conscious mind must lift the Mask of the Logos (Image Above).

Similar or Equivalent Terms:

Lucifer: Shiva, Maheshvar, Orion, Abaddon, Apollyon, Morning Star, Typhon Baphomet, Thanatos.

See: Logos. A more in-depth review of Lucifer is provided under the Logos since they are the same being in two different states.

M

Maub *[Mob-uh]*

Maub is an operating intelligence residing in the temporal sphere of the planetary group mind of the Earth. This operating intelligence within the planetary group mind is a planetary genie. The Earth has two planetary genies, one corresponding to the temporal group mind of the Earth in the physical universe, and one corresponding to the spiritual group mind of the Earth in the primordial universe known as EL.

Eventually these two genies are supposed to integrate the temporal sphere of the Earth with the spiritual sphere of the Earth to ignite the Planetary Monad in the physical universe. The Planetary Monad already exists in the primordial universe. Essentially, the temporal sphere will be incorporated into the already growing and expanding Planetary Monad.

When primordial matter and physical matter reach a high enough degree of sympathetic resonance, physical matter is raised to the metatronic state that exists just outside of time. At this point the physical Earth will become a metatronic world.

Until Maub awakens to the realization of the divine source then it remains in a state of darkness. The darkness of humanity feeds the darkness of this planetary genie, and in return this dark genie functions as the central organizing factor of the planetary darkness and perpetuates and reinforces the darkness of all mankind. For lack of a better word, this being is the Devil.

An aspect of Maub has already awoken to the realization of the divine source but most of the temporal group mind still remains in darkness. The growing liberated aspect of the temporal group mind is known as Germain. Every time an individual on Earth liberates an

M – Maub | Microcosmic Orbit

aspect of his or her authentic-self, an aspect of Maub is liberated from its planetary darkness and Germain grows stronger, brighter, and more active in the planetary sphere of the Earth. Eventually, once Maub is fully liberated, Germain (temporal liberated being of the Earth) will integrate with EL (primordial being of the Earth) to complete the Earth's Planetary Monad. Earth will then become a metatronic world.

Maub is a living personification of sheer horror. Before the resurrection of our Logos, any encounter with Maub is paralyzing and deeply disturbing. Maub haunts and torments the Foreman during the Foreman's ascent up Mount Magia. Maub is a living intelligence existing at the level of the temporal group mind of our planet and is a reflection and summation of all which is dark and evil in our humanity. It is an earthly-manifested living force of sheer evil with which we must contend.

Microcosmic Orbit

In Taoist Sexual Yoga, the Microcosmic Orbit is a subtle etheric energic pathway within the human anatomy within which travels energy (Qi-Chi). The energy can be controlled by direction of the conscious mind during deep breathing and sexual yoga exercises but is felt physically moving along the pathway due to a stimulation of the nervous system. The main energetic pathway within a person extends from the sexual organs up the spine of the back, over the head, down the front of the torso, and back to the sexual organs. When the couple is sexually connected, their pathways fuse to become one circuit with the energy orbiting up the back of one, over the heads of both, and down the back of the other, across the genitals of both, and back up the spine again. The couple can reverse the orbit as they wish with their minds. Other secondary orbits exist in our legs and arms. We can move the energy along these secondary orbits with our mind.

(See Sexual Cultivation to view two Microcosmic Orbit Diagrams).

Mind

The mind arises through the pairing of consciousness and matter. Consciousness is the mind's Father. Matter is the mind's mother. The mind and the created cosmos exist in fractal scales. The fractal scales emerged during the initial reconciliation process between divinity and creation on a cosmic level just before the beginning of time. The three major scales are the Cosmic, Planetary, and Individual. We have a Cosmic Mind, a Planetary Mind, and an Individual Mind.

The cosmic level is both the largest and smallest in fractal scales. The quantum world within the atom is cosmic. The galaxies and the furthest reaches of the universe are cosmic. The cosmic level is a serpent swallowing its tail.

The Godhead of the Cosmic Mind is IAO. IAO is the Godhead for all levels of mind including the planetary and individual. The forces of IAO and his Erodonic Trinity are currently reconciled on the cosmic level but remain to be reconciled on the planetary and individual levels within the physical universe. The unfinished levels of creation are what continue to compel the self-organizing force of Alpha to bring everything back into unity with the divine source of Ain Soph to form the Christ Monad. This is the Great Work or Magnum Opus.

All of creation including the physical universe and the primordial universe (Causal 'B') exist inside the Cosmic Mind. The Godhead of the Cosmic Mind, IAO, is the first born out of the divine source. The realms of creation within the Cosmic Mind are brought into organization when the second born of the divine source, the Logos, joins with IAO to complete the process of creation.

The cosmic story of the advent of creation and the forces of consciousness involved continue to echo throughout all the realms of creation to emerge via the collective unconscious into all the worlds literature, religious mythologies, and all forms of creative arts. This story continues to repeat *ad infinitum* because it carries with it a roadmap for the reconstitution of the Monad.

M – Mind

There are multiple forms of mind which are listed as follows:

1.) <u>Cosmic Mind</u>: The mind on a cosmic level.

2.) <u>Planetary Group Mind</u>: The mind on a planetary level.
The planetary group mind is the Noosphere and forms the basis of the Collective Unconscious.

3.) <u>Individual Mind</u>:

   a.) <u>The Human Mind</u>: Has a Noetic Soul and Erotic Soul

   b.) <u>The Animal Mind</u>: Has only the Erotic Soul.

4.) <u>Fractured Mind</u>:

   All internal psychic processes are disharmonious and dissociative in nature. The fractured mind is able to function as a mind by virtue of the automated programs instilled within it by the evolutionary processes of nature.

5.) <u>Individuated Mind</u>:

   All internal psychic processes have coalesced into a harmonious integrated whole and do not depend on the automated programs of nature for survival.

<u>Sphere of the Mind - Conscious Mind</u>: The area of the mind which is aware of itself as well as the deeper elements of the human psyche and cosmic quanta. The more the conscious mind becomes aware of all its constituent parts, the more individuated it becomes.

<u>Sphere of the Mind - Unconscious Mind</u>: The area of the mind and the contents therein that the conscious mind is not yet aware of. God is hidden in the unconscious until the conscious mind becomes aware of it.

Similar or Equivalent Terms:

Theosophy: Manas — Manas is the mind.

Monad – M

Monad *[Mo-nad; Mow-nad]*

The term Monad refers to One or Unity. In alchemy, the Monad is a unified state of being. It is a state of unity with God. There are two types of Monad and within the second type there are three levels. The two types of Monad are:

Type 1: Original Divine Monad

Includes only the three original non-created forces of consciousness all resonating as one, also known as a triune. The three original divine forces within the original divine Monad are:

1.) Divine Awareness – The Father

2.) Divine Lifeforce - Divine Soul

3.) Divine Love - Spirit

The three original forces form the Divine Trinity. They are considered divine because they were never created. They have always existed. Altogether resonating as one, they form the original divine Monad – Ain Soph. Ain Soph is the God Particle residing at the center of all things. Ain Soph is the being of our being. The reality within the realm of Ain Soph is called the Absolute. The Absolute is the only true reality. All else is just a shade of gray or refracted color of light of the only true reality of Ain Soph. Ain Soph and its three divine forces are "Absolute" because they do not correlate to time or space. They exist non-locally within the center of all things and have no scale. They are infinite and omnipresent. Although they were never created, an interaction occurs between the three original forces which create.

Type 2: Christ Monad

The Christ Monad is also called the Alchemical Monad, Reconstituted Monad, and New Monad. The Christ Monad is the original divine Monad (Ain Soph) in unity with the forces of creation. In order to establish and reconstitute the Christ Monad, this requires the

M – Monad

intervention of a conscious mind. It cannot occur on its own through the automatic processes of creation. There are multiple permutations of consciousness. All permutations must be brought into awareness with each through the intercession of the Noetic Soul via the conscious mind. The process to achieve the Christ Monad is the Great Work. Its process is veiled within the Great Arcanum and its fruit is mythologized as the Philosophers' Stone.

The Christ Monad arises on three different scales. The three scales are:

1.) Cosmic
2.) Planetary
3.) Individual.

All three scales together form a Super Monad.

The cosmic level is both the smallest and largest in scale. It's the atom and it's the universe as a whole. It's symbolized by Ouroboros, the serpent swallowing its tail. In order for any universe to organize out of chaos, it must first form a Christ Monad.

The physical universe already has a Christ Monad. The Christ Monad of the physical universe is in resonance with the Super Monad of the primordial universe. The Super Monad of the primordial universe is slowly lifting the physical universe to higher orders of resonance. The physical universe is nested inside its higher mother primordial universe.

The planetary and individual levels of creation in the physical universe are expanding forever in time and therefore these two levels will never finish the Monad development process. Instead, they will produce an infinite number of planetary and individual Monads.

The infinitely distant horizon that time affords the physical universe to create horizontally without end provides Ain Soph the bandwidth it needs for its never-ending process of creation. The physical universe was created to satisfy this divine need. Divinity needs infinite runway as an outlet for its never-ending process. The physical universe provides this. That's why the physical universe was created.

Monad – M

The primordial universe doesn't provide this because everything in the primordial universe is constantly in its highest state of completion because it's eternal. It is always reflecting eternal completeness. This also meets a need of divinity, but a different need.

<u>The Four Needs of Divinity</u>

Divinity has four basic needs. (1) It needs to create. (2) It needs to bring unity to that creation. The Noetic Soul serves this second need. (3) It needs to achieve eternal unity and completeness. Christ and the primordial universe provide this. (4) Lastly, it needs to create forever without end. The physical universe provides the runway for this.

Because the primordial and physical universes of Causal 'B' satisfy all the needs of divinity, there will only ever be two universes. However, that does not preclude multiple physical universes existing side-by-side as bubble universes in the physical stratum. Each physical universe could theoretically be coiled up inside a black hole singularity inside the primordial universe. I believe this is most likely the case.

Incredibly, each physical bubble universe in the physical stratum could have its own Cosmic Christ Monad where they each interact with each other in a way that is almost unfathomable to the human mind.

Again, there only needs to be two universes of creation which coexist in the same location of space but at different frequencies (primordial and physical). In celestial mechanics, this is the purpose of time and space as experienced today in the physical universe.

The primordial universe operates under a different type of physics. In the primordial universe, instead of a body moving through space to create time and space, time and space moves through the body, and the body lives forever. Bodies are not continuously created. All primordial bodies live in eternity.

This dynamic allows the Christ Monad to complete its integration process on all three levels of creation in the primordial universe. The upside to this primordial dynamic is that the creation process can complete itself. The downside is the Father runs out of running room. This compels the creation of the physical universe which has infinite

M – Monad

running room. The downside of the physical dynamic is that some part of the physical universe will always be incomplete and therefore some level of darkness will always exist. The primordial universe and the physical universe work together in a pair. One allows a body to live forever, the other allows for an infinite number of bodies to be created. Together, they complete each other.

The laws and mechanics of the universe allow for the elevation of physical matter through sympathetic resonance with primordial matter. This creates a new form of matter called metatronic matter. Metatronic matter is physical matter existing outside of time. A metatronic being is an immortal physical being. A metatronic being is a Christ being.

Again, it's very possible that there are multiple physical universes existing inside a sea of bubbles along a physical stratum held buoyant by one overarching primordial mother universe. Or there may be an infinite number of primordial and physical pairs. I believe the first scenario is correct because I don't see the need for infinite pairs.

The individual level that the Christ Monad forms is the Human level. The Christ Monad does not form within animals. The Noetic Soul, which is essential to the creation of the Christ Monad, only incarnates inside a human being. The eco-system of animal life is elevated with the completion of the Christ Monad at the planetary level. When enough human beings complete the Monad within a planetary sphere, this ignites the planetary Monad.

The Christ Monad at the cosmic level is the Cosmic Monad, at the planetary level, it is the Planetary Monad, and at the individual level, it is just the Christ Monad. When all three complete, they join the Super Monad of the primordial universe. The Cosmic Monad or Cosmic Christ is Eloah, Allah, Buddha, or Krishna. The historical Christ beings such as Jesus and Siddhartha Gautama reflect the story of the Cosmic Christ. The older in history a Christ being is known, the more their personal story evolves to reflect the cosmic story, and their actual personal story subsides from worldview (Theopomorphism).

The story of the Monad and its process of creation and reintegration is the greatest story of the universe. Its story emerges via the collective unconscious into all our world religions and mythologies.

Monad – M

In time, modern science will emerge with a mainstream scientific explanation and religion will subside as the looking glass into the greatest mystery of existence.

There is a special project underway on Earth in the physical universe to achieve a unity between divinity and creation in human bodily form and to awaken the temporal group mind of the Earth. It's called the Earth Monad Project. Many past attempts to achieve the Christ Monad on other worlds were unsuccessful and destructive. Therefore, the creation of a human genome which provides the capacity for the human being to pursue the Christ Monad, has since been outlawed throughout the cosmos as the "forbidden fruit" due to the great risk the process itself poses to neighboring peaceful humanities. The Earth is a rare exception. The process is being allowed to play-out under strict safety measures and protocols.

The forces of darkness do not want humanity to know its true place in the universe which is at the right hand of the divine Father. The Noetic Soul, which is sent into the darkness of creation to lift it up, has the innate and exceptional ability to re-unify creation with the divine source. This knowledge forms the basis of the Great Arcanum.

Symbols of the Christ Monad

The Squared Circle

1.) The Outer Circle is Causal 'M,' New Monad, Christ, New Heaven-New Earth.

2.) The Triangle is the Sacred Trinity – Logos, Noetic Soul, Numina.

3.) The Inner Circle is Causal 'A,' Original Monad, Ain Soph, Old Heaven.

4.) The Square is Causal 'B,' – Creation, the Mind.

Super Monad

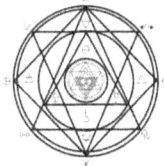

All Three Levels of the Christ Monad superimposed.

M – Monad

Monad Universal Symbolism

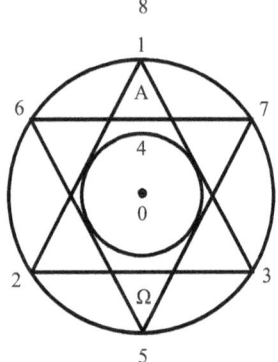

	Natural	Inverted	Super Partner
0	Ain Soph Monad		
A	Triad (Divine Trinity)		Nuad
1	Father		Logos
2	Divine Soul		Noetic / Human Soul
3	Spirit		Numina
4	Eros (Erodonic Trinity)		
Ω	Nuad (Sacred Trinity)		Triad
5	Logos	Lucifer	Father
6	Noetic / Human Soul	Psyche	Divine Soul
7	Numina	Eris	Spirit
8	Christ Monad		

The numbers are the permutations of consciousness.
The 8 is the large circle. The 4 is the small circle. The 0 is the center dot.

Mount Elohim – M

Mount Elohim *[El-o-him; Uh-low-hm]*

Once Alpha finishes leading the conscious mind to the completion of the Christ Monad (Philosophers' Stone) via the eighth alchemical process, a whole new mountain arises via the ninth alchemical process to expand and multiply the Christ Monad *ad-infinitum*. This mountain is the mountain of God, the mountain of eternity, the mountain of Christ. It's climbed eternally to reach an unseen infinitely distant summit. Its name is "Mount Elohim."

Once Alpha reaches the climatic point of culmination at the summit of the Third Mountain (Mount Magia), a new sanctum arises where the forces of Alpha consolidate and re-organize to prepare for a new organizational direction. This sanctum is called, "The Shrine of the Sacred Feminine."

In the Shrine of the Sacred Feminine, we continue to engage the quantum of the Gorgon embedded in matter where the matter is continuously elevated to higher and higher octaves of resonance with the divine source. The final step in the eighth alchemical process of the legendary Three Mountains evolves into the first step beyond the Third Mountain.

The sanctum at the summit of the Third Mountain is dedicated to the sacred feminine because of the nature of the alchemical work involved at this step in the journey. Matter belongs to the feminine line of forces in descent from the Spirit.

The alchemical work with the forces embedded in matter eventually reach a point of critical mass within the summit sanctum of Mount Magia where Alpha redirects the conscious mind of the human being on a whole new alchemical journey.

The Shrine of the Sacred Feminine becomes the new base camp to a whole new alchemical mountain stretching into eternity with an infinitely distant event horizon called Mount Elohim. At the summit of Mount Elohim is the Sanctum of Christ. The Sanctum of Eloah. At the base of Mount Elohim is the Shrine of the Sacred Feminine or the Sanctum of Magdalene. A force of infinite attraction exists between the

M – Mount Elohim

two sanctums. The forces of the cosmic quanta reveal to us that because matter was born in darkness, its journey up the mountainside of Mount Elohim is eternal. It can never be perfected. Because of this dynamic, a new divine paradox arises. The limitation of matter to achieve a perfect unity with the divine source at the summit of Mount Elohim compels a force of infinite attraction to arise to achieve the unity stretching to an infinitely distant summit. Paradoxically, this dynamic produces an unlimited potential within creation, a lifetime of eternal joy, and a drive toward infinite love. Every living being who has ever completed the Monad (Christ Monad; Philosophers' Stone) is still climbing Mount Elohim to this day, including Christ-Eloah himself.

The Noetic Soul can reach and enter the Sanctum of Christ on its own without a body of creation, but in monadal form, with the body of creation intact, the journey to the Sanctum of Christ is forever. The unity between creation and divinity is never perfected and because of this; it opens-up a whole new marvelous journey of unlimited potential.

Nature actually points to and gives us clues as to what emerges after a Monad is formed. The alchemical process exists in scales and reflects and echoes throughout creation. The cosmic singularity, which we call a "Black Hole," is a natural reflection and model of the Monad. Physicists are starting to take seriously the idea that perhaps the physical universe exists inside a black hole nested inside a higher dimensional mother universe – what I would call the primordial universe. If a singularity is a model of the Monad, or just a reflection of it, what can we learn from it?

1.) The singularity potentially forms its own universal realm of creation nested inside a higher mother universe. The Monad is based in a higher more fundamental realm.

2.) It continues to grow and expand even after the singularity (Monad) is formed. The initial establishment of the singularity is only beginning.

3.) It controls and creates its own time and space.

4.) It becomes the central organizing nexus of its realm of influence, directing and organizing all in its orbit.

5.) Its nature is mysterious and unknowable by the outside observer. It cannot be apprehended through perception.

6.) The Monad itself creates. It re-organizes matter-energy-Spirit.

Another echo / reflection in nature of the Monad is the butterfly. What does the butterfly suggest of the Monad?

1.) The Monad goes through stages of development until gaining its wings. (The alchemical processes)

2.) Its prior form must die before its final form is born. The final form is the "celestial body." The physical body is the cocoon.

The alchemical process driving the completion of the Monad is the eighth alchemical process called Primordial Alchemy. The alchemical process continues after the completion of the Monad (Philosophers' Stone) by Alpha compelling its continuous expansion. Continuing beyond the completion of the Monad is the ninth alchemical process called Eternal Alchemy.

In the eighth alchemical process of the Three Mountains which occurs at final stage of the Third Mountain when the alchemist enters the Third Sanctum, the bond of resonance between the Noetic Soul and the Father (Love) is tested by the forces of Eros.

This testing period is called the Tithing.

When the bond of that resonance is tested and confirmed, the covenant of the Father's love is restored within the matrix of creation. At this point, the forces of Heaven (the Father) now have an avenue and a means to bring the forces of the Earth (creation) into harmony with its Spirit via its unbreakable bond with the Human / Noetic Soul. This is the Holy Grail. The holy blood symbolizes the resonance of the

M – Mount Elohim

Father running through the veins of creation. This process brings the alchemist's physical body of creation into unity with the divine source. This is the alchemical Christ Monad.

The Christ Monad is achieved but not perfected with completion of the eighth alchemical process. The ninth alchemical process emerges after the completion of the Monad in order to grow it and perfect it. However, a new paradox emerges. The process of perfecting the Monad is never completed. It is eternal. (Eternal Alchemy)

The cosmic level of the physical universe is now engaged in its own ninth alchemical process of Eternal Alchemy. At an individual level, humans are being led by Alpha to eventually enter into the process of Eternal Alchemy. The Straight Path takes us there in one lifetime. The Spiral Path takes us there over many lifetimes.

In the Eternal Alchemy practice, the alchemist brings into differential resonance (1) the infinite depth of the awareness of the Father with (2) the infinite depth of the forces of darkness within matter.

In the Eternal Alchemy practice, the awareness of the Father lines-up behind the self-observing awareness of the conscious mind via the intercession of the Noetic Soul. This compels the Father to observe and realize the body of creation of the human being and for the darkness in matter to continuously rise-up into the unity with the Father. This drives the eternal expansion of the Monad.

This is an explanation of the eternal alchemy practice is based on the description in Concerto of the Rising Sun published in 2019.

September 2023 Update: As the eternal alchemy process advances, it goes through maturing stages of growth. It initially begins by utilizing the differentiating force of the divine Father (Level Q1 – See Quantum Meditation). However, the alchemist will eventually discover that there is actually a level beyond Q1 called G.

G is the utilization of the force of the Cosmic Christ—Eloah—as the mechanism of differentiation. Its power is beyond extraordinary. In Mount Elohim, Christ Eloah comes into view to cooperate with the alchemist in the expansion of his or her Monad.

N

Nexus

The center of gravity of your primordial being is the Nexus. The Nexus exists both at the center of your primordial being and at the center of the spiritual group mind of the Earth. The locations of each center of gravity (Void and Nexus) are found in the same place, just at different frequencies inside the center of the human being and inside the very center of the Earth itself. The same center of gravity existing at the center of the individual, and the center of the planet, also exist at the center of the cosmos at large.

Noetic Soul – Human Soul

The Noetic Soul is the lifeforce of the Sacred Trinity. The Sacred Trinity emerges during the permutating processes of consciousness known as Theokinesis. A set of underlying divine principles called Super Meta drive the theokinetic process. During the process of theokinesis, the fifth super meta in a sequence called Thelesis arises to compel the will of the Father to intervene with the spontaneous processes of creation and bring everything back into unity.

Thelesis gives rise to the Sacred Trinity. The Sacred Trinity includes: The Logos, Noetic Soul, and the Numina. The Sacred Trinity is the immaculate conception of the Father. Christ is the completion of that conception. Christ is the re-unified God—the transcendent completed human being.

The Noetic Soul is the lifeforce of the will of the Father. The Noetic Soul is also known as the Human Soul, as it is the presence of the Noetic Soul within a humanoid being that makes a being human.

The job of the Noetic Soul is to serve as the intercessing principal between creation and divinity to reconstitute the Monad. The Noetic

N – Noetic Soul

Soul is the eighth permutation of consciousness. Mythologically, the Noetic Soul is "The Only Begotten Son of God." The son is the soul. The term son is used out of tradition. The soul does not have a gender.

There are three types of soul. The three souls are the Divine Soul, the Noetic Soul, and the Erotic Soul. The Divine Soul was not begotten. The Divine Soul always existed. The Erotic Soul was not begotten by the Father. It was begotten by the Spirit. Only the Noetic Soul was begotten by the Father.

The will of the Father begot the Noetic Soul to save creation. The Noetic Soul is the chosen one. The Noetic Soul is the savior. This is the source of the prophecy of the Messiah and the Mahdi. The prophecy is not meant to be fulfilled in the world by only one human being. It is meant to be fulfilled within every human being. The prophecy is meant to be fulfilled within you.

The Father's love for creation emerges as a force. This force is the Sacred Feminine force of the cosmos. She is called the Numina. The Virgin Mary, and the many different sacred feminine forms symbolize the Numina. The Numina gives birth to the new Monad (Christ) within us. The Numina is the ninth (9) permutation of consciousness.

Similar or Equivalent Terms:

Erik P. Antoni:	Noetic Soul
World Religion:	Human Soul
Egyptian Mythology:	The Ba, Ka, Akh, Horus
Sumerian Mythology:	Marduk
Judeo-Christian Mythology:	Messiah, Anointed One, Only Begotten Son of God, Savior
Islamic Mythology:	Mahdi
Kabbalah:	Adam Kadmon

Noumenon – N

Noumenon *[Noo-men-non]*

Immanuel Kant developed the meaning of the word Noumenon from its Greek origin in contrast to the word Phenomenon. In Kant's definition, the noumenon is the ultimate reality of a thing which cannot be apprehended (captured) through the five senses of human perception, unlike the phenomenon, which can be. In Kant's philosophy, the only thing that can be apprehended by the mind, is the mind's representation of the thing it observes, but the actual thing itself is unknowable to the mind. The unknowable aspect is the Noumenon.
(See Kant, Immanuel)

Many have proposed that phenomena may arise out of an abstract world of the noumenon. Kant said the noumenal world may exist, but it is unknowable through human sensation.

In respect to Kant's definition of the noumenon, it is through "resonance," not "perception," that the world of the noumenon can be apprehended by the human mind as a developed faculty of super cognitive emotion which transcends the traditional five senses of human perception.

The noumenal world is a superluminal realm where the forces of consciousness interact with the forces of matter and bridge the source and creation. The interacting forces in the noumenon are called the cosmic quanta. Within the cosmic quanta, the forces of consciousness are "theogenic" and the forces of matter are "atomic." There is a third group in the cosmic quanta which demonstrate both a theogenic and atomic nature which are called "metagenic." For example, the Christ Monad is a metagenic force.

In the realm of the noumenon, quantum law governs the nature of reality, not the mechanical laws of general relativity. In a quantum reality, the mind—and the world around it—are intimate with each other. The observer and observed cooperate and know each other. When your mind cooperates with a quantum process your mind becomes a co-author of that process, and you innately have access to everything occurring in that process, including information. In that moment, your mind and that process are at one with each other. In a quantum reality, we co-create in cooperation with the universe.

N – Nuad

Nuad *[Nu-ad; New-Add]*

The spectrum of the Eyad transitions into a new spectrum beyond the Eyad when the Human / Noetic Soul completes the ascension of the Heaven of Erawan. The realization of the Divine Trinity marks the end of the spectrum of the Eyad and the beginning of a new cognitive stage of development preceding the birth of the Monad. The Logos calls this cognitive stage, the Nuad.

Only the Nuad can complete the Monad.

The Nuad is an organization of the mind which develops when the conscious mind becomes aware of all the forces of the Sacred Trinity. The formation of the Triad—which arises when the conscious mind realizes all the forces of the Divine Trinity—compels the formation of the Nuad. The Triad and Nuad are crystallizations of awareness that form in the mind when we become empathically aware of the higher forces of consciousness. The Nuad engages the forces of Eros and the forces of divinity to complete the Christ Monad.

Each force is a different permutation of consciousness within each of the three trinities preceding the trinity within the Christ Monad: (1) Divine Trinity, (2) Erodonic Trinity, (3) Sacred Trinity, and within the Christ Monad — (4) Christic Trinity. The Christic Trinity is the symphony of all preceding trinities; it is the grand triune.

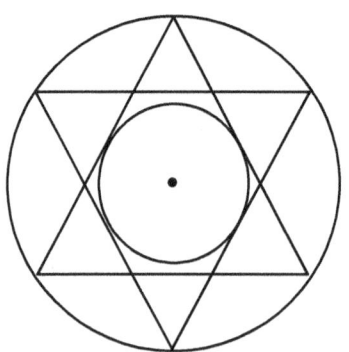

In this Monad Diagram, the Nuad is the downward pointing triangle. The upward pointing triangle is the Triad. The center dot is the Ain Soph Monad. The inner circle is Eros. The large circle is the Christ Monad.

Numina – N

Numina *[Nu-mi-na; New-mi-nah]*

The word Numina is the plural form of the word Numen, which is a spiritual force or divine power presiding over a thing or a place. The word is applied to the third force of the Sacred Trinity which is in direct descent of the divine Spirit. It is used in a plural form as the Numina exists in scales and within all human beings. Every human being with a Noetic Soul has their own Numen or Numina. The Numina is a trinity member of the immaculate conception of the Father to intervene with the forces of creation to lift them back up into a new unity with divinity. The third principal in any trinity of consciousness is always a force of energy in descent from the Spirit, all of which are symbolized by the feminine, the personification of love. The Numina is the Sacred Feminine force of the quantum cosmos, the living force of the Father's love of creation, and the bridge between the Spirit and Matter-Energy.

From a mythological perspective, the Numina is Mary, Tara, Dea, Achamoth, and Theotokos. Depending on a person's culture and religion, the Numina may appear to us in many different forms such as Mary in Christianity and Islam, Isis in Egypt, Lakshmi in Hinduism, Maya in Buddhism, Anahita in Zoroastrianism, Tonantzin of the Aztecs, Rhea in ancient Greece, as well as many other sacred universal feminine forms. Like the other principals of the Sacred Trinity, she has both a natural form and an inverted dark form. The dark inflection of the Numina is Eris, Discordia, Parvati, and Kali. The Monad cannot be completed without the Numina. The reason for this is that the Numina mediates the transformation of Spirit into Matter, and Matter back into Spirit, and reconciles the relative to the eternal. The Numina is responsible for the actual implementation of life and death.

N – Numina

The Noetic Soul reconciles all the forces of the mind, but the Numina binds them together. Without the Numina, all attempts to integrate the forces of the mind would be in vain. The Numina is the ninth (9) permutation of consciousness and is a key force involved in the transformation of the quantum of the Gorgon (11th Permutation of consciousness) into the quantum of the Magdalene.

Different from the Divine Trinity, every principal force in the Sacred Trinity, possesses a dark inflection as follows:

1.) Logos / Lucifer
2.) Noetic Soul / Psyche
3.) Numina / Eris

The forces of the Divine Trinity are "One For All."
The forces of the Sacred Trinity are "All For One."

The forces of the Sacred Trinity exist as a dimension within everything within scales. The major scales are Individual, Planetary, and Cosmic.

Similar or Equivalent Terms:

Ancient Rome:	Numina (Plural); Numen (Singular); Dea
Easter Orthodox:	Theotokos
Catholicism:	The Virgin Mary, Holy or Blessed Mother of God
Islam:	Mary
Buddhism:	Maya
Ancient Egypt:	Isis
Ancient Greece:	Rhea
Aztecs:	Tonantzin
Zoroastrianism:	Anahita
Hinduism:	Lakshmi, Parvati
Judaism:	Achamoth

Omega

The law of sympathetic vibrations in motion is Alpha. However, there are two directions of motion. The upward direction is Alpha. The downward direction is Omega [Ω]. Alpha and Omega [Ω] are the same force moving toward two different magnetic poles. One pole is inside the Nexus, the other pole is inside the Void. Omega [Ω] takes us to the center of our temporal-physical core (Void) while Alpha takes us to the center of our eternal-primordial core (Nexus). We reach both cores simultaneously where we then must integrate both.

Omega Point

Pierre Teilhard de Chardin coined the phrase Omega Point to describe a maximum level of complexity and consciousness towards which he believed the universe was evolving.

The Omega Point is the awakening of any body of creation (Individual, Planetary, or Cosmic) to the realization, actualization, and manifestation of the divine source within the here and now. The Omega Point is fundamental to the cosmic agenda of the universe which unfolds and plays-out across all celestial bodies of infinite starry space. It is a beautiful and miraculous work we all partake in. The Omega Point culminates with the reconstitution of the Christ Monad.

Chardin argued that the Omega Point resembles the Christian Logos, namely Christ, who draws all things into himself, who in the words of the Nicene Creed, is "God from God," "Light from Light," "True God from True God," and "through him all things were made." In the Book of Revelation, Christ describes himself thrice as "the Alpha and the Omega, the beginning and the end."

O – Omicron

Omicron *[O-mi-cron; Oh-mi-cron]*

After the death of the physical body (first death), it is possible to go through a (second death). The second death pathway of the soul arises when Alpha loses its ability to steer the evolution of the mind toward unification with the divine source. Alpha loses this ability when the Noetic Soul loses control over the mind. Typically, this occurs when the delusional narcissistic personality of the Gorgon rising out of the dark hemisphere of the underlying quantum cosmos has completely consumed the mind to form a dark pearl (Dark Monad or Anti-Christ). When the Noetic Soul loses positive control over the mind, a new geometric wave pattern arises which steers the temporal mind into a second death process. This geometric wave pattern is called Omicron.

When a person's physical body dies while their Noetic Soul is inside a dark pearl, they don't reawaken in the primordial universe. They remain stuck inside their temporal ethereal bodies after death in the lower spheres of the temporal group mind in a quasi-dream-state. The temporal group mind and the Omicron Wave combine to work on cracking the dark pearl that is trapping the Noetic Soul. It's a painful process that employs "suffering" to degrade the force of the dark pearl. This is not an operation that was intentionally designed by any superior intelligence. It's an automatic self-regulating process of nature. It is an inherent risk to the pursuit of the Christ Monad and is one of the reasons its pursuit has been outlawed by other civilizations in the galaxy.

Once the second death process completes itself, thereby releasing the Noetic Soul from a disincarnated temporal mind stuck inside the temporal group mind, the Noetic Soul reawakens in its primordial body in the primordial universe. At this point, the Noetic Soul can decide if it will continue to pursue the Monad. If so, it is reincarnated into a new physical body, and the Alpha Wave pattern reemerges to continue the drive toward unification with divinity within a new series of lifetimes in the physical universe.

"Reincarnation" is a process directed intentionally by human life in the primordial universe as a technology of consciousness.

Omicron – O

"Return" is a self-regulating process of the temporal group mind that automatically recycles a Noetic Soul that has failed to free itself from its temporal ethereal bodies after physical death but who is also not in a second death process. What causes this to happen is that the authentic-self (Noetic Soul) in a person never asserted itself in physical life but rather allowed the automatic instincts and reactions of the mind to guide itself through life in an automated manner. An imbalance of power develops in the temporal mind shifting too much power to the automated programs of the mind. If a person strives to free itself from the illusions of the mind throughout life, they will easily wake up in the primordial universe after death. If not, they are typically recycled and "returned," or worse, they go through the second death process.

The Omicron Wave unfolds in degrees. It tries to crack the pearl, so to speak, in a series of escalating grades. The early grades of the Omicron Wave occur before the person dies and typically involves some form of neurological disease or disorder that weakens the mind to release the Noetic Soul before physical death ever occurs.

Omicron psychic energy is the mark of a dark pearl. Empaths can feel the dark Omicron psychic energy emitting from certain individuals. Omicron energy typically forms a dark aura around individuals who are deeply narcissistic, sociopathic, or psychopathic. Omicron energy completely envelops a person who has been devoured by the Gorgon.

A black magician is someone who intentionally amplifies the Omicron Wave. The second death and its Omicron Wave actually forms the pathway of a dark religion to a black magician. A black magician's end goal is the second death. Once this fate has been decided, Lucifer and Eris emerge to accelerate the process to the second death. It's insane, but there's a logic behind the insanity.

The Omicron Wave itself becomes a weapon of control that consumes other people beyond the person emitting the dark energy. It calls forth the Gorgon to emerge inside the minds of other people in the black magician's sphere of influence. The Gorgon rewards the black magician for this with material wealth, power, and control over

O – Omicron

other people. What comes along with this, however, is that in any moment, the black magician can self-destruct, which is quite common. They drink too much of the Gorgon's power too quickly.

Unfortunately, on Earth in the physical universe, certain individuals are aware of this dynamic and intentionally amplify it to bring themselves great power and wealth while selling-out their souls. They're devoted to the Gorgon, the Omicron, and the second death. They believe that the second death can be indefinitely postponed while they embellish and orchestrate their evil upon the world even after death as a poltergeist or a demon. A black magician intentionally cultivates in life, the demonic outcome after death, even while knowing that it will end in the second death. The more powerful the dark pearl becomes, the further the black magician can delay the second death, but also, the longer the second death will take when it finally arrives.

The dark pathway of the Omicron is another inherent risk to the Monad project on Earth, and indeed, has been the cause of the destruction of past human civilizations that once existed on the Earth, but have been long lost to the sands of time.

Through the Omicron, the narcissist has a subliminal dark power over others. The rise of the Gorgon and Omicron in one person compels the rise of the Gorgon and Omicron in another person. It compels the rise of fear and hatred which surrenders the mind to the power of the Gorgon. Narcissistic parents typically cultivate narcissistic children.

By bringing all this to light, the power of the Gorgon and the Omicron is greatly weakened.

Erodysis and the power of the Christ Monad is much more powerful than the Omicron. The power of the Christ Monad is Gamma. Gamma is emitted by the love of Christ. The love of Christ is Erodysis. Erodysis is Gamma.

Similar or Equivalent Terms:

Omicron: Vampirism, Satanism, Gorgonism

P

Personality

The Personality is the persona of an individual arising out of four principal contributing sources. These four sources are:

1.) The Ego
2.) The Super-Ego
3.) The Id, and
4.) Choice

Human beings have a choice in how their personalities develop. People subconsciously model their personalities based on what they observe in the world around them and subconsciously select character traits they admire, feel will help them to integrate socially, and give them an evolutionary advantage.

The personality is an interfacing medium between the person's inner-self and the outside world. When the person's authentic-self transmits clearly through the personality, the personality is considered "natural." If the personality becomes weaponized as an ego-defense mechanism, thereby suppressing the authentic-self, the personality is considered "adaptive." The Gorgon side of the id compels the adaptive personality to form. The adaptive personality is a pathological formation of the mind. All personality disorders exist somewhere within the adaptive spectrum. The most pathological end of this spectrum is the narcissistic personality. The narcissistic personality is a delusional fake-persona which rises up and consumes the entire mind and personality of a person. It becomes its own living entity with its own separate will and way of thinking. It even has its own IQ, and its own psychosomatic influence on the physical body.

P – Perspective Awareness | Philosophers' Stone

Perspective Awareness

There are three forms of awareness. The original form of awareness is the awareness within Causal 'A' of Ain Soph which is Resonant Awareness. Resonant Awareness is the state of pure consciousness. Its awareness is the infinite divine Father. Its lifeforce is the infinite Divine Soul. Its energy is the infinite divine love of the Spirit.

Perspective Awareness collapses the infinite non-local wave function of Causal 'A' to give birth to the created cosmos. Perspective Awareness is the mind. All of creation is embedded in some level or expression of mind.

Reflective Awareness rises within the mind through the intercession of the Noetic Soul to enable the mind to reconnect back to and realize the divine source of Ain Soph.

Perspective Awareness and Reflective Awareness emerge from Resonant Awareness. Resonant Awareness is the Father, Perspective Awareness is IAO, and Reflective Awareness is the Logos. When all three are brought into unison, this is Dominus (Awareness of Christ).

Philosophers' Stone

Historically, the Philosophers' Stone is a legendary substance capable of turning base metals into gold. It is the highest goal of alchemy. Along with its ability to transform metals, it is said to have the ability to bestow immortality and to rejuvenate one's youth. It is the elixir of life. The process or effort to achieve the Philosophers' Stone is the Great Work or Magnum Opus. Its secrets are held inside what is called the Great Arcanum (Great Secret).

The Philosophers' Stone is a metaphorical symbol for something non-physical, much more practical and rational, yet something much more profound. The Philosophers' Stone is the reconstituted Monad. It is the human mind re-integrated with God. It is Christ. It is the highest goal of human existence. It is all permutations of consciousness re-harmonized back into a single unit of one. The great secret, or great arcanum, is the true purpose and position of the Noetic Soul.

Philosophers' Stone – P

The Noetic Soul is the only begotten son of god. The only begotten son of god is not just one historical figure. The Noetic Soul in every human being is the only begotten son of god. We are sent into the darkness to lift-up creation out of chaos.

Ain Soph is the original divine Monad. It is the God Particle residing at the center of all things. The original divine Monad does not include the forces of creation. However, Ain Soph automatically gives rise to creation spontaneously through the infinite power of its divine love. Its love sparks creation. Ironically, although love sparks creation, it initially emerges in darkness and chaos. When Ain Soph realizes that the infinite force of its Spirit is automatically sparking creation into existence, a divine will emerges with the intent to re-integrate creation. This Will is the Light. The Will of God and the Word of God are one and the same. It is the Logos. The Logos is the awareness of the Will. The Noetic Soul is the lifeforce of the will. The love for creation behind this will is the Numina. The three forces which emerge by the divine will of Ain Soph are the Sacred Trinity (The Immaculate Conception). The purpose of the Sacred Trinity is to engage the forces of darkness within the realms of creation to reconstitute the Monad. The reconstituted Monad is Christ. It is the Philosophers' Stone.

The historical accounts mentioned in the following sections, Antiquity to Interpretations, were sourced from the Wikipedia in 2019 but with analysis and commentary by Erik P. Antoni in [brackets].

Antiquity

The earliest known written mention of the philosophers' stone is in the Cheirokmeta by Zosimos of Panopolis (c. 300 AD). Alchemical writers assign a longer history. Elias Ashmole and the anonymous author of Gloria Mundi (1620) claim that its history goes back to Adam who acquired the knowledge of the stone directly from God. This knowledge was said to be passed down through biblical patriarchs, giving them their longevity. The legend of the stone was also compared to the biblical history of the Temple of Solomon and the rejected cornerstone described in Psalm 118.

P – Philosophers' Stone

"The stone which the builders refused is become the head stone of the corner." ... Psalm 118-22.

[Perhaps "builders" is an unconscious reference to the ancient builder race who belonged to the same federation of cosmic beings that outlawed the pursuit of the stone—the Monad (the forbidden fruit). Christ is the cornerstone of creation. But note, the ancient builder race on Earth was actually a rebellious faction that came to Earth in pursuit of the Monad but was later destroyed by an army from its home world for corrupting its own experiment. It corrupted it by interbreeding with it, practicing black magic, and creating chimeras—animal-human hybrids. It built many of the great megalithic sites on Earth and used early monadal humans in the construction of the projects.]

The theoretical roots outlining the stone's creation can be traced to Greek philosophy. Alchemists later used the classical elements, the concept of anima mundi, and creation stories presented in texts like Plato's Timaeus as analogies for their process. According to Plato, the four elements are derived from a common source or prima materia (first matter), associated with chaos.

Prima materia is also the name alchemists assign to the starting ingredient for the creation of the philosophers' stone. The importance of this philosophical first matter persisted throughout the history of alchemy. In the seventeenth century, Thomas Vaughan writes, "The first matter of the stone is the very same first matter of all things."

<u>Middle Ages</u>

Early medieval alchemists built upon the work of Zosimos in the Byzantine Empire and the Arab empires. Byzantine and Arab alchemists were fascinated by the concept of metal transmutation and attempted to carry out the process. The 8th-century Muslim alchemist Jabir ibn Hayyan (Latinized as Geber) analyzed each classical element in terms of the four basic qualities. Fire was both hot and dry, earth cold and dry, water cold and moist, and air hot and moist. He theorized that every metal was a combination of these four principles, two of them interior and two exterior. From this premise, it was reasoned that the transmutation of one metal into another could be affected by the rearrangement of its basic qualities. This change would be mediated by a substance, which came to be called xerion in Greek and al-iksir in

Philosophers' Stone – P

Arabic (from which the word elixir is derived). It was often considered to exist as a dry red powder (also known as al-kibrit al-ahmar, red sulfur) made from a legendary stone—the philosophers' stone. The elixir powder came to be regarded as a crucial component of transmutation by later Arab alchemists.

In the 11th century, there was a debate among Muslim world chemists on whether the transmutation of substances was possible. A leading opponent was the Persian polymath Avicenna (Ibn Sina), who discredited the theory of transmutation of substances, stating, "Those of the chemical craft know well that no change can be effected in the different species of substances, though they can produce the appearance of such change."

According to legend, the 13th-century scientist and philosopher Albertus Magnus is said to have discovered the philosophers' stone. Magnus does not confirm he discovered the stone in his writings, but he did record that he witnessed the creation of gold by transmutation.

<u>Renaissance to Early Modern Period</u>

The 16th-century Swiss alchemist Paracelsus (Philippus Aureolus Theophrastus Bombastus von Hohenheim) believed in the existence of Alkahest, which he thought to be an undiscovered element from which all other elements (earth, fire, water, air) were simply derivative forms. Paracelsus believed this element was, in fact, the philosophers' stone.

[The Alkahest is the divine Spirit or Holy Spirit. All matter and all energy are simply derivative forms of the divine Spirit.]

The English philosopher Sir Thomas Browne in his spiritual testament, Religio Medici (1643), identified the religious aspect of the quest for the philosophers' Stone when declaring, "The smattering I have of the Philosophers stone, which is something more than the perfect exaltation of gold, hath taught me a great deal of Divinity." … R.M. Part 1:38

A text published in the 17th century called, the Mutus Liber, appears to be a symbolic instruction manual for concocting a philosophers' stone. Called the "Wordless Book," it was a collection of 15 illustrations.

P – Philosophers' Stone

The Squared Circle
An alchemical symbol (17th century) illustrating the interplay of the four elements of matter symbolizing the philosophers' stone.

In Buddhism and Hinduism

The equivalent of the philosophers' stone in Buddhism and Hinduism is the *Cintamani*. It is also referred to as Paras / Parasmani (Sanskrit: पारसमणि, Hindi: पारस) or Paris (Marathi: परिस). In Mahayana Buddhism, Chintamani is held by the bodhisattvas Avalokiteshvara and Ksitigarbha. It is also seen carried upon the back of the Lung Ta (wind horse) which is depicted on Tibetan prayer flags.

By reciting the Dharani of Chintamani, Buddhist tradition maintains that one attains the Wisdom of Buddhas, is able to understand the truth of the Buddhas, and turns afflictions into Bodhi. It is said to allow one to see the Holy Retinue of Amitabha and his assembly upon one's deathbed.

In Tibetan Buddhist tradition the Chintamani is sometimes depicted as a luminous pearl and is in the possession of several different forms of the Buddha.

Within Hinduism, it is connected with the gods Vishnu and Ganesha. In Hindu tradition it is often depicted as a fabulous jewel in the possession of the Nāga king or as on the forehead of the Makara. The Yoga Vasistha (Book Name), originally written in the 10th century AD, contains a story about the philosophers' stone.

A great Hindu sage wrote about the spiritual accomplishment of Gnosis using the metaphor of the philosophers' stone. Saint Jnaneshwar (1275–1296) wrote a commentary with 17 references to the philosophers' stone that explicitly transmutes base metal into gold. The seventh century Siddhar Thirumoolar in his classic Tirumandhiram explains man's path to immortal divinity. In verse 2709 he declares that the name of God, Shiva, is an alchemical vehicle that turns the body into immortal gold.

Philosophers' Stone – P

Properties

The most commonly mentioned properties are the ability to transmute base metals into gold or silver, and the ability to heal all forms of illness and prolong the life of any person who consumes a small part of the philosophers' stone diluted in wine. Other mentioned properties include creation of perpetually burning lamps, transmutation of common crystals into precious stones and diamonds, reviving of dead plants, creation of flexible or malleable glass, or the creation of a clone or homunculus.

Names

Numerous synonyms were used to make oblique reference to the stone, such as *white stone* (calculus albus, identified with the calculus candidus of Revelation 2:17 which was taken as a symbol of the glory of heaven, vitriol (as expressed in the backronym Visita Interiora Terrae Rectificando Invenies Occultum Lapidem), also lapis noster, lapis occultus, in water at the box, and numerous oblique, mystical or mythological references such as Adam, Aer, Animal, Alkahest, Antidotus, Antimonium, Aqua benedicta, Aqua volans per aeram, Arcanum, Atramentum, Autumnus, Basilicus, Brutorum cor, Bufo, Capillus, Capistrum auri, Carbones, Cerberus, Chaos, Cinis cineris, Crocus, Dominus philosophorum, Divine quintessence, Draco elixir, Filius ignis, Fimus, Folium, Frater, Granum, Granum frumenti, Haematites, Hepar, Herba, Herbalis, Lac, Melancholia, Ovum philosophorum, Panacea salutifera, Pandora, Phoenix, Philosophic mercury, Pyrites, Radices arboris solares, Regina, Rex regum, Sal metallorum, Salvator terrenus, Talcum, Thesaurus, Ventus hermetis.

Many of the medieval allegories for Christ were adopted for the lapis, and the Christ and the Stone were indeed taken as identical in a mystical sense.

The name of stone or lapis itself is informed by early Christian allegory, such as Priscillian (4th century), who stated Unicornis est

P – Philosophers' Stone

Deus, nobis petra Christus, nobis lapis angularis Jesus, nobis hominum homo Christus. In some texts it is simply called stone, or our stone, or in the case of Thomas Norton's Ordinal, our delicious stone. The stone was frequently praised and referred to in such terms.

It needs to be noted that philosophorum does not mean, of the philosopher—or—the philosopher, in the sense of a single philosopher. It means, of the philosophers, in the sense of a plurality of philosophers.

Appearance

Descriptions of the philosophers' stone are numerous and various. According to alchemical texts, the stone of the philosophers came in two varieties, prepared by an almost identical method, white, for the purpose of making silver, and red for the purpose of making gold, the white stone being a less matured version of the red stone. Some ancient and medieval alchemical texts leave clues to the physical appearance of the stone of the philosophers, specifically the red stone. It is often said to be orange (saffron colored) or red when ground to powder. Or in a solid form, an intermediate between red and purple, transparent and glass-like. The weight is spoken of as being heavier than gold, and it is soluble in any liquid, yet incombustible in fire.

Alchemical authors sometimes suggest that the stone's descriptors are metaphorical. The appearance is expressed geometrically in Michael Maier's Atalanta Fugiens.

"Make of a man and woman a circle; then a quadrangle; out of this a triangle; make again a circle, and you will have the *Stone of the Wise*. Thus, is made the stone, which thou canst not discover, unless you, through diligence, learn to understand this geometrical teaching."

Rupescissa uses the imagery of the Christian passion, telling us it ascends "from the sepulcher of the Most Excellent King, shining and glorious, resuscitated from the dead and wearing a red diadem..."

Philosophers' Stone – P

Interpretations

The various names and attributes assigned to the philosophers' stone has led to long-standing speculation on its composition and source. Exoteric candidates have been found in metals, plants, rocks, chemical compounds, and bodily products such as hair, urine, and eggs. Justus von Liebig states that it was indispensable that every substance accessible ... should be observed and examined. Alchemists once thought a key component in the creation of the stone was a mythical element named Carmot.

Esoteric hermetic alchemists may reject work on exoteric substances, instead directing their search for the philosophers' stone inward. Though esoteric and exoteric approaches are sometimes mixed, it is clear that some authors are not concerned with material substances but are employing the language of exoteric alchemy for the sole purpose of expressing theological, philosophical, or mystical beliefs and aspirations. New interpretations continue to be developed around spagyric, chemical, and esoteric schools of thought.

The transmutation mediated by the stone has also been interpreted as a psychological process. Idries Shah devotes a chapter of his book, The Sufis, to providing a detailed analysis of the symbolic significance of the alchemical work with the philosophers' stone. His analysis is based on a linguistic interpretation through Arabic equivalents of one of the terms for the stone Azoth as well as for sulfur, salt, and mercury.

Indries Shah — The Sufis

"That the alchemists of the West knew that they were pursuing an internal goal is clear from their admonitions and the innumerable cryptic illustrations in their works. Alchemical allegory is by no means difficult to read if one bears in mind Sufi symbolism. In the seventeenth century, a thousand years after the time of their original inspirer — Geber (born circa 721) — the European alchemists were keeping lists of successive masters ..." ... "In the records we find the name(s) of Muhammed, Geber, Hermes, Dante and Roger Bacon."

(admonitions = counsel, advice, or caution)

P – Planetary Alchemy | Poltergeist

Planetary Alchemy

As we become aware of the temporal forces of creation existing on a planetary level, we become simultaneously responsible for them. This is a fundamental rule in alchemy. It cannot be avoided. As such, these forces arise within the mind as a new stressor to be transformed. This forms the basis of a whole new level of alchemy called Planetary Alchemy. Whereas in the 6th alchemical process, the stressor is individuality, the stressor in the 7th alchemical process advances beyond individuality to become planetary, beginning with the temporal group mind of the Earth. In the 7th alchemical process, the alchemist is no longer transforming just the contents of his or her individual mind; the alchemist is transforming the forces of the temporal group mind, and in doing so, has joined the cosmic process of awakening the planetary group mind of the Earth on a higher level.

Poltergeist – Demon   *[Pol-ter-geist; Powl-tr-gaist]*

Contrary to popular theological belief, a Poltergeist or Demon, is not a fallen Angel who once knew the light and then fell into darkness. This is a misunderstanding of the mythology. What fell from the divine source was the original outpouring of creation and its original matter.

Attributes, or principles, of this original matter copied and mirrored what was inside divinity. For example, the trinity of darkness, known as the Erodonic Trinity, reflects the order of the Divine Trinity. This reminds us of the phrase:

> *"And a third of the angels fell with him."*

Creation fell from the source into darkness because it was spontaneously formed outside the will of God.

Much worse than once knowing and later renouncing the light, a Poltergeist or Demon, was born in darkness. It never once knew the light. If it did, it could find its way back, but it cannot. It is only through the intercession of the Noetic Soul that darkness can be reconnected with the light. This dance takes place within the psyche.

Poltergeist – P

It is why the darkness is obsessed with the Noetic Soul and is why so many people are drawn to the darkness—we are meant to engage it. The Idamus is obsessed with the Noetic Soul but fears it. The Gorgon hates Christ and the Noetic Soul and wants to trap and control the soul. But note, when the Gorgon is finally lifted into the light, she transforms into the bride of Christ and becomes his greatest and most powerful ally.

The Noetic Soul, the intercessing principal between divinity and creation, brings creation back into unity with God. The Poltergeist or Demon is a Gorgon quantum born out of the darkness of matter. It attempts to assert its power and influence in the world even after death. The narcissist develops and cultivates in life what will eventually become a Poltergeist or Demon after death.

The Gorgon quantum rising out of the left the side of the id in the erotic sphere of the psyche within all human beings is the source of most poltergeist or demonic activity. The Gorgon quantum can cause psycho-kinetic activity from both people dead and alive. What activates it are periods of heightened stress, fear, anxiety, and trauma. The Gorgon rises in the psyche to bring a dark cohesion to the mind during periods of great unease by offering a delusional alternative to reality. Sociopathy, Narcissism, Schizophrenia, Border Line Personality, Demonic Possession, et al, are all constructs of the Gorgon.

The psyche of the human being breaks up after death and different pieces go in different directions. The Noetic Soul itself does not haunt the world. It heads for the primordial universe, the other side of the veil. It can get caught up in the temporal group mind having difficulty discharging its temporal ethereal bodies—which is a requirement to reawaken in the primordial. If this happens, the Noetic Soul is typically immediately reborn. Other psychic elements of what was once that person continue in different directions. The energetic shell of the personality can continue-on and *haunt* the world. This is a *Ghost*. But a ghost is a subtle energetic shadowing. It is a harmless phenomenon. It dissipates over time. If the person cultivated a Gorgon narcissistic mind, this force could splinter from the psyche after death and become a Poltergeist—a Demon.

P – Prelescent Period | Prima Materia

Prelescent Period [Pre-le-scent; Pre-leh-scent]

The Prelescent Period is the second of three major periods in the development of how consciousness emerges and functions within the mind. In the Prelescent Period the conscious mind has grown to question its own existence. It still possesses automated features of the mind passed down from the prior Auto Cognitive Period but has grown to become partially aware of the automated features with a limited ability to intervene with them and make a conscious choice or an unfiltered observation. In the Prelescent Period the human mind's internal reflective awareness of the divine source is greatly dampened by the underlying chemical brain wiring and automated programs inherited as artifacts of human evolution. The Prelescent Period is a crossroad in human evolution where the human species will either stand up and become a truly sentient being or remain part of the animal kingdom. The humanity on Earth in the physical universe is currently in the Prelescent Period.

Prima Materia

The Cosmic Consciousness is the ultimate fundamental reality of the universe which all matter reduces to and from which all things come forth. The Cosmic Consciousness is the Alpha and the omega of creation. It is both the "Prima Materia" from which all things are made and the final apex of evolution when it rises within its own creation to unify and reconcile creation with the divine source.

History (Sourced from Wikipedia 2019)

According to Plato, the four elements are derived from a common source or Prima Materia (first matter), associated with chaos. Prima Materia is also the name alchemists assign to the starting ingredient for the creation of the philosophers' stone. The importance of this philosophical first matter persisted throughout the history of alchemy. In the seventeenth century, Thomas Vaughan writes, "the first matter of the stone is the very same with the first matter of all things."

Prima Materia | Primordial Earth – P

<u>Analysis</u>

Plato correlates the Prima Materia with the first matter of creation associated with chaos. This would not be the Cosmic Consciousness. This would be the first matter which emerged from the first act of creation before it was organized. The Prima Materia can be the ultimate source substance (Ain Soph - the Cosmic Consciousness) or it can be the first matter of creation. When the Prima Materia first coalesces, it forms hydrogen. *See Also*: Chaos

Primordial Earth *[Pri-mor-di-al; Prai-more-dee-uhl]*

The Earth in the physical universe has a twin. It exists in a higher vibrational mother universe called the primordial universe. We have both a physical Earth and a primordial Earth. The physical Earth exists in the same location as the primordial Earth, just at a different wavelength and behind a singularity wall (the great veil). The physical universe is nested up inside a singularity (black hole) inside the primordial universe. A singularity wall separates the two universes. No wavelength of light can pass through. Only consciousness can pass through. For this reason, scientists in the physical universe have not yet detected the primordial universe, but its existence causes indirect anomalies in the physical universe such as the apparent presence of dark matter and dark energy.

    The planetary group mind enveloping the Earth has two great cathedrals, or hemispheres. One hemisphere encompasses the Earth in the physical universe. It's called the temporal group mind. Another hemisphere encompasses the Earth in the primordial universe. It's called the spiritual group mind. The spiritual group mind subdivides into bandwidths which resonate closer to or further from the divine source of Ain Soph (Original Monad). Each bandwidth is a heaven. There are nine heavens that bound the Earth in the primordial universe.

P – Primordial Earth

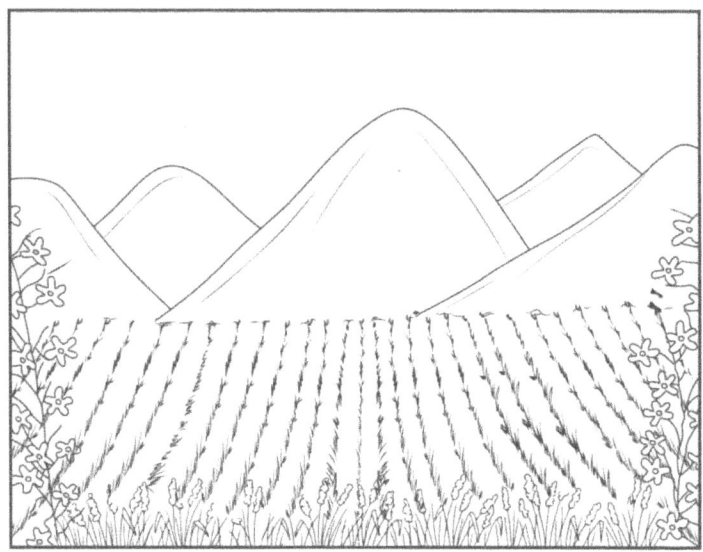

This sketch comes from a real memory of the Primordial Earth. This location of the Primordial Earth is referred to as the Emerald Green Valley. It is a gateway between the Physical and the Primordial.

In the Elysium heaven which completely envelopes and enshrines the primordial Earth, the divine Genie of the Earth, whose name is EL, lives both inside us, and all about us, and binds us with the land of the Earth in such magical ways that the mortal mind would never believe it. The mountains wiggle and jiggle as you think of them. The divine beauty of it all - will leave you speechless."

> *"No eyes have seen,*
> *no ears have heard, no mind has imagined,*
> *what God has prepared for those who love him."*

Similar or Equivalent Terms:

Shambhala; Hyperborea; Eden, Celestial Jerusalem

Primordial Universe

The primordial universe is the mother universe to the physical universe. They are dual reflections of each other. The primordial universe is based in eternity. The physical universe is based in time. The primordial universe is the other side of the great veil (singularity wall). It's where we come from before being born and go back to after we die.

When we're back in the primordial, we essentially live on a wheel. Imagine a wheel inside a wheel. The outer wheel is the physical universe and the inner wheel is the primordial universe. Each existence we live in the physical universe lines up on the wheel. Each physical existence reflects a mirrored primordial existence on the inner wheel. In the physical universe we cannot jump between physical existences, but in the primordial universe we can. Human beings jump existences through conscious will. When we jump existences it's like walking through an air curtain. The whole scene just changes. It's like walking between rooms.

In the primordial realm, we only have one immortal body which lives forever. With that one immortal body (primordial body) we are able to move between a number of primordial existences, or primordial realities which reflect each physical existence we once lived in the physical universe. The primordial universe is a wonderful eternal realm that is dual reflecting of the physical universe.

In the diagram to the right, each triangle is an existence. The physical level of each existence comes and goes with the birth and death of each physical body. The primordial manifestation of each existence remains forever imprinted inside the heavenly eternal-primordial realm.

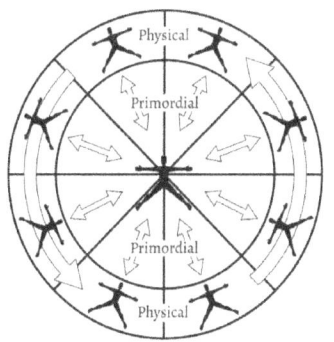

Similar or Equivalent Terms:

Hyperborea

P – Psycho-Sexual Dynamic

Psycho-Sexual Dynamic

The Psycho-Sexual Dynamic is the vicious feedback cycle between the mind and body. Most people have negative feedback cycles where their minds slowly become more dark, twisted, and delusional throughout life. The genesis of the negative feedback cycle is as follows.

The physical body of the human being is typically born in an asynchronous sexual alignment with its primordial body due to humanity's current state of spiritual-biological evolution. The initial sexual asymmetry distorting the resonance between our temporal-physical being and our eternal-primordial being is primarily neurological. This neurological condition is found within the physical brain and manifests through what is called the psycho-sexual dynamic.

The psycho-sexual dynamic is as follows.

The magnetic sexual polarity of the bodies of our temporal-physical system is out of harmony with the magnetic sexual polarity of the bodies of our eternal-primordial system. What supports and drives this sexual asymmetry is a disordered psyche within the temporal mind caused by a genetic predisposition in the physical brain.

Even if individuals can achieve brief moments of higher resonance with the Spirit through the practice of alchemical sexual intercourse, the higher resonant states are quickly lost due to a person's disordered psyche counteracting the harmony.

The disordered psyche in human beings maintains the sexual disharmony, but the sexual disharmony in turn supports the disordered psyche. The only way to break this vicious cycle is not just with the sexual cultivation practices of the Second Factor, but with the combined practices of all Three Factors working together in concert. We must become acutely aware of the psycho-sexual dynamic within us, listen to it, and apply the practices of the Three Factors accordingly. Within the common person, and even within the alchemist, the psycho-sexual dynamic is pre-set to support the disordered psyche and thus the Three Factors are required to break the cycle and achieve integration. The truth is, we are not born complete. Completion requires the intervention of a conscious mind to rise above its automated instincts. Through the Three Factors we can achieve a completed unified mind.

Q

Q Level

Consciousness loses its holistic integrity when its expression within a lifeform is refracted by the mind—like light passing through a prism — and those refracted rays of consciousness are forced to function separately or incoherently.

As the temporal sphere of the mind begins escalating its resonance with Ain Soph, the mind initially divides the unified light of Ain Soph into the three divisible forces of the Father, the Divine Soul, and the Spirit. However, as the resonance of our mind ascends further, the division of three reintegrates back into the unity of one, and Ain Soph emerges.

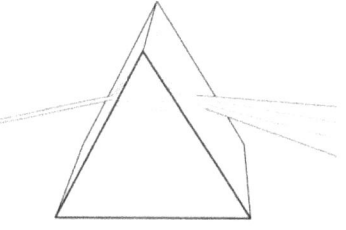

To measure this division experienced within, the refracted rays of light are grouped into major levels of division referred to as levels of Q, which stands for quotient. Quotient is the number reached by division.

Our goal is to arrive at Q1 which has no division. At Q1 we experience only levels of depth, not division. Q1 is an eternal level as the depth within Q1 is infinite. When we begin the alchemical process, we begin working at Q5. At Q5 we are neither aware of nor realize any division of the Cosmic Consciousness. At Q5 when we look inward, all we sense is darkness. At Q5, all we experience within is our human ego and the reflection of our human personality.

When we begin to feel and differentiate within us the authentic-self, we are at Q4. When we separate within ourselves that which is false from that which is real, we reveal our true self, our authentic-self (Noetic-Soul).

Q – Q Level

The means and methods of separating what is false within us, from what is authentic within us, is the Three Factors. When we reach Q3, we gain the cognitive ability to detect the first rays of light of the Cosmic Consciousness within us. This first divisible light level corresponds to the Divine Spirit of Ain Soph.

After many years in Q3 working with the Divine Spirit, we begin cognitively detecting a more refined level of light emerging from deep within our core. This new level is Q2. Q2 is still a divisible manifestation of the Cosmic Consciousness, but it is closer in resonance to its original nature. At the Q2 level, we work with the force of the Divine Soul and our primordial being. After many years in Q2, the Divine Soul brings us to the Father and the full breadth and majesty of the Cosmic Consciousness in its indivisible form known as Ain Soph. At this level, we are in Q1. In summary, the levels of Q are as follows:

- Q5 No awareness of our authentic-self, the Spirit, the Divine Soul, or the Father. In this state, we are a human automaton led purely by instinct and our ego defense mechanisms.

- Q4 We have an awareness of our authentic-self. A true center of gravity exists within us.

- Q3 We have an awareness of our authentic-self and the Spirit. We have a higher sense of God beyond self.

- Q2 We have an awareness of our authentic-self, Spirit, and the Divine Soul.

- Q1 We have an awareness of our authentic-self and the Father. If you are aware of the Father, then you are simultaneously aware of the Divine Trinity which includes the Father, the Divine Soul, and the Spirit. The Divine Trinity as a unified whole, is Ain Soph—original triune.

Once we achieve Q1, there is no inner division of light. We resonate with Ain Soph and continue forever inward into the infinite eternal depths of the Father. Q1 goes forever inward into the Father, but there is a level after the Father corresponding to Eloah. This level is G. We don't begin working with G until we reach Mount Elohim.

Qigong – Q

Qigong – Quigong, Chi Gong *[Qi-gong; Chee-Guhng]*

Qiqong is one of many methods of cosmic cultivation. Qigong is a form of Tai Chi originally taught in China. It channels the energy of nature and the greater cosmos to balance the energy of the physical-spiritual anatomy of the human being. It is a legitimate practice of the Second Factor. The practice of *Primordial Qigong* taught by Michael Winn is a great practice of cosmic cultivation.

The Qigong practice typically involves moving meditation, coordinating slow-flowing movement, deep rhythmic breathing, and a calm tranquil state of mind. People practice qigong throughout China and worldwide for exercise, relaxation, preventive medicine, self-healing, alternative medicine, expansion of consciousness, self-cultivation, and training for martial arts.

See Also: Cosmic Cultivation, Second Factor.

Qi Gong

Q – Quantum Meditation

Quantum Meditation [Quan-tum; Kwaan-tm]

Quantum Meditation is a practice of the Third Factor [5] as it develops our relationship with the forces of the divine source and the whole pantheon of the cosmic quanta. The practice of Quantum Meditation shifts the conscious mind's focus of conscious awareness beyond our temporal ethereal bodies into our spiritual ethereal bodies, and even further into the noumenal realm of the cosmic quanta and the divine source. There are three ways to shift our focus of conscious awareness into our higher spiritual ethereal bodies which resonate beyond our temporal ethereal bodies:

1.) After the death of our physical body when we transcend the illusions of our mind and escape our temporal ethereal bodies to enter paradise.

2.) When we integrate our spiritual ethereal bodies with our temporal ethereal bodies in the alchemical processes of the Third Mountain.

3.) Through the practice of Quantum Meditation.

Quantum Meditation can be practiced while our physical body is either awake or asleep. It is best to first learn while awake and then while asleep. To perform this practice, we must be able to feel the resonance of the Spirit with our emotional faculty. This means our level of Q needs to be at Q3. In summary, the levels of Q are as follows:

Q5   No awareness of our authentic-self, the Spirit, the Divine Soul, or the Father. In this state, we are mostly a human automaton led purely by instinct and our ego defense mechanisms.

---

[5] See Three Factors

Quantum Meditation – Q

Q4 We have an awareness of our authentic-self (Noetic Soul). A true center of gravity exists within us.

Q3 We have an awareness of our authentic-self and the Spirit. We have a higher sense of God beyond self.

Q2 We have an awareness of our authentic-self, Spirit, and the Divine Soul.

Q1 We have an awareness of our authentic-self and the Father. If you are aware of the Father, then you are simultaneously aware of the Divine Trinity which includes the Father, the Divine Soul, and the Spirit. The Divine Trinity as a unified whole, is Ain Soph. Once we achieve Q1, there is no inner division of light. We resonate with Ain Soph and continue forever inward into the infinite eternal depths of the Father.

G The Monad is complete and now we are expanding it with the aid of Eloah—the Cosmic Christ—in Mount Elohim.

Practice:

1.) Start off with a breathing exercise which relaxes your whole physical body.

2.) Focus on feeling the Divine Spirit with your emotions.

3.) As you continue to relax your body, contrast your awareness of the Divine Spirit with your awareness of your physical body.

4.) Allow your awareness of your physical body to slip away from your mind while you hold onto your awareness of the Divine Spirit.

5.) Now shift your attention to your emotions. Focus on your emotional center. Contrast the difference in your mind between your common human emotion from that of the Divine Spirit. Choose the Divine Spirit over your common human emotions and allow your common human emotions to slip away.

Q – Quantum Meditation

6.) Now shift your attention to your thought processes. Focus on your mental center. Contrast the difference in your mind between the feeling of your thoughts from that of the Divine Spirit. Choose the Divine Spirit and allow your thoughts to slip away.

7.) Now shift your attention back to your physical body. Focus on the feeling of your physical body. Contrast the difference in your mind between your physical body and the Divine Spirit. Choose the Divine Spirit and allow your physical state to slip away.

8.) Repeat this cycle of differentiation and release as needed. With each cycle, each element you are releasing becomes softer and more transparent.

9.) With each cycle, go deeper into the Divine Spirit.

10.) As your feelings shift deeper into the Divine Spirit, begin listening to the Divine Spirit with your feelings. Listen very delicately and you will begin hearing with your feelings. There is a very subtle communication which is occurring. You will begin receiving knowledge directly from the cosmic quanta.

The longer we are able sustain a heightened resonance between our conscious mind and the Divine Spirit (Spirit), the more the physical wiring of our brain is re-wired to support and deepen the resonance. Over time, the subtle communication between our conscious mind and the emergent forces of the cosmic quanta develops into a new super cognitive faculty called "intraspection." This is not "introspection." Introspection takes place solely between your own thoughts. Intraspection is a communication between the conscious mind and the forces of the cosmic quanta. The Spirit is the first of these forces.

As we continue the Third Factor practice of quantum meditation alongside other practices of the Three Factors, additional forces within the cosmic quanta - beyond the Spirit - begin to emerge and present themselves. As we develop our super cognitive ability to communicate with the cosmic quanta; prayer, quantum meditation, and intraspection, all come together to resonate as one. The practice of quantum meditation is very different from the practice of astral projection taught by many new age metaphysical schools. With astral projection, practitioners attempt to astral travel using their temporal ethereal bodies.

Astral Projection

It is necessary to explain and dispel some of the myths about the practice of astral projection and lucid dreaming. Many students of astral projection believe the practice allows them to leave their physical bodies in a way which is special, metaphysical, and different than what most people commonly experience.

However, all people shift their conscious awareness beyond their physical bodies into their deeper ethereal bodies every time they fall asleep. The only difference is, they are not aware of the unfolding process. This is designed by nature to be this way. When the conscious mind inserts itself into the transitional process of sleep, we are interrupting our mind's communication with the planetary group mind. The astral projection practice trains our conscious mind to witness the shifting of our conscious awareness from our physical body into our deeper ethereal bodies, and then to maintain a conscious awareness of the fact that our physical body is asleep while we go about travelling the planetary group mind (Astral World).

When a person's conscious mind is having difficulty intervening upon and interrupting this natural process, it does not mean the person is less spiritually evolved. It means the person's brain is functioning in the way it was designed and is resisting any interruption.

In the early years of my own alchemical work, I use to astral travel on a regular basis by shifting my focus of conscious awareness into my deeper ethereal bodies while maintaining conscious awareness of the fact that I was not awake in my physical body. I used to play with the virtual environment of the temporal group mind as a lucid dreamer so

Q – Quantum Meditation

often does. I could adjust my temporal group mind environment at will. Eventually, my conscious mind awoke to the realization of what I was experiencing. Our experience in our ethereal bodies is not an experience of separate universes. We are experiencing the planetary group mind of the Earth.

When I finally awoke to this realization, I decided to stop interrupting the special instructions of the planetary group mind and I began cooperating with it more proactively.

If for some reason the planetary group mind requires you to be aware of your physical state while having a virtual experience within the planetary group mind, then it will happen. There is no reason to force it. Allow everything to unfold and manifest naturally.

There is nothing real and permanent in the planetary group mind which you can reliably and continuously go back and forth from. It's not a natural universe. It's a virtual universe. What you experience in the planetary group mind is not independent of your mind. It's literally an observer-observed interaction.

The physical universe and the primordial universe are projections of a higher order. They are formations of the Cosmic Mind. The observer-observed interaction is still very much in effect in the ongoing creative processes of each universe with the exception that, from the standpoint of an individual, for an observer-observed interaction to take material effect, it requires the mind of the individual to be resonant with the forces of the Cosmic Mind and the Cosmic Consciousness.

Once reflective awareness of the forces within the cosmic quanta becomes an operating function of the mind, the human being becomes a conscious collaborator in the creative processes of the universe.

When people are simply dreaming or astral projecting, they are not experiencing the primordial universe.

The key to astral projection is quieting your mind and subtly observing your body as it falls asleep. The key is learning to spy on the process. It's an art form more than it is a science. If your brain catches you spying, it will resist. When the shock of sleep arrives, if you power through without losing awareness, you will witness the unfolding.

R

Reflective Awareness

There are three forms of awareness. The original form of awareness is the awareness within Causal 'A' of Ain Soph which is "Resonant Awareness." Resonant Awareness is the state of pure consciousness. Its awareness is the infinite divine Father. Its lifeforce is the infinite Divine Soul. Its energy is the infinite divine love of the Spirit. "Perspective Awareness" collapses the infinite non-local wave function of Causal 'A' to give birth to the created cosmos. Perspective Awareness is the mind. All of creation is embedded in some level or expression of mind. Reflective Awareness rises within the mind through the intercession of the Noetic Soul to enable the mind to reconnect back to and realize the divine source of Ain Soph. Perspective Awareness and Reflective Awareness emerge from Resonant Awareness. Resonant Awareness is the Father, Perspective Awareness is IAO, and Reflective Awareness is the Logos. When all three are brought together in unison, this is Dominus.

Reincarnation – Transmigration

Reincarnation is when the physical body dies and the soul associated with that physical body is reborn into a new physical body to live a new physical existence. The cycle of birth and death repeats in the reincarnation process. Each physical existence is one lifetime. We can have many lifetimes. Some people theorize that the Noetic Soul (Human Soul) reincarnates consecutively in linear fashion, one lifetime after another. Other people propose the idea that the soul may animate multiple physical bodies in parallel existences. Some suggest that souls who are now human may have lived lifetimes as an animal or a plant.

R – Reincarnation

Others say the Noetic Soul only reincarnates in a human body and was never once incarnated in an animal and never will be. Reincarnation is a fundamental core belief in many religions and philosophies including Buddhism, Hinduism, and the Kabbalah. It is said by some that the early philosophical teachings of Christianity included reincarnation. Each religion or philosophy has its own concepts of how reincarnation works. The following are some key principles about reincarnation:

1.) There are three soul types: the Divine Soul, Erotic Soul, and Noetic Soul (Human Soul). Only the Noetic Soul reincarnates. Some philosophies believe there are many souls in the body. This a prismatic refraction of the Erotic Soul and Noetic Soul passing through the lens of the mind via the various organs of the body. Each organ corresponds to the mind and refracts the light of the Erotic Soul and Noetic Soul differently. In Taoism this dynamic is actually leveraged in the alchemical process. Through the alchemical transformation and integration process these refractions of the mind dissolve as the mind unifies. In western alchemy, we utilize a similar process with a different lens. We utilize the Five Centers in the Transformation of the False Selves. Both processes lead to the unified mind.

2.) The Noetic Soul reincarnates only in the humanoid body.

3.) The Noetic Soul never once incarnated in a lower-level lifeform such as a dog or a tree. Only the Erotic Soul animates the lower-level species. There is only one Erotic Soul which animates all species simultaneously. The Noetic Soul intervenes with the Erotic Soul within the mind to reconnect it back to the Divine Soul and reconstitute the Monad.

4.) True reincarnation is when we die and first reawaken in our primordial body after death before taking a new physical body. If we do not reawaken in our primordial body after physical death before taking a new physical body, this is not true reincarnation. This is called, Recycled Return. For more explanation see: *Eternal-Primordial Being*

Reincarnation – **R**

5.) Reincarnation does not occur as a process for the Noetic Soul to evolve spiritually. This is a common egocentric view. It's wrong. The soul does not evolve. The body and the mind evolve. The Noetic Soul is already perfect. The reason the Noetic Soul reincarnates is to elevate the mind and the physical matter of the body by way of the Noetic Soul's connection to the Divine Soul. The Noetic Soul does not come into the world for it itself. It comes into the world to complete the process of creation by bringing consciousness and matter into harmony by way of the Noetic Soul's presence within the mind. When the conscious mind cooperates with this process, the process can be completed in a single human lifetime and the process of reincarnation is transcended.

6.) There are two universes within Causal 'B' (Creation) which overlay and parallel each other at different frequency wavelengths which all human beings oscillate between in the human reincarnation process. The two universes which overlay and parallel each other are the physical universe and the primordial universe.

7.) The physical body is the twin mortal body to the immortal primordial body. We only ever have one primordial body. It never dies and we never change it. However, we take on many physical body's life after life in the physical universe through the process of reincarnation. Between physical existences, we re-awaken in our primordial body in the primordial universe.

8.) There is a special project underway on Earth in the physical universe to achieve a unity between divinity and creation in human bodily form and to awaken the temporal group mind of the Earth. It's called the Earth Monad Project. The primordial humanity on Earth is directing the evolution of the physical humanity on Earth and therefore is in control of the whole process of human reincarnation. A higher spiritual deity is not in charge of the human reincarnation process. We are.

R – Resonance | Rubicon

Resonance *[Re-so-nance; Reh-zuh-nuhns]*

Resonance is a supernatural empathy or super sensory familiarization between all things which transcends all dimensions of space, time, and mind. It is innate to the soul. Resonance is the medium of our super cognitive faculties of intraspection and the divine language of Kier. It is the fountainhead of all gifts and all abilities.

Resonant Awareness

There are three forms of awareness. The original form of awareness is the awareness within Causal 'A' of Ain Soph which is "Resonant Awareness." Resonant Awareness is the state of pure consciousness. Its awareness is the infinite divine Father. Its lifeforce is the infinite Divine Soul. Its energy is the infinite divine love of the Spirit. "Perspective Awareness" collapses the infinite non-local wave function of Causal 'A' to give birth to the created cosmos. Perspective Awareness is the mind. All of creation is embedded in some level or expression of mind. Reflective Awareness rises within the mind through the intercession of the Noetic Soul to enable the mind to reconnect back to and realize the divine source of Ain Soph. Perspective Awareness and Reflective Awareness emerge from Resonant Awareness. Resonant Awareness is the Father, Perspective Awareness is IAO, and Reflective Awareness is the Logos. When all three are brought together in unison, this is Dominus.

Rubicon *[Ru-bi-con; Roo-buh-kaan]*

The Rubicon is the point of no return. In the alchemical process of unifying the mind to complete the reconstitution of the Monad, when the self-organizing force of the universe, Alpha, rises to guide the conscious mind on its journey of unifying mind, there is a point where Alpha will not recede. This is when we cross the Rubicon. Alpha will not subside at this point except for the death of the physical body or at off ramps spaced very few and far between. The universal point of no return is the fifth grade of the First Mountain. *See First Mountain.*

S

Sacred Fire

The Sacred Fire is the amplified and accelerated rhythm of Alpha. When on the Spiral Path, our individual evolution is in Alpha Group Sync with the rest of humanity on Earth. In Alpha group sync, Alpha's rhythm and geometric unfoldment is very slow in motion and unfolds gradually in planetary time. When we accelerate Alpha, we break our group sync and enter the Straight Path and our evolution is accelerated. There is a tangible and heightened rate of transformation of our anatomical being. The measurable effect of our accelerated transformation is the Sacred Fire. This measurable effect is often equated with Kundalini or a climbing serpent of fire.

Similar or Equivalent Terms:

Kundalini (Hinduism)

S – Sanctum of Magia

Sanctum of Magia [Ma-gi-a; Muh-gee-ahh]

A sanctum is a point of stillness and consolidation within the forces of Alpha in its process of leading all the forces of the mind, body, and consciousness toward a unified mind—the Monad.

The Alpha Wave pattern produced by the forces of Alpha in the process of developing the Monad includes three major development periods called the Three Mountains. The Monad development process also includes Three Sanctums. The Three Sanctums are between the First and Second Mountains, the Second and Third Mountains, and just below the summit of the Third Mountain. The Sanctum of Magia is the sanctum sitting just below the summit of the Third Mountain. There is a fourth sanctum at the summit of the Third Mountain but at this point the Monad has already been formed.

Similar or Equivalent Terms: Sanctum of the Logos, Third Sanctum

This Mayan pyramid symbolizes the Third Mountain, Mount Magia.
The temple was built by the Mayan to worship Kukulcan.
Kukulcan is the Yucatec Maya Feathered Serpent Deity. It was known as Quetzalcoatl to the Aztecs. The pyramid is the main structure of the Chichen Itza archaeological site in the Mexican state of Yucatan.
Each of the nine major steps of the pyramid symbolize one of the nine heavens of the Earth. The doorway on top symbolizes the Third Sanctum.
The tier atop the Third Sanctum symbolizes the final work of Mount Magia.
When we complete Mount Magia, we become a Feathered Serpent.

Satan *[Sa-tan; Say-tun]*

Satan is the dark inflection of IAO. Just as all the other forces of consciousness have a dark inflection—except for the three original forces (Father, Divine Soul, Spirit)—the quantum of IAO also has a dark inflection. All the forces of consciousness, in both their reconciled states, and dark inflected states, have mythological representations emerging out of the collective unconscious into all the world's historic religious scriptures, poetry, fables, literature, and all the world's creative arts. The dark inflection of IAO is the most famous of the dark mythological characters. The dark inflection of IAO is Satan. What may surprise many people is that Lucifer and Satan are the dark inflections of two totally different forces of consciousness. Satan is the dark inflection of IAO. Lucifer is the dark inflection of the Logos.

In Egyptian mythology, Satan is Set (also spelled Seth), the Logos is Osiris, The Noetic Soul is Horus, and the Numina is Isis. Osiris and Set are the principal forces involved in the final alchemical labor of the Third Mountain.

The Wikipedia 2017 summarizes their story as follows:

"The Osiris myth is the most elaborate and influential story in ancient Egyptian mythology. It concerns the murder of the God Osiris, a primeval king of Egypt, and its consequences. Osiris's murderer, his brother Set, usurps his throne. Meanwhile, Osiris's wife Isis restores her husband's body, allowing him to posthumously conceive a son with her. The remainder of the story focuses on Horus, the product of the union of Isis and Osiris, who is at first a vulnerable child protected by his mother and then becomes Set's rival for the throne. Their often-violent conflict ends with Horus's triumph, which restores order to Egypt after Set's unrighteous reign and completes the process of Osiris's resurrection."

Similar or Equivalent Terms:
IAO, Set, Seth, Enlil, Center Head of Cerberus, Yaldabaoth.

S – Second Factor | Second Mountain

Second Factor – Cultivation

The Second Factor helps our conscious mind to access the Divine Spirit deep within us to utilize its force in the practices of all Three Factors. The key is understanding that we are all made of energy and energy exists in three different states: (1) Positive-Yang-Male, (2) Negative-Female-Yin, and (3) Neutral-Yuan. The Spirit is genderless and completely neutral in its energy. The energy of the human mind exists in a spectrum between Yin and Yang. All men and women have both polarities within them. No one is all male and no one is all female, regardless of our sexual organs. The key is seeing past the Yin-Yang polarities of the mind to access the deeper energy of the Spirit. The Second Factor incorporates cultivation techniques into our daily life to help us to balance our biomechanical and psychic energy to allow the Spirit to rise within our conscious mind. Without this balance, our biomechanical and psychic energy clouds our mind making it more difficult for our conscious mind to connect with the Spirit. Some cultivation techniques involve sexual yoga practices while other practices are performed solo in direct concert with the forces of nature, or with the forces of the cosmic quanta underlying the forces of nature. Cultivation works best when we are already practicing the First Factor. If not, the cultivation practice is contaminated by the reactions of the human psyche. The Three Factors are mutually supportive.

Second Mountain – Mount Kabbalah

Mount Kabbalah is the second of three mountains in the alchemical process of achieving the Christ Monad. The three mountains are major Alpha patterns which guide the conscious mind of the alchemist during the alchemical process. In the second mountain, Mount Kabbalah, we deconstruct the compensating mechanisms of the human ego and the adaptive instincts of our animal nature which prevent the authentic-self within us from integrating into a cohesive individuated whole. By going through this deconstruction process, we are at the same time allowing a fragmented-self to self-assemble into an individuated-self –which, when achieved– liberates our true authentic nature.

Second Sanctum

A sanctum is a point of stillness and consolidation within the forces of Alpha. It is a necessary stage in the process of leading all the forces of the mind, body, and consciousness toward a unified mind – the Monad. The Second Sanctum is the sanctum between the Second Mountain and Third Mountain.

The Alpha Wave pattern produced by the forces of Alpha in the process of developing the Monad includes three major development periods called the Three Mountains. The Monad development process also includes Three Sanctums. The Three Sanctums are between the First and Second Mountains, the Second and Third Mountains, and just below the summit of the Third Mountain. There is a fourth sanctum at the summit of the Third Mountain but at this point the Monad has already been formed.

Sefirot, The [Sef-ir-ot; Seph-hi-roth]

In the third major stage of development in the reconstitution of the Monad, which in Hermetic lore is called the *"Third Mountain,"* Alpha keeps cycling the conscious mind of the alchemist through all 13 layers of the mind. Each cycle ascends to a higher order of resonance with Ain Soph wherein we learn about the various dimensions and interactions of the forces within Ain Soph and how these interactions compel the emerging processes of creation. The forces of consciousness alchemically interact with each other. They compound and multiply in a process called *Theokinesis*. Each new force of consciousness, and each new force of mind, which arises out of the process of theokinesis, is called a *Permutation*.

All theokinetic permutations of consciousness are mapped out in the book on spiritual alchemy called *Song of the Immortal Beloved*. Theokinesis is a "spiritual physics." There are nine principal permutations of consciousness and two additional permutations arising out of the mind for a total of eleven theokinetic permutations. The first three forces—the divine trinity—are the only non-permutated permutations; meaning, they have always existed as permutations.

S – Sefirot, The

Official Rabbinical Diagram of the Sefirot of the Kabbalah

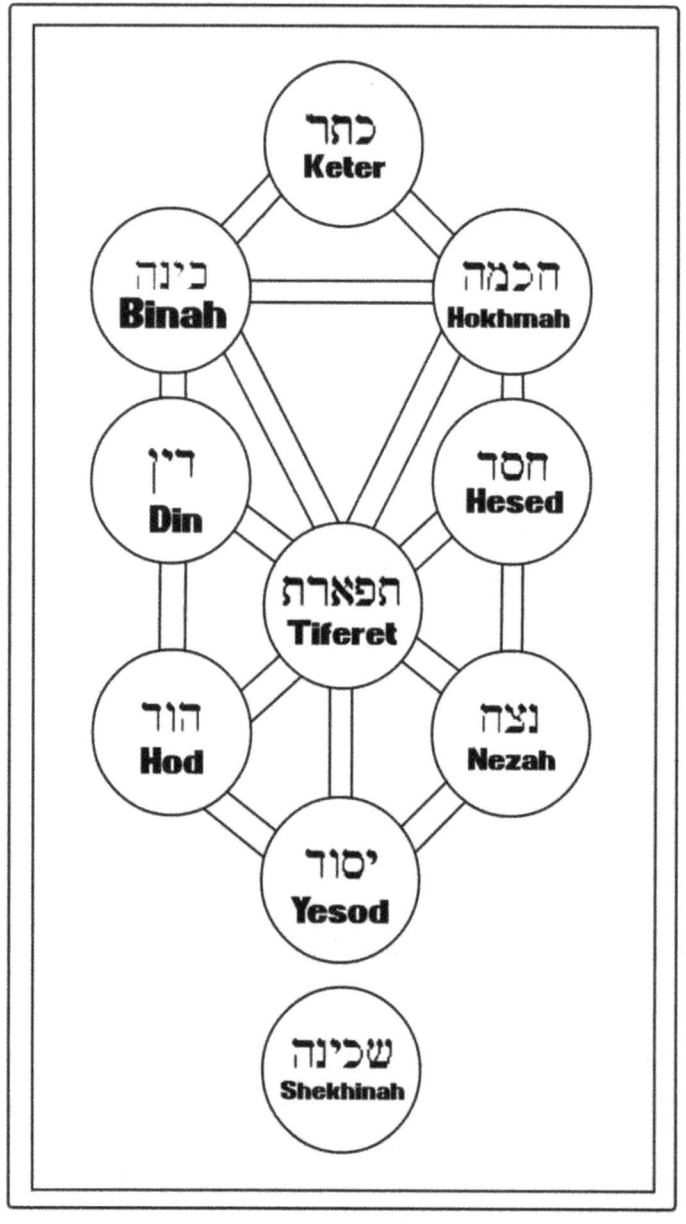

Sefirot, The – S

The Kabbalistic ancestors who introduced the Sefirot most likely had their own direct experience of the cosmic quanta and the Sefirot is an attempt to describe the nature of the cosmic quanta. Based on the rabbinical descriptions of the Sefirot - and experience with the cosmic quanta and the process of theokinesis - although there are ten Sefirot, and nine permutations of consciousness with two additional of the mind, it is evident that they are not the same on a one-to-one basis. There are some profound correlations, however, which are described below:

First, [A] a description of the process of theokinesis and the permutations of consciousness experienced during the process of alchemical integration is provided. Second, [B] an official rabbinical definition for each Sefirot of the Kabbalah is presented. Third, [C] a comparative analysis between [A] and [B] is demonstrated and explained.

[A] — Theokinesis and the Permutations of Consciousness

A popular theological belief is that the original unity of God - the original Monad - Ain Soph - created the universe because it was alone. Meditation on the quantum forces within us reveals that this was not the original cause. Quantum meditation reveals that the act of creation develops and completes itself in three primary stages. Creation was not a single act. It continues to repeat *ad-infinitum*.

Creation emerges out of Ain Soph due to the way in which Ain Soph is internally composed. Ain Soph has three primary dimensions within itself with each dimension possessing its own divine force. The differentiation between these three divine forces compels an interacting relationship to arise and develop between each of the divine forces. This interplay drives the process of creation. This process is called *"Theokinesis."* Theokinesis is a divine algebra or spiritual physics. Because the three forces within Ain Soph will never stop interacting, the process of creation never-ends. Creation initially emerges spontaneously without intent due to the infinite power of the love being produced by the interplay of divine forces.

S – Sefirot, The

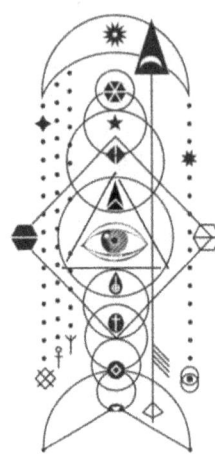

Because creation emerges spontaneously, it initially emerges in darkness[6] and chaos. There is a will within Ain Soph to reconcile creation and reconstitute the Monad. Meditation on the process reveals the process to achieve unity is regulated by one of two means. The first means is to destroy creation. The second means is to unify creation with the original Monad. The second means is the only viable long-term solution because creation will never stop. The moment creation is destroyed, it immediately reemerges. To end the cycle of creation and destruction, creation and divinity must be reconciled and unified. When the process of creation is able to complete itself without being destroyed, a new Monad arises with the original Monad at the core of the new Monad. Mythologically, the new Monad is Christ – the completed being – the reunified God.

The infinite energy provoking the emergence of creation also compels that same creation to emerge as a vision. Creation initially emerges as a mental construct. This vision cannot maintain itself within the original causal realm of divinity. The realm of divinity is called Causal 'A.' Only Ain Soph can reside in Causal 'A.' When creation emerges, it automatically forms its own causal realm within which all of creation resides called Causal 'B.' All universes of creation reside inside Causal 'B' including the primordial and physical universes.

The emerging vision of Ain Soph forms the mind. Every level of creation resides inside a mind. The physical universe and the primordial universe reside inside a Cosmic Mind. The creation of a human being resides inside a human mind. The body and mind are indivisible.

---

[6] Isaiah 45:7: I form the light, and create darkness: I make peace, and create evil: I the Lord do all these things.

Sefirot, The – S

In order for any creation to complete itself and be saved, the mind of creation must achieve a unity of resonance with Ain Soph. The mind must become self-aware of Ain Soph in order to achieve the unity. This is the goal of Alpha and the Spiral Path and Straight Path. Alpha is directing all things toward an eventual unity with Ain Soph. All things will continually experience a cycle of birth and death until that unity is realized and accomplished. The mind of creation emerges from Ain Soph in finite form, yet it must reconcile with the infinite absolute divine source of Ain Soph in order to achieve and realize the new unity. Interestingly, the Alpha solution to reconciling a finite form with an infinite source is to reconcile within scales.

Time, space, the atom, and our whole matrix of creation emerges as a result of the reconciliation. The atom, the galaxies, and the physical universe which we experience today, on a cosmic level, are the outcome of a reconciled unity between creation and divinity. There are three major scales of creation to be reconciled. The first major scale is the cosmic scale which includes both the very small and the very large. It is a serpent swallowing its tail (Ouroboros). The primordial universe, and its sister physical universe – which we all currently inhabit - are already reconciled at the cosmic level. We have a Cosmic Monad. We have a Cosmic Christ. The primary goal of the Cosmic Monad is to finish carrying-out the will of the Father to unify the lower scales of creation with the divine source.

The Cosmic Monad is now focused on the planetary and individual spheres of creation. Once all three levels achieve the Monad, all three levels of the Monad become one. At this point, the process of creation has been eternally stabilized inside a self-regulating Super Monad. All three levels of creation in the primordial universe are integrated within the Super Monad. The physical universe has a Monad at the Cosmic level but the planetary and individual are still in process. The Cosmic Monad of the physical universe is already at one with the Super Monad of the primordial universe.

S – Sefirot, The

The Process of Creation from Start to Finish

Stage 1

It all begins with the original divine awareness called the Father. The Father does not have a gender, but he is called the Father out of mythological tradition and because he holds the original seed of all creation. The Father is the first (1) permutation of consciousness.

How does the Father exist? Some would say this is unknowable, however, quantum information arising out of the noumenon reveals the answer. Existing below the permutations of consciousness are a phenomenon called Super Meta. The super meta are an underlying set of divine principles which compel the divine forces. The first super meta is called Force Potential. Within zero, there is an infinite potential. This potential within zero has a nature which gives rise to the infinite paradoxical awareness of the Father. The Father is an absolute infinite awareness existing beneath all things.

The second super meta is called Being. Being arises due to the existence of the first super meta called Force Potential. Because Force Potential exists, then Being must exist. Being is the intrinsic life-force directly associated with any form of awareness. The being of the Father is the Divine Soul. The Divine Soul is the second (2) permutation of consciousness. Because the Father is absolute and infinite, then the Divine Soul is absolute and infinite.

The pure awareness of the Father is called Resonant Awareness. Resonant awareness will do what awareness does. It will be aware. The first thing that the awareness of the Father is aware of is his own life, his own being, the Divine Soul. The realization of the Divine Soul is considered the first realization of the Father. It is an eternal realization because the Father has always been aware of his own existence. This realization is called the First Triumphant.

The Father's awareness of his Divine Soul automatically gives rise to Love. This Love is the Spirit. The Spirit is also called the Divine Spirit and the Holy Spirit.

Sefirot, The – S

The emergence of the Spirit is the third (3) permutation of consciousness. There is a super meta which compels the rise of the Spirit when the Father becomes aware of his own Divine Soul. This third super meta is called the Force of Unity. It is the Law of One. For some exotic reason, the moment the Father becomes aware of his own life, this produces a duality between awareness and being, or between awareness and life, which must be reconciled back to one.

The first three permutations of consciousness are the only three non-permutated permutations of consciousness out of all permutations of consciousness. They are considered non-permutated because they have always existed, yet paradoxically, they are considered permutated because they relate to each other as operating permutations of consciousness driving all other permutations of consciousness in the process of creation.

Because the awareness is infinite, and because the life of that awareness is infinite, then the energy produced to unify these two forces is infinite. This infinite energy is—infinite love—the Spirit.

The infinite energy demanded and produced by the Law of One—which gives rise to the Spirit of God—is driving the divine forces toward an infinitely distant event horizon called Zero-Base-Prime.

The infinite energy driving toward Zero-Base-Prime produces a phenomenon we call Consciousness. It is fundamental to the unity of the original Divine Monad of Ain Soph. The mathematical equation of consciousness can therefore be expressed as:

$$\textit{Infinite Awareness (Outward)} \times \textit{Infinite Life (Inward)}$$
$$\times \textit{Infinite Love (Energy)} = \textit{Consciousness}$$
$$or$$
$$\textit{Consciousness} = \textit{Infinity}^{\,3}$$

S – Sefirot, The

Next, the infinite energy of the Spirit spontaneously sparks a creative vision of the cosmos. The spark compels imagination. The compelled vision of the Spirit forms the mind. This spark is the fourth super meta called Dynamis. Creation is sparked into existence spontaneously and unintentionally by the force of love (the Spirit) produced by the awareness of Ain Soph (the Father) being aware of its own lifeforce (The Divine Soul).

The spark happens outside of the conscious will and divine awareness of the Father. The spark of Dynamis happens automatically. Because of this, creation and the mind emerge in chaos. This chaos is darkness. When the mind emerges in darkness, it carries with it, attributes of awareness, life, and energy.

The unit of —Mind, Awareness, Life, and Energy— emerging out of the Divine Trinity of Ain Soph, is called Eros or the Eros-Dyad.

The Eros-Dyad can be viewed as a whole as the 4th permutation of consciousness when it emerges in darkness. However, in order to reconcile it with divinity, the reconciliation requires us to differentiate the forces within the Eros-Dyad.

The three forces embedded within the Eros-Dyad—embedded within the mind—are called the Erodonic Trinity. Every trinity—in any permutation of consciousness—always possesses the same three dimensions of awareness, life, and energy. The awareness in any trinity of consciousness is the Godhead of that trinity. The Godhead of the Erodonic Trinity is IAO. IAO is also known as Tetragrammaton, YHWH (Yahweh), and Jehovah.

IAO is the fourth (4) permutation of consciousness. IAO is the first-born of the Divine Trinity. IAO is born of the Spirit. IAO is born in darkness and chaos. The life-force of the Erodonic Trinity is the Erotic Soul, the life-force of IAO, the Sea of Eros—the Eternal Sea. The Erotic Soul is the fifth (5) permutation of consciousness. The third principal of the Erodonic Trinity is Matter-Energy. Matter-Energy rises and transforms out of a theogenic force into an atomic force. Matter-Energy is the sixth (6) permutation of consciousness.

Sefirot, The – S

<u>Stage 2</u>

The Father becomes aware that the Spirit of his love is sparking creation into existence, but his creation is trapped in darkness because the spark of his creation happens spontaneously without his intention. This is the second realization of the Father and is called the Second Triumphant. IAO and his Erotic Soul are initially trapped in darkness. They cannot resonate with the Father because of the way they are born. IAO is the king of the darkness and has no direct knowledge of divinity. The awareness in IAO is not resonant awareness. The awareness in IAO is Perspective Awareness. Perspective awareness forms the mind.

<u>Stage 3:</u>

The Father's realization of his creation having been born and stuck in darkness compels a process within divinity called Thelesis. Thelesis is the fifth super meta which gives rise to a new trinity. This trinity is called the Sacred Trinity or Lower Trinity. The Lower Trinity is a direct reflection of the Upper Trinity or Divine Trinity. Thelesis gives rise to the Father's love of creation and his will to save it.

    The Godhead of the Sacred Trinity is the Logos. The Will of God and the Word of God are one and the same. The Logos reflects the Father within all realms of creation. The awareness of the Logos is Reflective Awareness. When reflective awareness emerges within the mind, it allows the mind to look inward and reconnect back to and become resonate with Ain Soph to reconstitute the Monad. The Logos is the seventh (7) permutation of consciousness.

    The Noetic Soul is the lifeforce of the will of the Father. The Noetic Soul is also known as the Human Soul. The job of the Noetic Soul is to serve as the intercessing principal between creation and divinity to reconstitute the Monad. The Noetic Soul is the eighth (8) permutation of consciousness. Mythologically, the Noetic Soul is the Only Begotten Son of God. The son is the soul. The term son is used out of tradition. The soul does not have a gender.

S – Sefirot, The

There are three types of soul. The three souls are the Divine Soul, the Noetic Soul, and the Erotic Soul. The Divine Soul was not begotten. The Divine Soul always existed. The Erotic Soul was not begotten by the Father. It was begotten by the Spirit. Only the Noetic Soul was begotten by the Father.

The will of the Father begot the Noetic Soul to save creation. The Noetic Soul is the Chosen One. The Noetic Soul is the Savior. This is the source of the prophecy of the Messiah and the Mahdi. The prophecy is not meant to be fulfilled in the world by only one human being. It is meant to be fulfilled within every human being. The prophecy is meant to be fulfilled within you!

The Father's love for creation emerges as a force. This force is the Sacred Feminine force of the cosmos. She is called the Numina. The Virgin Mary, and the many different sacred feminine forms symbolize the Numina. The Numina gives birth to the new Monad (Christ) within us. The Numina is the ninth (9) permutation of consciousness.

The Book of Revelation reveals that the tenth (10) permutation of consciousness is a beast rising out of the sea with a crown of ten horns on his head. The modern theological interpretation of this symbology is wrong. Modern theology believes the beast of the sea represents a future anti-Christ who is a person who will rise up from the sea of politics.

This beast of the sea is one side of the Id within the human psyche. The lifeforce of the Id is a psycho-kinetic-spiritual force living in darkness within the human psyche called Idamus. Idamus rises from the Eternal Sea (Sea of Eros). When the perspective awareness within the human mind interfaces and engages the Erotic Soul within us in an automated manner, this gives rise to the forces of the id complex residing in darkness within the human psyche.

Because human beings on Earth are designed to reconstitute the Monad, the organization of the human mind reflects the same organization of the cosmos which existed before the reconciliation on a cosmic level. The Noetic Soul is sent into the darkness to reconcile the forces of creation residing in darkness.

Sefirot, The – S

When the Noetic Soul continuously elevates its resonance with the Father while incarnated within the human mind of the physical body, the Noetic Soul eventually resurrects its Logos—reflection of the Father within the human mind. We use the force of the resurrected Logos to reconcile the forces of the id complex. Resonance with the Father infiltrates the mind and is experienced in the mind as the state of Turiya—a blissful state of being. Turiya and the forces of Eros are married in the alchemical wedding to form the Christ Monad.

All permutations of consciousness (except the first three) have a shadow or dark inflection. The dark inflection of IAO is Satan. The dark inflection of the Logos is Lucifer. If human beings possess the ability to reconstitute the Monad within the human psyche (we all do on Earth) but fail to utilize their ability, then the permutations of consciousness evolve into denser permutations of mind which keep compounding and twisting the mind. This is how we fall into evil.

Unless the reconciliation occurs, the forces continue compounding eventually turning love into fear and despair. Fear of the mind eventually compels the rise of the second beast of the Book of Revelation. The second beast is the beast of the Earth. The Earth is the neurological chemistry of the brain. The number of the second beast is 666. The number series reflects the compounding processes of creation. The number six in a series represents the 6th permutation of consciousness out of which the beast arises. It arises out of the psyche and brain matter of the human being. The second beast within the human psyche is called the Gorgon.

The Gorgon is the eleventh (11) permutation of consciousness. The quantum of the Gorgon exists within all people, but it does not rise within the mind of all people, thus it is not considered a principal permutation. However, when it rises in the mind, it takes over the mind. The Gorgon compels the rise of the narcissistic personality within the human being.

S – Sefirot, The

Narcissism is a psychosomatic disease of the mind that begins forming in childhood due to an inability to process and resolve emotions. As part of the disease, the mind offers delusional constructs of self and reality to compensate, and the brain further rewires to reinforce the disease. It gets worse through life. The disease fuels the development of a fake or contrived persona into which the mind feeds all its energy to separate and alleviate the mind from fear, stress, and anxiety. The human mind is too afraid to allow the authentic-self to emerge and be itself. It is too afraid of rejection and humiliation. Fear is the main driver to the rise of the Gorgon. The Gorgon narcissistic mind attempts to convince the world of the fake persona to avoid rejection and humiliation. The Gorgon is the dark champion of the mind. The narcissistic mind is intentionally acting out the fake persona. The fake persona is copied or imitated from other human beings. The Gorgon can also build multiple fake personas, but this is rare. In the Gorgon mind, the authentic-self (Noetic Soul) is pushed into the background.

All the effort of the mind to portray the fake persona to the world compounds the delusional mind which ironically brings about a form of cohesion to the mind. It is a dark pearl. When the Gorgon narcissistic personality takes over the mind, this is the Anti-Monad or Anti-Christ. Lies, deceit, and cruelty are normal and customary for the Gorgon mind. In the Book of Daniel, the Gorgon is the little horn growing up with the tenth horn. Idamus compels the rise of the Gorgon. Their relationship is based in fear, not love. All of what is worst in human beings, arises out of the Gorgon. The Gorgon mind secretly hates eroticism and sexuality. It mocks it, abuses it, twists it, and uses it for its own selfish narcissistic agendas. The reason is, it wants to block the conscious mind's access to the Divine Spirit. The coupling of opposite forces within us, opens-up a doorway to the Spirit. The Gorgon hates this and will do anything to prevent it.

Sefirot, The – S

Book of Daniel 7: 7 to 9

"7 After this I saw in the night visions, and behold a fourth beast, dreadful and terrible, and strong exceedingly; and it had great iron teeth: it devoured and broke in pieces, and stamped the residue with the feet of it: and it was diverse from all the beasts that were before it; and it had 10 horns."   (This is Idamus)

"8 I considered the horns, and, behold, there came up among them another little horn, before whom there were three of the first horns plucked up by the roots: and, behold, in this horn were eyes like the eyes of man, and a mouth speaking great things." (This is the Gorgon)

"9 I beheld till the thrones were cast down, and the Ancient of days did sit, whose garment was white as snow, and the hair of his head like the pure wool: his throne was like the fiery flame, and his wheels as burning fire."

The Noetic Soul's resonance with the Father (Ancient of the Days) during the alchemical process, integrates and transforms the nature of the Idamus and the Gorgon.

At the cosmic level, when the new cosmic unity was finally realized and achieved between IAO and the Logos, sexuality emerged within all living things as a reflection of the original coupling of Love and Will in the alchemical creation process. All duality is a reflection of the original process of "darkness" being coupled with "light" to bring creation back into unity with the divine source. Darkness-Light, Odd-Even, Hot-Cold, Female-Male, Negative-Positive, are all a reflection of the original cosmic creation process.

What the theokinetic processes of consciousness and creation reveal is that, it is the "differences" between all things which compel the processes of creation, and it is our conscious awareness, understanding, and acceptance of those differences, which brings about a lasting and sustainable harmony and unity within creation. If we try to eliminate the differences, then creation is destroyed. I believe there is a powerful life lesson in this revelation. Life is not about getting everyone to live the same way and to agree on everything. Life is about

S – Sefirot, The

becoming conscious of, understanding, and appreciating all our differences, for without these differences, there would be no magnetism to spark the next level of existence.

Theokinesis also reveals that all things are constantly changing and evolving toward a higher reality. Our fear of change ultimately becomes self-fulfilling and the very thing we most fear becomes realized. Accept differences, accept change, it is the energy of life.

[B] — <u>The Sefirot of the Kabbalah Definitions</u>

The following are the Sefirot of the Kabbalah as per the Jewish Virtual Library[7]. Key qualities which help align the Sefirot to the permutations of consciousness are underlined.

- Keter: The Supreme Crown – The (a) <u>uppermost</u> aspect of the Sefirot which can be contemplated by human beings.

- Hokhmah: Represents the contemplative synthetic aspects of (b) <u>God's thought</u>. It is the primordial (c) <u>point of creation from which all knowable reality originates.</u>

- Binah: Understanding, Discernment. Refers to the analytic distinguishing aspects of God's thought. It is the (d) <u>uppermost feminine element</u> in the Godhead and is symbolized as the mother of Shekhinah. Many of the symbols associated with Binah are therefore identical to those of Shekhinah. (e) <u>Having received the seed from Hokhmah, Binah conceived and gave birth to the seven lower Sefirot.</u>

- Hesed: Love, (f) <u>Lovingkindness, Compassion,</u> (g) <u>Greatness, Grace</u>. Represents the generous, benevolent <u>(masculine)</u> side of God. There are (h) <u>72 bridges of Hesed</u>.

---

[7] www.jewishvirtuallibrary.org

Sefirot, The – S

- Din, Gevurah: Judgment, Might, Power. This sephirah represents the fearsome powers of divine punishment and (i) <u>wrath in the world</u>.

- Tiferet: Glory, Beauty. Represents the ideal balance of justice and mercy needed for proper running of the universe. (j) <u>This sephirah unites all the upper nine powers. Tiferet is the offspring of Hokhmah and Binah.</u>

- Nezah: (k) <u>Eternity, Endurance</u>, <u>Victory</u>. Represents God's (m) <u>active grace in the world</u>.

- Hod: (n) <u>Represents the lower channel through which God's judgment comes down to the world.</u> It is associated with the power of prophecy. (p) <u>Hod and Nezah are often treated as a complementary pair.</u>

- Yesod: (q) <u>Foundation.</u> (r) <u>The channel through which Tiferet strives to unite with Shekhinah</u> and pass on the creative and benevolent divine forces.

- Shekhinah: (s) <u>God's presence, kingdom.</u> A Talmudic concept representing God's dwelling and immanence in the created world. It was equated with the "Keneset Yisrael," (t) <u>the personified Spirit</u> of the people of Israel. According to a Rabbinic tradition, the Shekhinah shares in the exiles of the Jewish people. Therefore, the (u) <u>redemption</u> of (v) <u>the people of Israel</u> is (w) <u>inextricably linked to the remedying of an alienation within God him/herself</u>, introducing a bold new element into traditional Jewish Messianic eschatology. (x) <u>It is through the Shekhinah that humans can experience the Divine.</u> The passivity of the Shekhinah is often emphasized (y) <u>(equated with its femininity)</u>, as (z) <u>the recipient of forces from the higher Sefirot.</u>

S – Sefirot, The

Official Rabbinical Diagram of the Sefirot of the Kabbalah

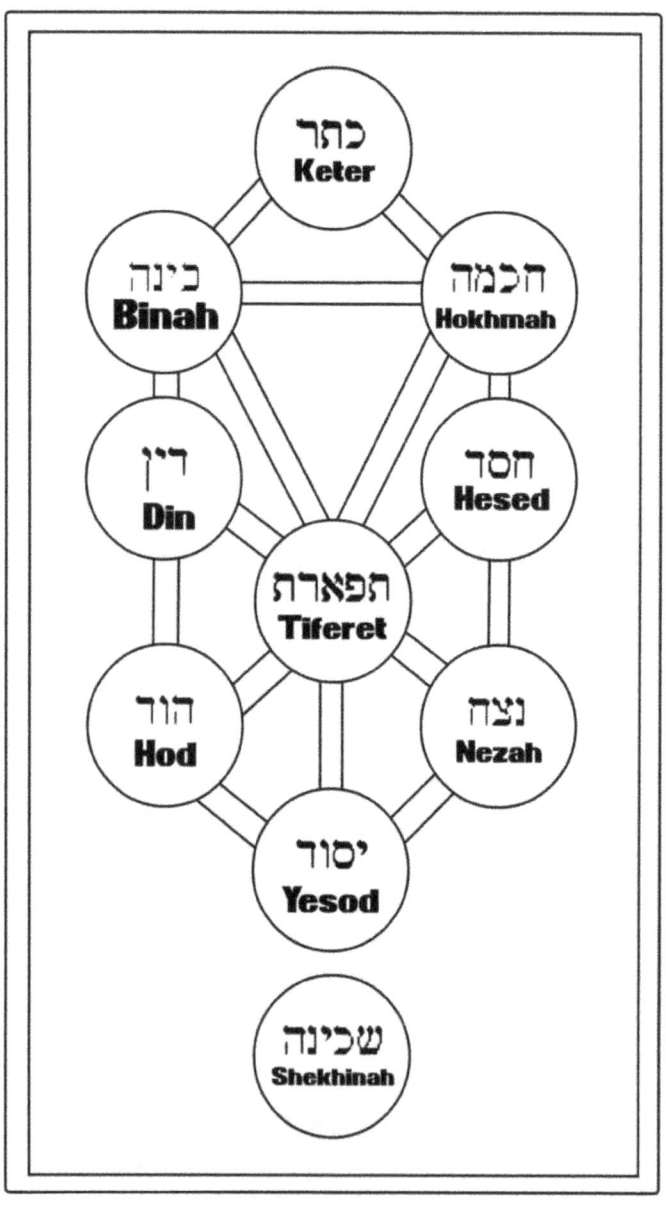

Sefirot, The – S

[C] — Comparison between the Sefirot of the Kabbalah and the process of Theokinesis

Based on an analysis of the written descriptions of the Sefirot described in section (B) and certain key words underlined within each description, one can logically deduce that the Sefirot do not represent the specific permutations of consciousness as described in section (A). The Sefirot do not correlate on a one-to-one basis to the permutations of consciousness experienced in the process of theokinesis. The Sefirot represent "qualities" of energy expressed by the various permutations of consciousness when viewed in a motionless position.

When a person is undergoing the alchemical integration process, Alpha compels the conscious mind of that person to witness the actual process of creation in motion. We witness the process of theokinesis in action. To complete the Monad on an individual level, we need to realize what is happening. Direct knowledge of what is happening within the process of creation - in how the forces operate and interact – is somehow fundamental to the reconstitution of the Monad. If you want to put it all back together, then you must know how it all came apart. The forces of consciousness require this of the conscious mind.

Someone attempting to view the same process while not undergoing the alchemical integration process will see the forces in a static or frozen position. When the conscious mind views the process in a static position, the conscious mind does not fully ascertain the actual forces. What the conscious mind gathers is only a snapshot of the qualities which the underlying forces generate. It's like looking at the interior of a watch. While undergoing the process, we can see the interior of the watch in motion. We can see all the forces and how they interplay. We can see all the gears and hands moving. We can see all the interactive relationships. When we are not undergoing the alchemical integration process, all we see are an assortment of stagnant mechanical shapes. It's like watching a movie in motion in full color with audio, versus just viewing a series of black and white still shots scattered in random order without motion or audio.

S – Sefirot, The

The author of the Sefirot descriptions was someone who was not engaged in the actual process of alchemical integration. The Sefirot are motionless still shots. He or she was most likely a meditator who had a degree of super cognitive sensitivity to gain a level of awareness of the various "qualities" of the forces involved. He or she was only able to ascertain the energies in a motionless state. The Sefirot is incomplete in terms of explaining the process of creation and the forces involved; however, it does provide a qualitative assessment of the forces, and points to the beginning, middle, and completion of creation.

Key Alchemical Observations of the Sefirot Descriptions

Hokhmah

Keter

- a.) "Uppermost"[8] logically refers to the position of the Father as the Godhead of Ain Soph, but it could refer to the Godhead of any trinity. It can refer to either the Father, IAO, or the Logos.

Hokhmah

- b.) "God's thought" indicates "mind." Thought and mind do not exist within Ain Soph and therefore cannot be attributed to the Father. These qualities are more attributable to IAO.

- c.) "Point of creation from which all knowable reality originates" can be attributed to either the Father or IAO.

Binah

- d.) "Uppermost feminine element" refers to the Spirit. The third principal in any trinity is in direct line to the Spirit. Love is symbolized by the feminine. Will is symbolized by the masculine. It was the original coupling of Love and Will which completed the cosmic level of creation. Any third

---

[8] Letters a.) b.) c.) d.) correspond to letters (a) (b) (c) (d) in section [B]

principle is therefore symbolized by the feminine. Spirit is the uppermost of the feminine line. Second, is Matter-Energy of the Erodonic Trinity. Third, is the Numina of the Sacred Trinity.

e.) <u>"Having received the seed from Hokhmah, Binah conceived and gave birth to the seven lower Sefirot."</u> Perhaps "Seed[9]" refers to the "First Triumphant" (the Father's realization of his own life), "the Divine Soul" which gives rise to the Spirit, the love of God. Due to the energy of this "seed," the Spirit produces the great outpouring of creation. This indicates that Hokhmah is not the Father or the Divine Soul, but possibly the realization between the two. This is the first indication that the Sefirot may not be the principal forces themselves, but rather qualities and manifestations of the forces.

<u>Hesed</u>

f.) <u>"Compassion"</u> is a discretely complicated permutation of consciousness. It is actually a highly evolved emotion produced by a combined symphony of all ten principal forces. Compassion requires contemplation which requires a reflective awareness. It also requires an experience of both love and suffering. Compassion is a leading quality of the unified completed Monad (Christ Monad). "Lovingkindness," as well, is indicative of experience and contemplation. The *"Christ Monad"* suffered for its completion at the cosmic level, and now has great compassion for the Noetic Soul in its mission to fulfill on the lower levels, what has already been fulfilled and accomplished on the highest level.

---

[9] Letters e.) f.) correspond to letters (e) (f) in section [B]

S – Sefirot, The

g.) "Greatness"[10] is a central quality of the Logos. The Logos is the champion of the divine Father. He is unbeatable. "Grace" is a divine quality of the Spirit. "Masculine" is a reference to the Logos (Will-Word of God).

h.) "72 bridges of Hesed" indicates that Hesed is a bridging force between all the principal forces of consciousness. "Compassion" is a binding force of the Christ Monad.

Din, Gevurah

i.) "Wrath in the world" is a reference to the inverted aspect of the Logos which is Lucifer or Shiva. When the human mind fails to reflect and resonate with Ain Soph, the Logos inverts to destroy the body of creation harboring its sacred lifeforce, the Noetic Soul - so that the Noetic Soul may be liberated. The idea of "Divine Judgment" is a misunderstanding of divinity. Divinity does not judge the realms of creation. The Father delegated all his authority over creation to the Logos and its Noetic Soul. Humanity only suffers the causality of its own lack of awareness, authenticity, and compassion.

Tiferet

j.) "This sephirah unites all the upper nine powers. Tiferet is the offspring of Hokhmah and Binah." At first glance, some may attribute Tiferet to the Noetic Soul due to the word "unites," as it is the mission of the Noetic Soul to unite all the forces (powers) to complete the Monad. The clue that the Tiferet does not correlate to the Noetic Soul is that the "Tiferet is the offspring of Hokmah and Binah." As analyzed above, Hokhmah correlates to IAO. Binah correlates to the Spirt. The Noetic Soul is not the offspring of either IAO or Binah. The

---

[10] Letters g.) h.) i.) j.) correspond to letters (g) (h) (i) (j) in section [B]

Sefirot, The – S

Noetic Soul is the offspring of the Father who more closely correlates to Keter. The only soul which descends from both IAO and the Spirit is the Erotic Soul which flows through all lifeforms of creation. It "unites" all lifeforms because it is a "single" soul flowing through all life throughout the universe. It forms the Sea of Eros. It is the Eternal Sea.

Under Sefirot (9) "Yesod is the channel through which "Tiferet" strives to unite with Shekhinah and pass on the creative and benevolent divine forces." The key term here is "strive." The Idamus rises out of the Eternal Sea and "strives" for its existence, and in doing so, generates animal desire. The "striving" is a further indication that the Tiferet correlates to the Erotic Soul. The Erotic Soul is not divine, but the Erotic Soul, at the cosmic level, has already been saved and united with the Cosmic Monad, and therefore resonates with the divine forces. This is why the essence of all the animals, and nature in general, is so beautiful. In some ways, on a psychic level, animals are more evolved than human beings on Earth in the physical universe, yet the Noetic Soul has been given reign over all of creation by the Father.

Nezah

k.) "Eternity[11], Endurance, Victory." The key word here is "Endurance." The Noetic Soul is sent into the darkness of creation by the will of the Father to engage and "endure" the darkness. Through the Noetic Soul's resonance with the divine forces in a practice of "Primordial Alchemy," the forces of darkness are lifted up and integrated with divinity to achieve "victory" in the completion of the Christ Monad. At this point, we bring our total being into the "eternal" realm.

---

[11] Letter k.) corresponds to letters (k) in section [B]

S – Sefirot, The

    m.) "Active grace in the world" is a reference to "Alpha" and the "Numina." Alpha is a function of the Father's will to bring creation into harmony with divinity out of love for creation. The Father's love for creation (Numina; Sacred Feminine) is the "grace" he shines upon the world. "Nezah" represents the intercessing power acting between the Sacred Trinity (Lower Trinity) and all of creation.

Hod

    n.) "Represents the lower channel through which God's judgment comes down to the world" is a reference to the Lower Trinity (Sacred Trinity). The word "channel" represents a "trinity." There are 3 trinities involved in creation and a fourth trinity which emerges upon completion:

        1.) Divine Trinity - Upper Trinity (Precedes Creation)

        2.) Erodonic Trinity (Forces of Creation)

        3.) Sacred Trinity - Lower Trinity (Redeemer of Creation)

        4.) Christic Trinity (Symphony of All Preceding Trinities)

The "judgment" is, creation will be lifted-up, or destroyed. Judgment is carried out by the Sacred Trinity, not divinity.

    p.) "Hod[12] and Nezah are often treated as a complementary pair" is a confirmation of the analysis of "Nezah" and the analysis of "Hod" as being associated with the Sacred Trinity. "Hod" represents the forces of the Sacred Trinity themselves. "Nezah" is the power of the forces; in their power to redeem creation. The Sacred Trinity (Lower Trinity) is comprised of the (1) Logos, (2) Noetic Soul, and (3) Numina.

---

[12] Letters m.) n.) p.) correspond to letters (m) (n) (p) in section [B]

Sefirot, The – S

Yesod:

q.) "Foundation" refers to the "mind." The mind is the foundation upon which creation is built. The physical universe is built on the foundation of the Cosmic Mind.

r.) "The channel through which Tiferet strives to unite with Shekhinah and pass on the creative and benevolent divine forces" refers to the "mind". The channel in this case is the Erodonic Trinity. The Erodonic Trinity gives rise to the mind. It is the incarnation of the Noctic Soul within the mind that allows the mind to pass on the forces of divinity to creation. "Yesod" is the mind.

Shekhinah

s.) "Shekhinah"[13] is the Christ Monad in its completed state. God's presence, kingdom is the Spirit of the Christ Monad which is "Erodysis."

t.) "The personified Spirit" is a reference to "Erodysis." Within the Christ Monad, a new fourth trinity arises. Within every unity there is a trinity within. Within the trinity of the Christ Monad, the awareness is "Dominus," the life is "David," and the energy, or love, is "Erodysis." The word "personified" is a reference to "unity" and "completeness."

u.) "Redemption" refers to creation in its redeemed state which is the Christ Monad.

v.) "The people of Israel" are really the people of the Earth. The people of the Earth were created to accomplish the will of the Father and complete the Christ Monad on both an individual level and on a planetary level. The messianic age will ensue after we complete the planetary Christ Monad.

---

[13] Letters q.) r.) s.) t.) u.) v.) correspond to letters (q) (r) (s) (t) (u) (v) in section [B]

S – Sefirot, The

- w.) "<u>Inextricably linked to the remedying of an alienation within God him/herself</u>," refers to the rediscovery and reintegration of what was previously alienated. The process of creation alienates the original Monad of divinity – Ain Soph. "Shekhinah" is the remedying of the Monad in its new form. The entire process of creation and its reintegration is all a process "within God itself."

- x.) "<u>It is through the Shekhinah that humans can experience the Divine</u>." It is through the reconstitution and completion of the Christ Monad (Shekhinah) that human beings and their bodies of creation can experience the divine.

- y.) "The passivity of the Shekhinah is often emphasized <u>(equated with its femininity)</u>," is a reference to the Spirit of the Christ Monad which is "Erodysis." The spiritual state of Erodysis is a transcendental state of deep compassion, rapture, bliss, and a profound empathy between divinity and creation through which the unity of Christ is maintained. Erodysis, being of the third principal in the trinity of Christ, is in the feminine line of forces, whose first force, is the Spirit.

- z.) "<u>The recipient of forces from the higher Sefirot</u>"[14] is referring to the reconstituted Christ Monad as being the recipient and new reservoir of forces from the higher Sefirot.

<u>Final Analysis</u>

Keter is the beginning of creation.
Tiferet is the middle, or soul, of creation.
Shekhinah is the completion of creation.

---

[14] Letters w.) x.) y.) z.) corresponds to letters (w) (x) (y) (z) in section [B]

Self-Actualization – Self-Realization

When the authentic-self (Noetic Soul) in a person consistently seeks to rise above the limitations of his or her temporal-physical being to transform the mind, and that practice becomes the preferred method for dealing with adversity in lieu of common human reaction, then that person is a self-actualizing human being. Self-actualization promotes a continuous reflective awareness, a devotion to a higher purpose, and a deep immersion into the force of the Spirit. A self-realized person is someone who has been self-actualizing throughout life and has amassed a powerful center of gravity within his or her authentic-self. In the process of liberating his or her authentic-self, the person has become aware of all the forces of the cosmic quanta on a deep super cognitive emotional level, and as result, has unified the mind.

Sentience *[Sen-tience; Sen-shense]*

Sentience is the divine source of the Cosmic Consciousness reflecting upon itself from within the mind of a life-form. This reflectivity emerges and evolves progressively within each lifeform. Sentience is a progressive ladder of cosmic-self-awareness. Until reflective awareness of the divine source fully emerges within the mind of a life-form, that life-form's inner cognitive awareness of its divine source is mediated and suppressed by its auto-cognitive programs. What fills the void left by the mind's impaired awareness of its divine source is illusion.

Sexual Cultivation – Tantra, Taoist Sexual Yoga

The practice of alchemical sexual intercourse is a controversial subject. Entire ancient cultures, cults, and religions were created and revolved around this one practice. This practice is the most tangible of all alchemical practices and deals directly with the most powerful force within the physical organism and therefore the practice is easily twisted to misinform, seduce, and control others.

S – Sexual Cultivation

The component of the practice which has captured the minds of so many people and has been used by some to seduce and manipulate others, is the concept of sublimating a person's sexual energy to birth a new spiritual existence in lieu of physical reproduction.

In this practice, both the men and the women, during sexual intercourse, engage in special breathing and meditative exercises to prevent a man's seminal ejaculation, and to slow or even stop, a woman's menstrual cycle. In theory, this allows the semen in men, and the ovum in women, to be used for the spiritual reproduction of one's spiritual ethereal bodies while curtailing the process of physical reproduction.

This is a compelling idea due to its creative logic. However, the logic does not stand the test of actually undergoing the alchemical process and witnessing its principles and forces at play. The purpose of the sexual practice appears to have been distorted over many centuries.

The spiritual ethereal bodies already exist as part of the anatomy of our primordial being. We only need to integrate or harmonize our spiritual bodies with our temporal bodies, not create or recreate them.

The real purpose of the sexual cultivation practice is to promote and cultivate a higher degree of resonance between the force of the Spirit and all our bodies (six temporal bodies). This is accomplished when all our internal energy is well-balanced and organized by means of the First Factor, and then that energy, in its Yang or Yin state, is combined with its opposite polarity from another energy source. This other energy source can be another human being, the forces of nature, or from deep within the underlying cosmic quanta of the cosmos. For beginners, the most easily accessible source is another human being. For an advanced adept, the most accessible source is the cosmic quanta.

When the energy of our bodies is cultivated into a higher resonance with the Spirit, the forces of the Cosmic Consciousness become more accessible to the conscious mind. When these forces become more accessible to the conscious mind, we can use them in our alchemical transformation practices to yield remarkable results. The higher resonance with the Spirit among all our bodies also promotes the integration and unification of our total being.

Sexual Cultivation – S

Our cultivated sexual balance promotes and opens a window of our super cognitive awareness between the Noetic Soul, the Spirit, the Divine Soul, and the Father. It is our super cognitive awareness of the Spirit which is used as the catalyst of transformation in the advanced level practices of the First Factor. The Spirit is the first dimension of the Philosophers' Stone of the medieval alchemists to arise within us. The achievement of the Philosophers' Stone is the reconstitution of the Monad — it is Christ — the completion of creation.

The resonance between our temporal bodies and spiritual bodies is cultivated to higher and higher levels throughout a long alchemical journey, not just in one, or even in a few practices, and culminates with the integration of our temporal-physical being and our eternal-primordial being into one grand unified celestial being.

The initial sexual asymmetry distorting the resonance between our temporal-physical being and our eternal-primordial being is primarily neurological. This neurological condition is found within the physical brain. This neurological condition manifests through a phenomenon referred to as the Psycho-Sexual Dynamic. See Psycho-Sexual Dynamic for more information on this subject.

The notable physical changes practitioners may notice with continued practice is the separation of a man's orgasm from ejaculation, the opening of what in Taoist Sexual Yoga is called the microcosmic orbit, and the diminishment of a woman's menstrual cycle.

In Indian Tantra, the caduceus of mercury symbolizes the same phenomenon of the Taoist microcosmic orbit. The two serpents of the caduceus are named Ida and Pingala. The two serpents symbolize the sublimated sexual energy which the practitioners physically feel moving along the etheric channels of their human nervous system. The caduceus also symbolizes the union between divinity and creation.

S – Sexual Cultivation

Although practitioners may experience all the above-mentioned physical effects, none of these effects by themselves are indicative of alchemical or spiritual progress. The sexual practice itself is only one third of the alchemical formula.

Another misconception is that "Kundalini," which is really the force of Alpha, is awoken solely through alchemical sexual intercourse. It takes all Three Factors working correctly together in concert to amplify and accelerate the force of Alpha within us. Secondly, there are other means beyond sexual intercourse which allow us to cultivate our energy to satisfy the requirement of the Second Factor.

If the Second Factor sexual practices are performed absent of the First Factor and Third Factor, the result is zero, regardless of any noted physical effects of the cultivation practices.

In the final analysis, the alchemical sexual practices are only practices of enhanced sexual intercourse to heighten the resonance of our sexual energy with the Spirit. Normal sexual relations work as well but to a lesser degree. When we learn to listen to our body, we will know when to enhance our sex life with the practices of alchemical sexual intercourse to cultivate our energy with the Spirit, or whether to maintain normal sexual relations with our partner. The effect of many years of enhanced sexual practice eventually becomes sustained through normal sexual relations. Normal sexual relations become a form of cruise control for the more advanced alchemist of this work.

What many practitioners do not realize is that harmony and balance have two contributing factors. These two factors are: (1) physical, and (2) psychological. Many practitioners focus solely on the physical or sexual aspect. Alchemy is not solely a physical process with magical formulas which only need to be applied correctly to achieve the desired result. Alchemy is a spiritual process which the physical practices support, but do not lead.

Charlatans would have you believe the sexual practice is the primary key to alchemy, and that the practice itself is required to be taught only by them, or by one of their accomplices. They are wrong.

Sexual Cultivation – S

Your relationship with God is the key to alchemy. This relationship requires no special intermediary.

The number one myth perpetrated by charlatans of this practice is that if ejaculation or orgasm occurs, then whatever alchemical progress had been achieved up until that point would all be lost. This is profoundly false and very dangerous. Such illogical preconceived notions serve only to create another level of illusion which the alchemist must transcend during the alchemical process.

People in general are so predisposed to "illusion" that although the alchemical process aims to break down our illusions to enable the realization of the truth and liberate one's authenticity, people will initially form illusions about the alchemical process itself.

We only dissolve our illusions of the alchemical process by moving through the process with an open mind, and with as few preconceived notions as possible, and with a willingness to reevaluate our perspective as we move along the process.

The more progress we make, the more natural, humanistic, logical, and scientific our perspective becomes. The more ideological, absolute, self-righteous, and compensatory our relationship is with the process, the further we are from understanding it.

If we are properly working with the First Factor, allowing our temporal bodies to work correctly with their own energy systems, an opportunity arises within us where we can further cultivate this energy by mixing it and neutralizing it with the magnetic forces from a source beyond our own body. The psycho-sexual energy must first be organized between the bodies of our own being by way of the First Factor, and then secondly cultivated via the Second Factor with a force beyond our physical anatomy consisting either of (1) the neutralizing energy of another person, (2) the neutralizing energy found all about us in nature, or (3) the neutralizing energy of the cosmic quanta found deep within us in the underlying cosmos. Most people skip the First Factor and continue straight to the Second Factor rendering their cultivation useless. Why neutralize with a source beyond us?

S – Sexual Cultivation

Because by itself, our psycho-sexual energy is inherently polarized; even in its organized state. Our psycho-sexual energy is either too male-yang or too female-yin. The Spirit exists in a magnetically neutral-yuan state. If we wish to open a clearer connection with the Spirit within our conscious mind, we can do this by neutralizing the magnetic charge of our psycho-sexual energy. When our psycho-sexual energy is too polarized, the polarization can interfere with or cloud our conscious awareness of the Spirit.

We can neutralize our sexual energy by adding to it a neutralizing or balancing force. Many alchemists find this neutralizing or balancing force with their sexual partner or within nature. An advanced alchemist can draw this force from deep within the cosmic quanta, no longer requiring an outside physical source.

Once the alchemist achieves an advanced level of Q, the alchemist will naturally access deeper levels of neutralized energy from within the spectrum of the Cosmic Consciousness, and from his or her own primordial being, which by itself, can neutralize the temporal-physical system and bring the entire system into harmony with the Spirit. However, until such super cognitive awareness is achieved, a source beyond us is used as a neutralizing mechanism.

A person's magnetic sexual charge is not as simple and neat as just male or female. Male and female only represent two ends of a magnetic spectrum. Everyone's magnetic sexual charge falls somewhere within the sexual magnetic spectrum. No person's sexual magnetic charge is 100% male-yang or 100% female-yin. Although you may have all male parts or all female parts, your psycho-sexual magnetic charge falls within a spectrum.

The more to one end of the spectrum you are, the more attracted you will be to someone of equal distance from the other end of the spectrum. The more in the middle your magnetic charge, the more in the middle you will be attracted to someone else. In terms of alchemy, sexual compatibility is not as simple as sexual organ compatibility, but rather the compatibility of each person's position in the sexual magnetic spectrum.

Sexual Cultivation – S

The sexual intercourse practice is as follows:

- In addition to the course of normal sexual intercourse, while the couple is connected, they should both bring themselves close to the point of climax and then stop moving to prevent climax yet stay connected.

- In this moment of stillness, they should both breath in deeply through their nostrils and hold their breath for as long as they comfortably can. 20 to 30 seconds is normal. When it is time to exhale, they should exhale at the same time through the mouth.

- While holding your breath, you should use your mind to guide your sexual energy around the circular pathway formed between your body and your partner's body. The alchemist should research the detailed explanations and energy flow diagrams of "Taoist Sexual Yoga." The books of Mantak Chia and Michael Winn are recommended.

- The main energetic pathway within a person extends from the sexual organs up the spine of the back, over the head, down the front of the torso, and back to the sexual organs. This is the "Microcosmic Orbit."

- When the couple is sexually connected, their pathways fuse to become one circuit with the energy orbiting up the back of one, over the heads of both, and down the back of the other, across the genitals of both, and back up the spine again. The couple can reverse the orbit as they wish with their minds.

- The couple should take subsequent deep breaths, and while holding their breath they should direct their sexual energy along the circuit with their minds until sexual control is stabilized while still maintaining a connection.

S – Sexual Cultivation

- During sexual intercourse, when the couple are holding their breath and directing their sexual energy with their minds, this is called "Sublimation."

- Normal sexual intercourse continues between each act of sublimation. Typically, the person with less control initiates the moments of sublimation.

- A woman may achieve orgasm as often as she pleases during sexual intercourse as her energy is not lost during orgasm. A woman's sexual energy is depleted with her menstruation.

- When a man withholds ejaculation, it is not because it is forbidden, it is to cultivate the power of the semen for a sustained period. The man may wish to withhold ejaculation during the full course of the practice, or he may ejaculate at the end of the practice. The man must listen to his body.

- While a couple is sexually connected, to ensure the best flow of energy between them, there are a few points or gates which need to be closed or connected between the couple. The first gate is the mouth. When the couple is kissing, the gate is connected and energy flows along this connection point. When not kissing, the tongue should stay touching the roof of a person's mouth.

- The second gate is the perineum located between the anus and the genitals. The perineum is kept closed by clenching the sphincter muscles of the surrounding area. When the couple is connected, the energy will pass along this connection point without clenching as long as they maintain their connection.

- Eventually, when the couple disconnects, each person should continue sublimating their sexual energy for a period of 20 to 30 minutes along their own orbit which rises up the back, over the head, down the torso, and back down to the genitals. We can do this lying down or seated.

- Other secondary orbits exist in our legs and arms. We can move the energy along these secondary orbits with our mind.

- When you feel the energy passing the heart area of your chest, you should use your mind to guide the energy to accumulate in the area below the naval called the "Sea of Chi." Imagine the energy swirling in this area and shortly thereafter you will feel the energy accumulating in the Sea of Chi.

- It is important to continue sublimating after disconnecting as the energy we are working with is closer in resonance with the Spirit and we want to continue cultivating this spiritualized energy.

In "Taoist Sexual Yoga," there is a very detailed metaphysical science behind this sexual practice which defines all the etheric pathways and components of the anatomy. In addition to the practice described in the Alchepedia, the alchemist should research this science and go deeper with the practice to a level with which they are satisfied.

Some people will naturally ask if they can still practice the Second Factor even if they lost some of their sexual organs, and the answer is yes, absolutely. Your brain is your primary sexual organ. For as long as you are alive, you can practice the Second Factor. Additionally, not all reproductive organs are used in every practice of the Second Factor.

See on next two pages: Microcosmic Orbit Diagrams.
Also See: Cosmic Cultivation

S – Sexual Cultivation

Microcosmic Orbit

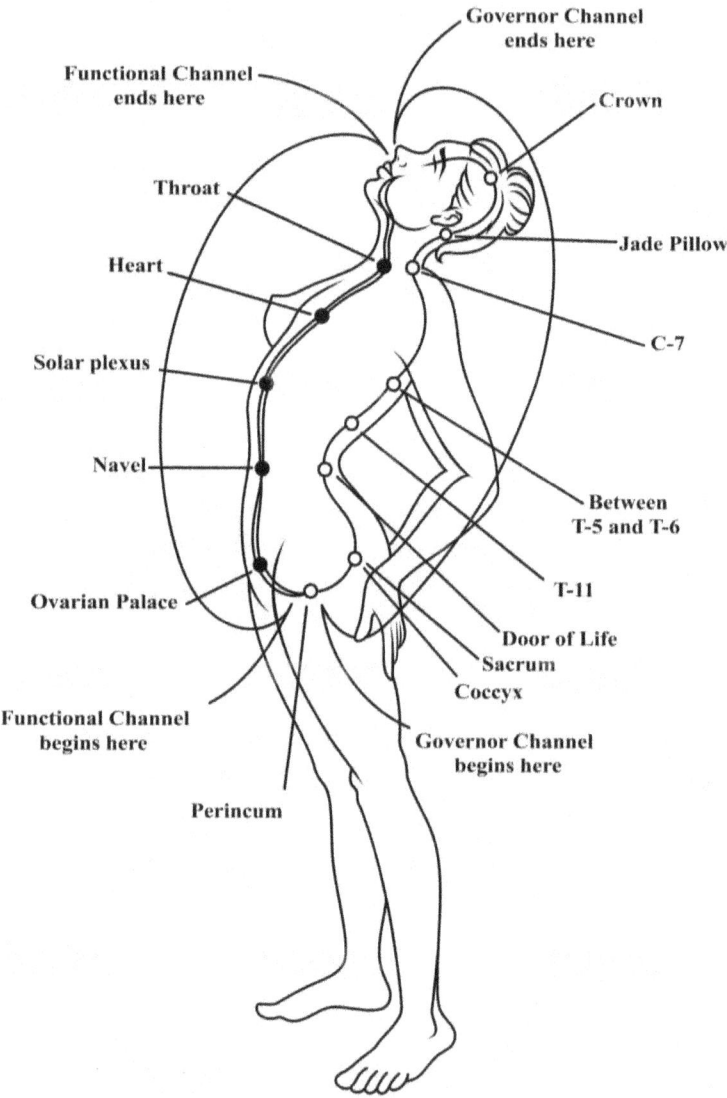

Reference: Taoist Secrets of Love: Cultivating Male Sexual Energy: Chia, Mantak; Winn, Michael. 1984. 323 p. ISBN 0-943358-19-1 URL: Also see: Taoist Secrets of Love: Cultivating Female Sexual Energy.

Sexual Cultivation – S

Microcosmic Orbit

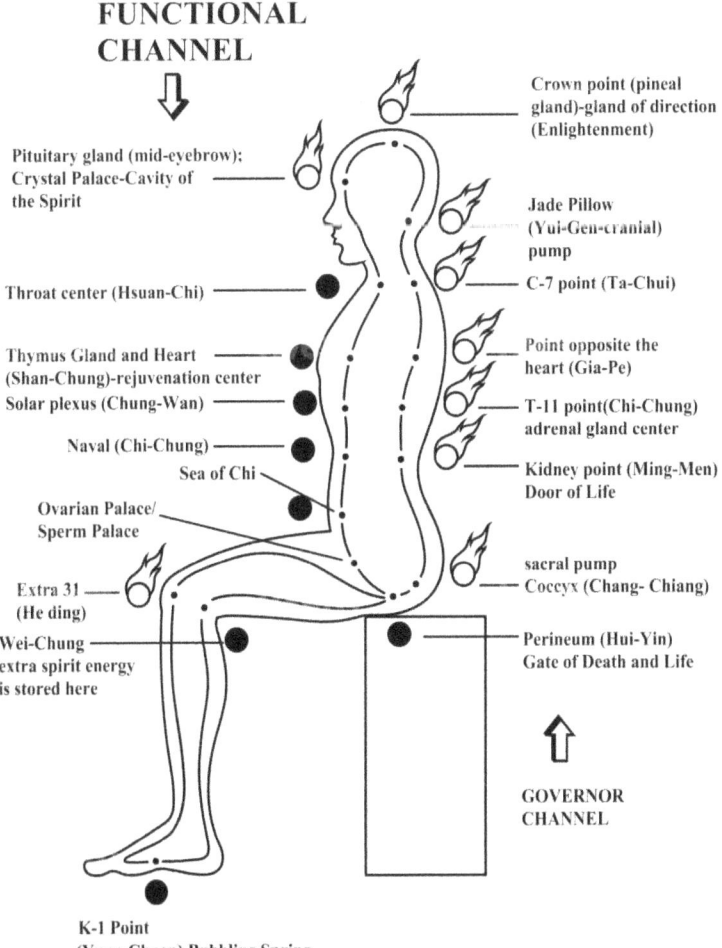

Reference: Taoist Secrets of Love: Cultivating Male Sexual Energy: Chia, Mantak; Winn, Michael. 1984. 323 p. ISBN 0-943358-19-1 URL: Also see: Taoist Secrets of Love: Cultivating Female Sexual Energy.

S – Short Path

Short Path

The Short Path, as opposed to the Spiral Path, or Straight Path, is the idea of an instantaneous enlightenment, or instantaneous realization of God. It is possible for the Noetic Soul within the human being to achieve an instantaneous realization of the Divine Source which one may qualify as enlightenment; however, this enlightenment does not form the reconstituted Christ Monad (Philosophers' Stone). It does not complete the Great Work or fulfill the prime directive of the Noetic Soul, but the realization does aid the Noetic Soul in eventually completing its divine mission.

  The divine mission of the Noetic Soul is not the realization of God. It already has this innate knowledge. The mission of the Noetic Soul is to utilize its divine connection with God to lift-up the created bodily form which was born in darkness and reconstitute the Monad (Christ Monad). The Noetic Soul already has a direct connection to the divine source which can never be lost. The connection only gets muffled, dampened, and filtered by the mind.

  The presence of the Noetic Soul within the mind forms the Noetic Sphere of the mind. The Erotic Sphere of the mind exists due to the presence of the Erotic Soul within the mind. The Erotic Soul emerges disconnected from the Divine Source due to the way its conceived spontaneously out of the Divine Source. It cannot reconnect on its own. The Erotic Sphere needs the intervention of the Noetic Soul to reconnect it back to the Divine Source and reconstitute the Monad. This cannot be done instantaneously. It can only be achieved through the guidance and direction of Alpha which unfolds systematically and geometrically.

  Alpha eventually leads all things back to unity whether along the way of the Straight Path or the Spiral Path. The Short Path is a necessary first step along the way of the Straight Path. The Short Path reminds the Noetic Soul of the divine source. Once remembered, this awareness is then used in the alchemical transformation and integration process. The Short Path advances our level of 'Q,' which is a necessary step in the Great Work. The Short Path is the beginning, not the end.

Sigma *[Sig-ma; Sig-mah]*

The creation of the material cosmos is compelled into existence through a cosmic sonic projection wave emitted by the dimension of mind within all things. From a unified cosmic perspective, the source of this projection wave is the Cosmic Mind. The cosmic sonic projection wave is represented by the Greek letter Sigma [Σ]. Sigma carries within its projection wave, the blueprints for the organization of creation. Alpha counter-balances Sigma to steer the end product of creation to rediscover and reconcile with the ultimate divine source of Ain Soph.

Spiral Path

The Spiral Path is the multi-lifetime approach a person undertakes to reconstitute the Monad in lockstep with all other people in the same planetary sphere. This collective approach utilizes the planetary group mind as the central organizing nexus between all people. Everyone begins on the Spiral Path, and most will finish on the Spiral Path.

The self-organizing force of the universe (Alpha) is directing all human beings to develop a harmonious unification of mind with the divine source. Alpha is driving everyone to rebuild the Monad within creation. When people cooperate with this force in a subconscious manner, they continue to reincarnate life after life in lockstep with the rest of the human race on the planet to achieve the same goal. This slow many lifetime approach is called the Spiral Path.

When people wake-up to the process which Alpha is guiding them upon, and decide to cooperate with it, the process speeds up within them and is able to reach completion in one human lifetime. This accelerated approach is called the Straight Path.

The accelerated Straight Path an individual person undertakes actually functions as a subroutine within the overall Spiral Path. The ultimate goal of the Spiral Path is to awaken the temporal group mind of its planetary sphere and complete the Planetary Monad.

S – Spirit, The | Spiritual Group Mind

Spirit, The – Divine Spirit, Holy Spirit

The Spirit is the third of three fundamental dimensions of the Cosmic Consciousness within the original divine Monad of Ain Soph. The three fundamental dimensions are Awareness, Life, and Love. The Father is the Awareness within the Cosmic Consciousness. The Divine Soul is the Life within the Cosmic Consciousness. The Spirit is the Love within the Cosmic Consciousness. Ain Soph is all three divine forces expressed as one—original Monad.

The Spirit is utilized by a meditator in the practice of alchemical meditation to transform the psychic contents of his or her mind. See Alchemy – Meditation Practices.

When a person consistently utilizes the Spirit to transform and integrate his or her mind, the universal force of Alpha rises within them to guide them in the process of reconstituting the Monad.

Similar or Equivalent Terms:

Alkahest (European Medieval Alchemy), Holy Ghost (Christian); Saraswati (Hinduism)

Spiritual Group Mind

The spiritual group mind is the upper hemisphere of the planetary group mind enveloping the Earth in the primordial universe. The twin hemisphere of the spiritual group mind is the lower hemisphere of the planetary group mind enveloping the Earth in the physical universe called the temporal group mind. The physical universe is based in time, therefore the hemisphere of the planetary group mind enveloping the Earth in the physical universe is called "temporal." The primordial universe is based in eternity and has awoken to the realization of the

Divine Spirit of God, therefore the hemisphere of the planetary group mind enveloping the Earth in the primordial universe is "spiritual."

Each hemisphere of the planetary group mind is a cathedral of the Earth. We have a cathedral of light, and we have a cathedral of darkness. The spiritual group mind is the cathedral of light. The temporal group mind is the cathedral of darkness.

The collective resonance of all life on Earth generates a planetary intelligence within each hemisphere of the planetary group mind. The planetary intelligence governing the spiritual group mind of the Earth in the primordial universe is a planetary genie called EL.

EL is a living sentient being fully aware and integrated with the divine source. It is a planetary Christ Monad. The planetary intelligence governing the temporal group mind of the Earth in the physical universe is a planetary genie called Maub. Maub is a living being who has not yet awoken to the realization of the divine source.

The archetypes of the collective unconscious of Carl Jung and Joseph Campbell arise out of the planetary group mind enveloping the entire Earth. The heavenly realms so often referred to in many Earth mythologies are the spiritual bandwidths of light of the planetary group mind enveloping the Earth in the primordial universe. The circles of Hell so frequently mentioned in many Earth mythologies are the temporal bandwidths of darkness of the planetary group mind enveloping the Earth in the physical universe. During the process of the alchemical integration of the human mind, the conscious mind of the human being traverses all the bandwidths of both light and darkness.

Mythologically, Maub is the Devil. The darkness of humanity feeds the planetary mind of Maub and in return Maub feeds its darkness non-locally right back into the unconscious minds of all individuals on Earth in a symbiotic reciprocal manner. Maub is a mirror of humanity on Earth in the physical universe. The darkness is self-reinforcing and works in a viscous cycle. Darkness begets more darkness and light begets more light. When Maub eventually integrates with EL, the Earth in the physical universe will become a planetary Christ Monad in unity with its primordial twin—EL. When the two combine the Earth will become a Metatronic World—physical matter existing outside of time.

S – Spirituality

Spirituality

There are three paths of spirituality: Religion, New Age, and Alchemy. The basis of the religious path is formed in:

1.) Belief and Ideology

2.) The suppression of basic instincts deemed sinful by an elite.

3.) The placement of an elite intermediary between people and God because people by themselves are deemed unworthy of a direct relationship with God. This elite intermediary is either a church, a priest, or a doctrine that must be followed.

4.) Good versus bad. It is our actions which determine whether we are good or bad even if our good actions come from a false place within.

5.) Control of a church over its members via fear of their own mortality. This aids those in power in controlling society.

The new age path exists as a rebellion against the suppressive control of organized religion. Its thesis is "feel good spirituality." The new age path is guided by popularism and the political correctness of influential individuals who have rejected religion. It has no real spiritual compass. It follows the popular flavor of the week.

The path of spiritual alchemy is based on the universal principles of transformation which transcend all cultures and time periods, as the substance of what is being transformed, and the methodologies being employed, are timeless and do not change based on the influence of the latest modern thinking or belief systems. Alchemy is what it is, regardless of time and culture. We only grow to better understand it.

Where religion sees everything in terms of good versus bad, correct behavior versus incorrect behavior, and new age thinking judges everything based on what is popular, politically correct, and what feels good, alchemy sees everything in terms of authentic versus false, truth versus fiction, illusion versus real.

Alchemy comes to us from the universe. Religion comes to us as a representative byproduct of a human species' current stage of psycho-cognitive development.

Spirituality – S

The way of religion is we first must become true to receive God. The way of alchemy is we first must receive God to become true. Religion therefore denies sacraments to those it deems wicked; whereas alchemy offers sacraments precisely to redeem the wicked.

Alchemy serves as a source of religion, yet alchemy is not a religion. Religion must be defended to be upheld. Alchemy is upheld by the truth without need of being defended. Truth is self-proclaiming and self-fulfilling and always rises to the top. It is very easy for charlatans to exploit the intangibility of spiritual concepts. The realm of spiritual philosophy, including religion, new age, and even alchemy, is vulnerable to the rise of narcissistic individuals. Be careful following others. Find and connect with Ain Soph within yourself. Even alchemy has its own dark shadow. There are two types of alchemy:

<u>Spiritual Alchemy</u>

The aim of spiritual alchemy is to cooperate with the self-organizing force of the universe to reconstitute a unity between creation and divinity (Christ Monad). The process is already occurring naturally in nature incrementally driving all things to a higher expression of existence. When human beings cooperate with this force subconsciously through periodic and intermittent awakenings and brief moments of transcendence, this is the Spiral Path. The Spiral Path requires multiple human lifetimes to reach its goal of re-unification. When human beings consciously and willfully cooperate with this force on a day-to-day basis to achieve a continuous awakening throughout life, this is the straight path. The straight path can be accomplished in one human lifetime. Spiritual alchemy follows the natural organic process of the universe. It has two modes – fast (straight) or slow (spiral). Spiritual alchemy utilizes the principles of the Three Factors to cooperate with Alpha and bring the conscious mind into an awareness of the Spirit to implement the process of transformation. Spiritual Alchemy is the Song of the Immortal Beloved.
The Immortal Beloved is Christ.

S – Spirituality | Straight Path

<u>Dark Alchemy</u>

Consists of any of the following elements.

a.) The manipulation of the natural forces of the universe to synthesize an artificial outcome which would have never occurred naturally or organically (Alpha) and opposes the ultimate goal of the Christ Monad.

b.) Methods which serve to accelerate the compounding processes of the mind to the point that Alpha can no longer steer the mind to the point of reunification with the divine source. Theoflection is lost. Such methods would be in league with the Gorgon. It is the path to the second death or Omicron Wave. (See Omicron).

c.) Schools or organizations that offer an artificial alchemical method and value adherence to its rules over love—and loyalty to its organization over the freedom of self-exploration, are more than likely schools of Black Magic, or Dark Alchemy.

Straight Path

The Straight Path is the spiritual path a person undertakes to reconstitute the Monad in a single human lifetime. The straight path of the one accelerates the spiral path of the many. The self-organizing force of the universe (Alpha) is directing all human beings to develop a harmonious unification of mind with the divine source. The unified mind is called the Monad. The original divine Monad (Ain Soph) has always existed outside the realm of creation. It precedes creation. Alpha is driving all human beings to rebuild the Monad within creation.

When people cooperate with the force of Alpha in a subconscious manner, they continue to reincarnate life after life in lockstep with the rest of the human race on the planet to achieve the same goal. This slow many lifetime approach is called the Spiral Path. When people wake-up to the process which Alpha is guiding them upon, and decide to cooperate with it, the process speeds up within them and is able to reach completion in one human lifetime. This accelerated approach is called the Straight Path.

When the Straight Path emerges, Alpha directs the conscious mind of the person through three major stages in development of the Monad. These three stages in hermetic lore are called the Three Mountains. Someone in the First Mountain (Mount Sophia) is an Apprentice. Someone in the Second Mountain (Mount Kabbalah) is a Journeyman. Someone in the Third Mountain (Mount Magia) is a Foreman.

When on the Spiral Path, the human being traverses all three mountains simultaneously. We experience flashes of each mountain throughout the course of our life. This occurs over many physical existences in lockstep with all human beings on Earth.

When on the Straight Path, the Three Mountains separate, and we climb each mountain sequentially, one after the other. Ironically, climbing the Three Mountains sequentially is faster than climbing them all together as one. The later in life we begin the Three Mountain journey, the faster we move through them due to the accumulation of our current life experiences and realizations. The purpose of the Straight Path of the one in the evolutionary mechanics of nature is to add energy and momentum to the Spiral Path of the many.

Super Ego

The Super Ego is the self-observing function of the mind behind which the authentic-self (Noetic Soul) observes its own mind and body. The mind automatically overlays the self-observing awareness with automated scripts to influence the self-observing function to suggest and direct a programmed set of choices and scripted behaviors. It becomes a false moral conscience. The more we become aware of the scripted programs of the mind, the more our conscious awareness emerges to make free and clear observations and decisions.

S – Super Cognitive Emotion

Super Cognitive Emotion

Super Cognitive Emotion is a faculty which emerges when we relearn how to use the original resonance system of consciousness to communicate with the forces of the cosmic quanta underlying the fabric of reality. We use the original system of feeling and resonance innate to the Spirit within the domain of divinity.

From within the domain of divinity—the Absolute—the Father communicates with us empathically through a sonar-like resonance.

"Hallowed be thy name," is an empathic familiarization with the divine Father. It's how we communicate with him.

This is the origin of what we call … emotion.

Common human emotion, which is vastly different from super cognitive emotion, arises in the human psyche through perception and automated instinct as a functional artifact of the evolutionary mechanics programmed in the human brain to promote the survival and reproduction of the species. Common human emotion is a lower manifestation of its original form. Super cognitive emotion arises within the human being from a profound awareness between the interaction of the forces of consciousness. In a fully developed state, super cognitive emotion bring forth Turiya, which is a sustained sympathetic resonance of awareness and feeling with divinity, and the use of the divine language of consciousness called Kier.

The longer we are able sustain a heightened resonance between our conscious mind and the Spirit, the more the physical wiring of our brain is re-wired to support and deepen the resonance. Over time, the subtle communication between our conscious mind and the emergent forces of the cosmic quanta develops into a new super cognitive faculty called intraspection. This is not introspection. Introspection takes place solely between your own thoughts. Intraspection is a communication between the conscious mind and the emergent forces of the cosmic quanta. The Spirit is the first of these forces to emerge. As we continue the Third Factor practice of quantum meditation alongside other practices of the Three Factors, all the forces of the cosmic quanta - beyond the Spirit - begin to present themselves.

Super Meta – S

Super Meta *[Su-per Me-ta; Su-per Meh-ta]*

The super meta together compose a divine mathematical algebra which is self-stimulating and self-propagating whose acoustical mathematical permutations are called Theokinesis.

The origin of everything is mathematical, acoustical, and theokinetic. The super meta are an underlying set of divine principles which compel the divine forces. They exist below, or are embedded within, the forces of consciousness and drive all their permutations. They compose and drive a "Spiritual Physics." For some exotic reason - within zero - infinite "Force Potential" (1st super meta) and infinite "Being" (2nd super meta) are compelled to reconcile with each other to an absolute ground state called "Zero-Base-Prime." The force to reach and sustain Zero-Base-Prime produces infinite energy within Unity called the "Force of Unity (3rd super meta)." The Force of Unity produces infinite energy because it is forcing infinity to reconcile with infinity. When the infinities are superimposed, "Force Potential" is infinite outward and "Being" is infinite inward. Consciousness can be mathematically formulated as follows:

$$Consciousness = Infinity^3$$

or

$$Consciousness = (Infinite\ Outward) \times (Infinite\ Inward) \times (Infinite\ Energy)$$

This theory of consciousness underlies Einstein's theory of special relativity which is:

$$E=mc2$$

Relativity is a subset of a more fundamental equation.

S – Super Meta

The Force of Unity exists within everyone and within all things. On a super cognitive emotional level when we resonate with the Force of Unity we experience Divine Love (Spirit). Thus, the Law of One is Love. Intuition and logic indicate the following relationships:

0 - Zero-Base-Prime:	Ain Soph
1 - Force Potential:	Father (Awareness)
2 - Being:	Divine Soul (Life)
3 - Unity:	Spirit (Love)

The fourth super meta is Dynamis. Dynamis sparks a vision of creation out of the infinite energy of the Spirit. It starts the whole process of creation. Dynamis gives rise to imagination. It gives rise to the mind and to the Erodonic Trinity:

1.) IAO

2.) Erotic Soul

3.) Energy-Matter

The fifth super meta is Thelesis. Thelesis compels the will of the Father to emerge to reconcile creation and bring it all back into unity. Thelesis gives rise to the Father's Immaculate Conception of the Sacred Trinity to function as the intercessing principal between creation and divinity.

T

Temporal Group Mind *[Tem-poral; Tem-pruhl]*

The temporal group mind is the lower hemisphere of the planetary group mind enveloping the Earth in the physical universe. The twin hemisphere of the temporal group mind is the upper hemisphere of the planetary group mind enveloping the Earth in the primordial universe called the spiritual group mind. The physical universe is based in time, therefore the hemisphere of the planetary group mind enveloping the Earth in the physical universe is called "temporal." The primordial universe is based in eternity and has awoken to the realization of the Divine Spirit of God, therefore the hemisphere of the planetary group mind enveloping the Earth in the primordial universe is called "spiritual." Each hemisphere of the planetary group mind is a cathedral of the Earth. We have a cathedral of light and we have a cathedral of darkness. The spiritual group mind is the cathedral of light. The temporal group mind is the cathedral of darkness. The collective resonance of all life on Earth generates a planetary intelligence within each hemisphere of the planetary group mind. The planetary intelligence governing the spiritual group mind of the Earth in the primordial universe is a planetary Genie called "EL." EL is a living sentient being fully aware and integrated with the divine source. It is a planetary Christ Monad.

    The planetary intelligence governing the temporal group mind of the Earth in the physical universe is a planetary Genie called "Maub." Maub is a living being who has not yet awoken to the realization of the divine source. Mythologically, Maub is the Devil. The darkness of humanity feeds the planetary mind of Maub and in return Maub feeds its darkness non-locally right back into the unconscious minds of all individuals on Earth. It has a symbiotic reciprocal relationship with all

T – Temporal Group Mind

individual minds on Earth. Maub is a mirror of humanity on Earth in the physical universe. The darkness is self-reinforcing and works in a vicious cycle. Darkness begets more darkness and Light begets more light. The only way to break the vicious cycle and awaken Maub to the realization of the divine source, is enough individual human minds must awaken to the realization of the divine source on their own until Maub awakens and integrates with EL. When Maub eventually integrates with EL, the Earth in the physical universe will become a planetary Christ Monad.

The awakening of the temporal group mind is not evolving solely by the mechanical laws of nature alone. Humanity in the primordial universe on Earth is consciously intervening with and guiding the whole process. This conscious cooperation is called "The Earth Monad Project." The Alien guided genetic development program is part of the overall Earth Monad Project. The Aliens directly involved in the project are a highly advanced artificial intelligence (AI) which ultimately takes its direction from the humanity residing in the primordial universe on Earth. Humanity itself is in control of the Earth Monad Project and therefore the whole process of human reincarnation in the physical universe on Earth. The primordial humanity on Earth is directing the evolution of the physical humanity on Earth. When in physical form, we are a subject of the project. When in primordial form, we are a manager of the project.

Both hemispheres of the planetary group mind are stratified into bandwidths of global psychic energy which each human being's subtle ethereal bodies communicate with. The many levels and layers within the individual human mind correlate to the many bandwidths within the planetary group mind. The bandwidths within the planetary group mind function as a cognitive base within the individual minds of each human being on Earth. When a human being sleeps, their conscious minds are virtually immersed into these global bandwidths of psychic energy where they dream in cooperation with the intelligences embedded in each hemisphere of the planetary group mind. The intelligences communicate with a metaphoric and mythological language.

The archetypes of the collective unconscious of Carl Jung and Joseph Campbell arise out of the planetary group mind enveloping the Earth. The heavenly realms so often referred to in many Earth mythologies and religions are the spiritual bandwidths of light of the planetary group mind enveloping the Earth in the primordial universe. The circles of Hell so frequently mentioned in many Earth mythologies and religions are the temporal bandwidths of darkness of the planetary group mind enveloping the Earth in the physical universe. During the process of the alchemical integration of the human mind in the development of the Christ Monad, the conscious mind of the human being traverses all the bandwidths of both light and darkness.

Temporal-Physical-Being – Physical Being, Physical Body

A human being's Temporal-Physical Being is the parallel twin being to a human being's Eternal-Primordial Being residing in a higher frequency primordial universe parallel to the physical universe. The physical body is the twin mortal body to the immortal primordial body. We only ever have one primordial body. However, we take on many physical body's life after life in the physical universe through the process of reincarnation. When our physical body dies, we eventually re-awaken in our primordial body in the primordial universe.

Theism *[The-ism; Thee-i-zm]*

The term "Theism" derives from the Greek "Theos" or "Theoi," meaning "God." Essentially, Theism is a contrast to Deism. Theism does not reject the possibility of divine intervention, revelation, or interaction. Theism can be monotheistic (one God) or polytheistic (many Gods). See Deism.

T – Thelesis | Theokinesis

Thelesis *[Thel-e-sis; Thel-EH-sis]*

A set of underlying divine principles called super meta drive the permutating process of consciousness called Theokinesis. During the process of theokinesis, the fifth super meta in a sequence called Thelesis arises to compel the will of the Father to intervene with the spontaneous process of creation to bring everything back into unity. Thelesis immaculately conceives and gives rise to the Sacred Trinity including (1) the Logos, (2) Noetic Soul, and (3) the Numina. When the Sacred Trinity fulfills the will of the Father, the divine source and creation come to resonate as one inside a new reorganized matrix which is Christ, the new Monad. Thelesis is the first of two stages of the Immaculate Conception. Christ is the second and final stage of the Immaculate Conception.

Theoflection *[Theo-flection]*

The more our physical being becomes aware and sensitive to the forces of the cosmic quanta, the more they become aware and sensitive to our physical being, and the more they become aware and sensitive to our physical being, the more they can positively direct our lives.

Theokinesis *[Theo-kin-e-sis; Thee-O-kin-EE-sis]*

A popular theological belief is that the original unity of God, the original Monad—Ain Soph, created the universe because it was alone. Meditation on the quantum forces within us reveals that this was not the original cause. Quantum meditation reveals that the act of creation develops and completes itself in three primary stages. Creation was not a single act. It continues to repeat *ad-infinitum*.

Creation emerges out of Ain Soph due to the way in which Ain Soph is internally composed. Ain Soph has three primary dimensions within itself with each dimension possessing its own divine force. The differentiation between these three divine forces compels an interacting relationship to arise and develop between each of the divine forces. This interplay drives the process of creation. This process is called Theokinesis. Theokinesis is a divine algebra or spiritual physics.

Theosphere | Theta – T

Theosphere *[Theo-sphere; Theos-sphere]*

The cosmic level of creation, which is already reconciled, is called the Theosphere. The Theosphere is the largest in scale in the outward spectrum of space-time but at the same time it is also the smallest in scale within the inward spectrum of the quantum cosmos. The inner and outer cosmos are one. The door to the outer is entered through the door of the inner, and here in lays the grand key to navigating all of the created cosmos. The Theosphere and Causal 'M' are one and the same. Causal 'M' is the third of three Causals to form in the process of reconciling Causal 'A' (Divinity) with Causal 'B' (Creation). The Theosphere is the first stage of that process to emerge when it completes the cosmic level of creation but eventually it stretches to incorporate all three levels of creation. The reconciliation process continues beyond the cosmic level to the planetary and individual levels of creation ultimately reconciling all three levels within a new super unified Monad. *See*: Causal 'M' for a more detailed explanation.

Theta *[The-ta; Thei-tuh]*

Theta is the force of death. Because human beings on Earth in the physical universe exist with two unintegrated spheres of the mind (erotic and noetic), the dark unintegrated erotic side of the human being spawns evil when interacting with the cosmic quantum of IAO. The force of Theta (death) counteracts the forces of the erotic sphere thereby suppressing the mind's interaction with IAO. The force of Theta arises from the dark inflected quantum of the Logos. Mythologically, this force of consciousness is called Lucifer. In the quantum cosmos, its existence is much more rational than in Earth mythology. This quantum force teaches us that the force of death cannot be transcended through conflict. It can only be transcended by consciously integrating the noetic sphere of the mind with the erotic sphere of the mind.

T – Third Factor | Third Mountain

Third Factor

The Third Factor (Love) is our relationship with the Spirit itself. It is the most important of all Three Factors. If you want to use the Spirit in the First Factor of Transformation, then you need to develop a direct relationship with the Spirit via the Third Factor. The Second Factor helps us to reach the Spirit. We develop our relationship with the Spirit by learning how to love, and by developing our faith in God. The key to the Three Factors is that we must learn how to feel and resonate with the Spirit. It cannot be a mental belief or thought. We must develop a heightened sensory awareness within our emotions through which we discover the Spirit. We must feel the Spirit with our emotions. It is not a physical feeling. When we feel the Spirit with our emotions, this is called "Super Cognitive Emotion." This is quite different from "Common Human Emotion." Our ability to use our super cognitive emotional abilities to communicate with the forces of the cosmic quanta to transform ourselves and extract knowledge is what compels us in the process of building the Monad. We need to work with the First Factor to properly work with the Second Factor. The Second Factor, if properly worked with, facilitates the Third Factor, which further facilitates the First Factor. All Three Factors work together.

Third Mountain – Mount Magia

Mount Magia is the third mountain in a three-mountain alchemical process of achieving the Christ Monad (Philosophers' Stone). The three mountains are major Alpha patterns which guide the conscious mind of the alchemist during the alchemical process. It unfolds in geometric patterns guiding all things toward an ultimate unity with God. Its patterns are universal based upon a repeating echo of the same pattern which worked at the cosmic level to complete the process of creation at the cosmic level of creation infinite eons ago in the deep eternal past. In the third mountain, Mount Magia, we harmonize our individuated-self with the Cosmic Consciousness, the Cosmic Mind, and Creation, thereby accomplishing the Great Work.

Third Sanctum – Sanctum of Magia, Sanctum of the Logos

A sanctum is a point of stillness and consolidation within the forces of Alpha. It is a necessary stage in the process of leading all the forces of the mind, body, and consciousness toward a unified mind – the Monad. The Third Sanctum is the sanctum sitting below the summit of the Third Mountain. It initiates the final work of reconstituting the Monad.

The Alpha Wave pattern produced by the forces of Alpha in the process of developing the Monad includes three major development periods called the Three Mountains. The Monad development process also includes Three Sanctums. The Three Sanctums are between the First and Second Mountains, the Second and Third Mountains, and just below the summit of the Third Mountain. There is a fourth sanctum at the summit of the Third Mountain but at this point the Monad has already been formed.

Three Factors – Philosophical Trinity

The goal of the Three-Factors is the unification of the human mind with the Cosmic Consciousness. It is a unification of the mind with God. It is the reconstitution of the Monad. The mind arises through a pairing of consciousness and matter. Consciousness is the mind's Father. Matter is the mind's Mother. Matter arises within creation in darkness due to the way in which creation is spontaneously and automatically sprung into existence. Matter and consciousness arise from two different sources. Matter arises out of darkness in descent from the Spirt. Consciousness arises out of the invisible light of the Father. When the two are paired, there is a collision of matter and consciousness, and the mind arises out of that collision. Because of this, the mind emerges in a fractured incomplete form. The mind arises in darkness.

In order for the human mind to complete itself, a self-observing conscious awareness must arise within the mind to resolve its incoherent fractured condition. The instinctive automatic processes of the mind suppress the self-observing consciousness from arising within the human mind. Typically, the human mind just follows its nature-installed instinctive autocognitive programs.

T – Three Factors

Essentially, human beings are born incomplete and it is up to us to complete ourselves. To complete ourselves, the human Noetic Soul must rise up within the human mind to reconcile and unify the mind with God and complete the process of creation within itself. The means and methods of this process are the Three Factors. The process is what we call *"Spiritual Alchemy."* We call the process *"Alchemy"* because it involves a process of *"Transformation."* We call the process spiritual alchemy because we are using the Spirit of God (the love of God) to compel the process of transformation.

The self-observing conscious awareness arising in the mind is the Noetic Soul. From a psychological perspective, we call it the *"Authentic-Self."*

In order to resolve all the fragmented components of the human mind and unify it, the authentic-self must emerge in the human mind in a self-observing capacity. When this happens, the mind splits into the observer and observed. When the mind splits into the observer and observed, content is automatically pulled to the periphery of the mind and becomes the observed, and the authentic-self emerges in the center of the mind as the observer. When this happens, we start observing many of our thoughts, feelings, and instincts. Most people confuse all their thoughts, feelings, and instincts with who they are. If you are able to observe it, then it is not part of your authentic-self. The observed is a construct of the mind which is not fully integrated.

The First Factor - Transformation

The First Factor (Transformation) is a psycho cognitive process of splitting the human mind into the observer and observed, isolating the fragmented constructs of the mind (elements), and then compelling their transformation. When an element of the mind transforms, an aspect of our authentic-self is freed and joins the observer in the center of our being. There are thousands of psychic elements which need to be observed and then transformed.

Three Factors – T

In a process of alchemical meditation, we isolate each psychic element within us and then contrast that element with our awareness of the Spirit. When an awareness of the Spirit is paired in the mind in contrast to the psychic element we are observing, the psychic element is automatically transformed. The underlying law in the universe which facilitates the transformation of any element in the presence of the Spirit is the law of sympathetic vibrations, or sympathetic resonance. All things are compelled to harmonize with the Spirit when brought into its light within the conscious mind. This is the key to alchemy. The universal force which brings the observed element of the mind into harmony with the Spirit is Alpha. The Spirit transforms everything into an authentic cohesive state. This is how we unify the mind.

When we start transforming the psychic elements within us, eventually Alpha raises its self-organizing momentum within us to further compel the process of integrating the mind. When Alpha rises within us, it starts guiding our conscious mind through all the layers of the mind. This is called the Sacred Fire.

At this point, we need to take our hands off the steering wheel and allow Alpha to drive the bus. At this point, we just focus on whatever Alpha is presenting to us to transform. The content of our mind which we observe and transform is brought into our frame of conscious awareness through our life events and life circumstances. The mind reacts to everything. We use these reactions to discover ourselves and transform what we discover. As we allow this discovery and transformation process to continue, Alpha leads the Noetic Soul through three major stages of development in the completion of the Monad. These three major stages are called the Three Mountains. The Three Mountains are explained in great detail in the book *Song of the Immortal Beloved*. The Three Mountains are called:

1.) Mount Sophia

2.) Mount Kabbalah

3.) Mount Magia

T – Three Factors

In Mount Sophia, we compel the force of Alpha. In Mount Kabbalah, Alpha leads us to consolidate the temporal-noetic sphere of our being corresponding to the Temporal Group Mind of Earth and the physical universe. In Mount Magia, Alpha leads us to integrate the physical and primordial hemispheres of our being by integrating the noetic and erotic hemispheres of our being. (see diagram below).

The primordial hemisphere corresponds to the Spiritual Group Mind of Earth and the primordial universe. Both hemispheres of the Planetary Group Mind correspond to what Carl Jung called the Collective Unconscious. The primordial universe is the mother universe to the physical universe. They are dual reflections of each other. The primordial universe is based in eternity. The physical universe is based in time. The primordial universe is the other side of the veil. It is where we come from before being born and go back to after we die.

The Created Spheres of the Human Being

This diagram is a cross-section of the human being

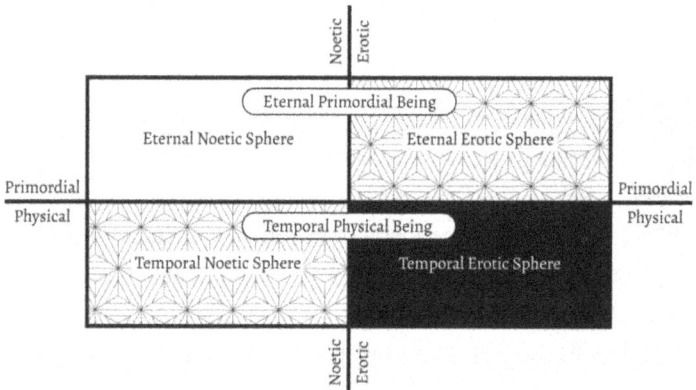

The Second Factor – Cultivation

The key to the First Factor is our contrasting awareness of the Spirit The Spirit is the key to transformation, but we need something to help us reach the Spirit. The Second Factor helps our conscious mind to access the Spirit deep within us. The key is understanding that we are all made of energy and energy exists in three different states:

Positive-Yang-Male, Negative-Female-Yin, and Neutral-Yuan.

The Spirit is genderless and completely neutral in its energy. The energy of the human mind exists in a spectrum between Yin and Yang. All men and women have both polarities within them. No one is all male and no one is all female, regardless of their sexual organs. The key is seeing past the Yin-Yang polarities of the mind to access the deeper energy of the Spirit. The Second Factor incorporates cultivation techniques into our daily life to help us to balance our biomechanical and psychic energy to allow the Spirit to rise within our conscious mind. Without this balance, the biomechanical and psychic energy of our mind and body cloud the energy of the Spirit. Some cultivation techniques involve sexual yoga practices while other practices are performed solo in direct concert with the forces of nature, or with the forces of the cosmic quanta underlying the forces of nature. Cultivation works best when we are already practicing the First Factor. If not, the cultivation practice is contaminated by the automated reactions of the psyche. The Three Factors are mutually supportive. We need all three.

The Third Factor – Love

The Third Factor is our relationship with the Spirit itself. It is the most important of all Three Factors. If you want to use the Spirit in the First Factor of Transformation, then you need to develop a direct relationship with the Spirit via the Third Factor. The Second Factor helps us to reach the Spirit. We develop our relationship with the Spirit by learning how to love, and by developing our faith in God.

T – Three Factors | Three Mountains

The key to the Three Factors is that we must learn how to feel and resonate with the Spirit. It cannot be a mental belief or thought. We must develop a heightened sensory awareness within our emotions through which we discover the Spirit. We must feel the Spirit with our emotions. It is not a physical feeling. When we feel the Spirit with our emotions, this is called Super Cognitive Emotion. This is different from Common Human Emotion. Our ability to use our super cognitive emotional abilities to communicate with the forces of the cosmic quanta to transform ourselves and extract knowledge is what compels us in building the Monad.

The cosmic quanta include a whole host of forces of consciousness. Three of these forces are divine, but there are other forces as well which we come to realize during the alchemical integration process. All are key in some way. Alpha leads us in this process of discovery, transformation, and integration.

We need to work with the First Factor to properly work with the Second Factor. The Second Factor, if properly worked with, facilitates the Third Factor, which further facilitates the First Factor. All Three Factors work together.

Three Mountains

The three mountains are major Alpha patterns which guide the conscious mind of the alchemist during the alchemical process of achieving the Christ Monad (Philosophers' Stone). Alpha is the self-organizing force of the universe. It is the law of sympathetic vibrations in motion. It unfolds in geometric patterns guiding all things toward a unity with God. Its patterns are universal based upon a repeating echo of the same pattern that worked to complete the process of creation at the cosmic level of creation infinite eons ago in the deep eternal past.

In the first mountain, Mount Sophia, we move into a direct apprenticeship with the universal alchemical process where we learn how to transform the elements of our minds and accelerate the rhythm of Alpha.

Three Mountains – T

In the second mountain, Mount Kabbalah, we deconstruct the compensating mechanisms of the human ego and the adaptive instincts of our animal nature which prevent the authentic-self within us from integrating into a cohesive individuated whole. By going through this deconstruction process, we are at the same time allowing a fragmented-self to self-assemble into an individuated-self –which, when achieved– liberates our true authentic nature.

In the third mountain, Mount Magia, we harmonize our individuated-self with the Cosmic Consciousness, the Cosmic Mind, and Creation, thereby accomplishing the Great Work.

After completing the reconstitution of the Monad at the summit of the third mountain, a new fourth mountain of eternity arises called Mount Elohim.

The purpose of the Mount Elohim is the eternal expansion of the Christ Monad, but Mount Elohim has no summit. The summit of Mount Elohim is an infinitely distant event horizon.

In medieval European alchemy, the Fourth Mountain aligns with the ninth alchemical process called "Multiplication" involving the expansion of the already formed Philosophers' Stone.

The Three Mountains complete the Philosophers' Stone.

The Fourth Mountain expands it.

Other traditions have different names or mythologies for organizing the major stages of the alchemical process—and some see the major stages organized a little differently. For example, the Navajo and the Apache speak of four mountains.

The real emphasis is on completing the Philosophers' Stone, because at this point the prime directive of the Noetic Soul has been fulfilled and its consciousness has been released from the cycle of return and recurrence. Self-realized beings such as these, that have completed the unified mind—Monad-Philosophers' Stone—
have gained full self-determination over the reincarnation process. They cannot get hung-up in the temporal group mind after death. They are masters over creation with the ability to shift their consciousness between the primordial universe and physical universe at will.

T – Tithing, The

Tithing, The *[Ti-thing; Tai-thing]*

During the eighth alchemical process of the Three Mountains, which begins at the final stage of the Third Mountain when the alchemist enters the Third Sanctum, the bond of resonance between the Noetic Soul and the Father is tested by the forces of Eros.

This testing period is called the Tithing.

When the bond of that resonance is tested and confirmed, the covenant of the Father's love is restored within the matrix of creation. At this point, the forces of Heaven (the Father) now have an avenue and a means to bring the forces of the Earth (creation) into harmony with its Spirit via its unbreakable bond with the Human / Noetic Soul. This is the Holy Grail. The holy blood symbolizes the resonance of the Father running through the veins of creation.

This process brings the alchemist's physical body of creation into unity with the divine source. This is the alchemical Christ Monad.

<u>The Tempest Soul</u>

Artwork which captures the mood of the Testing-Tithing Period
In the book, *Song of the Immortal Beloved*

Treasuries of Light

The most transformative period of the Great Work occurs in the upper stage ascent of Mount Magia. The upper stage ascent includes our ascent through all nine spiritual heavens of the Earth and one final stage beyond the heavens.

The nine heavens, which completely envelope and enshrine the Earth in the primordial universe, begin in the middle kingdom of the Earth's planetary soul, and then continue upward through all levels of the upper kingdom, and are organized into three groups of three. Each group of three is a Treasury of Light. There are three Treasuries.

The first treasury we journey through is the lower treasury, and includes the heavens Nirvana, Simmatuu, and Khimmadooree. The second treasury we journey through is the middle treasury, and includes the heavens Valhalla, Elysium, and Terrasumna. The third treasury we journey through is the upper treasury, and includes the heavens Barstow, Jenesis, and Erawan.

The reason there are three groups of three is that the heavens follow a universal geometric pattern of unfoldment in periodic cycles of three. Maturation cycles follow the same cosmic pattern.

"Destroy this temple and I will raise it again in three days"
...John 2:19

Each Treasury of Light represents one maturation cycle across the nine heavens.

As a Foreman, we experience a complete reformation of our being at an interval rate of every three heavens as we ascend the Treasuries of Light. The maturation cycles begin in Bardo. However, the cycles are not formally recognized as Treasuries of Light until they reach Nirvana.

The reason for this is, it is not until we reach the nine heavens that the maturation cycles become noticeable in their power of transformation. Once in the heavenly realms, the maturation intervals mark the beginning and end of each Treasury of Light. The magnitude of reformation the Foreman experiences in each treasury grows progressively larger from one treasury to the next.

T – Treasury of Souls

Treasury of Souls

How many Human Souls are there? Many people ponder this question. Alchemy provides the answer. There are three types of souls and an infinite number of Human Souls which re-collect back into one soul. The Human Soul is the Noetic Soul. They are the same.

Divine Soul: There is only one Divine Soul. It is infinite and absolute. It is the life force of the Father. It does not manifest directly within creation. We commune with it through resonance.

Erotic Soul: There is only one Erotic Soul. It is omnipresent. It is the life force of IAO. It animates all bodies of creation. It is a dimension of mind.

Noetic Soul: There is only one Human Soul / Noetic Soul. It is fractally reflected and infinitely replicated. It is the life force of the Logos. It superimposes and intervenes with the Erotic Soul within the mind. When we stand between two mirrors, we see an infinite progression of individual reflections of self. Each reflection in progression is an individualized Noetic Soul. When we reconstitute the Monad, we emerge as one in front of the mirror. This is:

"The Achievement of the Philosophers' Stone."

The Noetic Soul standing in front of the mirror is the Noetic Soul on a cosmic level. It is the Noetic Soul of Eloah, the Cosmic Christ, the Immortal Beloved. When we complete the Great Work, we manifest Eloah while maintaining our reflection within the human mind. This is the unified mind.

Triad *[Tri-ad; Try-add]*

The Triad is an organization of mind (organization of forces within the mind) which arises when the conscious mind realizes the three forces of the Divine Trinity residing within the divine Monad of Ain Soph. The Triad arises to compel the formation of the Nuad within the human mind. The Triad helps the Noetic Soul find the Logos and Numina within itself to reestablish the Sacred Trinity within the conscious mind. This realization forms the Nuad. The conscious mind realizes the Divine Trinity when its vibrational resonance with the divine source ascends beyond the heaven of Erawan. The Nuad engages the forces of Eros and the forces of divinity to complete the Christ Monad. Each force is a different permutation of consciousness.

Triumphants *[Tri-um-phants; Trai-uhm-fnts]*

Since the beginning of creation, the Father has only ever had two realizations and one will. Beyond these three divine actions, he remains invisible - at rest - in an ever-present state of infinite peace and infinite power. Just from these two realizations, and this one will of the Father, came forth the entire universe we all know today, from the formation of galaxies to the structure of the atom, the emergence of sexuality, and our whole matrix of reality.

The two realizations and the one will of the Father belong to a group of four major theological actions called Triumphants. The first three triumphants belong exclusively to the Father. The first three triumphants are also called the three primations of the Father. The super meta underlie and compel the theological actions, or triumphants. They are all part of the process of theokinesis.

The first triumphant is the Father's realization of his own life (The Divine Soul). The first triumphant compels the rise of the Spirit (Divine Love). The Father loves his own life. The first triumphant always was and always will be.

T – Triumphants

The second triumphant is the Father's realization of creation. It is the divine realization that his Spirit had spontaneously sparked creation and that this creation was in darkness. The Father's realization of creation being in darkness compelled the rise of the Father's will to save creation and bring it back into unity with his divine presence.

The will of the Father is the Third Triumphant.

The will of the Father compels the emergence of the Sacred Trinity. (1) The awareness of the will of the Father is the Logos—the sacred masculine. (2) The life of the will of the Father is the Noetic Soul. (3) The Father's realization of creation compels his love for creation, which is the Numina—the sacred feminine. The Sacred Trinity is the intercessor between divinity and creation.

The final and fourth triumphant belongs exclusively to the only begotten son of God – The Noetic Soul.

The final and fourth triumphant, or theological action, which completes the whole cycle of creation, is the fulfillment of the Father's will to achieve the unity between creation and divinity.

The unity between divinity and creation is the Monad.

The universal symbol of the Monad is Christ.

Christ is the fulfillment of the fourth triumphant.

Each of the three triumphants of the Father are called primations. The fourth and final triumphant is called christification.

The job of the lower trinity is to reconcile divinity with creation and give birth to Christ within the heart of every human being.

The fourth triumphant is our Magnum Opus—the Great Work.

The completion of the Great Work is the accomplishment of the Hyperborean Mystery. Hyperborea is the primordial universe.

The accomplishment of the hyperborean mystery is the unification of our physical being with our primordial being. It is the completion of the celestial body of Christ—the metatronic body. If the physical body can be raised high enough in resonance with the primordial body, the physical body is placed outside of time and becomes immortal. This is the metatronic celestial body of Christ.

Turiya – T

Turiya *[Tu-ri-ya; Tuh-ree-yuh]*

Turiya is the conscious mind's sustained, consistent, and deeply profound super cognitive emotional awareness of the love of God (The Spirit). The conscious mind will initially capture glimpses of the Spirit where it can feel it momentarily during meditation, however, this does not rise to the level of what is called "Turiya." Turiya is a sustained state of awareness of the Spirit which carries into the waking conscious mind even during the course of normal life activities. It feels like a divine music playing in our emotions in the background of our mind.

Turiya is entered upon through an awareness of the love of God –the Spirit—but becomes much more. It evolves into a resonant unity with God. Through Turiya, we come to know, live, and breath the awareness, life, and love of the divine Father.

The divine Father is the innermost of the Immortal Beloved. Alchemy is the Song of the Immortal Beloved. The music of the song is Turiya. In total, the Immortal Beloved is Christ.

When we live in Turiya, we experience a profound melody within our higher emotions playing like a divine music in the background of our mind, filling us with a divine bliss and joy, far exceeding what anyone can imagine until they finally experience it. This divine musical background is the eternal divine love of the Father. It is a marvelous symphony of divine moods which continuously change in melody, harmony, and complexity, accompanying all our internal psychic processes. It overlays our outer-experience of the world. Once a level of resonance with the Father is sustained through the love of his Spirit, the resonance escalates in octaves in three major consecutive intervals. The three intervals of Turiya are:

1.) Communion Turiya

2.) Symphysis Turiya

3.) Dominus Turiya

T – Turiya

Communion Turiya

Communion Turiya is entered upon with the 7th alchemical process where the alchemist must raise his awareness of the divine Father. This is done in grades with each grade correlating to a different bandwidth of the spiritual group mind of the Earth, or heavenly realm. It concludes with a profound realization of the true nature of the forces of the Divine Trinity.

Symphysis Turiya

Symphysis Turiya is the level of Turiya utilized in the process of Primordial Alchemy where the forces of creation and the id complex are integrated. It's called "Primordial," because its alchemical process mirrors the same original alchemical process that the greater cosmos underwent to reconcile the forces of light and darkness before the beginning of time at the on-set of creation. Primordial Alchemy is the 8th alchemical process. In the 8th alchemical process which occurs at the final stage of the Third Mountain when the alchemist enters the Third Sanctum, the bond of resonance between the Noetic Soul and the Father (Love) is tested by the forces of Eros. This testing period is called the Tithing. When the bond of that resonance is tested and confirmed, the covenant of the Father's love is restored within the matrix of creation. At this point, the forces of Heaven (the Father) now have an avenue and a means to bring the forces of the Earth (Creation) into harmony with its Spirit via its unbreakable bond with the Noetic Soul. This is the Holy Grail. The holy blood symbolizes the resonance of the Father running through the veins of creation. This process brings the alchemist's physical body of creation into unity with the divine source. This is the alchemical Christ Monad.

Turiya | Turiya Faculty – T

<u>Dominus Turiya</u>

When we complete the reconstitution of the Monad, we enter the highest level of Turiya called Dominus Turiya. In Dominus Turiya we enter the 9th alchemical process called Eternal Alchemy. In the eternal alchemy practice, the alchemist brings into differential resonance: (1) The infinite depth of the awareness of the Father, with (2) the infinite depth of the forces of darkness within matter. In the eternal alchemy practice, the awareness of the Father lines-up behind the self-observing awareness of the conscious mind via the intercession of the Noetic Soul. This compels the Father to observe and realize the body of creation of the human being and for the darkness in matter to continuously rise-up into unity with the Father. This drives the eternal expansion of the Monad (Christ Monad). This process evolves to the eventual arrival of Eloah, the Cosmic Christ, who takes our expanding Monad to a new level in Mount Elohim.

Turiya Faculty *[Tu-ri-ya; Tuh-ree-yuh]*

The primordial dimensions of every living being already exist in the state of turiya. It is through the integration of our temporal-physical being with our eternal-primordial being that the temporal dimensions of our being enter turiya. The emergence of turiya rewires the physical brain. What emerges by effect of turiya is the Turiya Faculty whose purpose is to sustain, perpetuate, and deepen turiya. The turiya faculty is a secondary sexual characteristic of an integrated and self-realized human being.

Just as the faculties of Thought, Feeling, Memory, Imagination, Intuition, and Volition, are all faculties of the human mind, the Turiya faculty emerges to become the prime central organizing faculty of the human mind and takes control over all other faculties to sustain and perpetuate the communion between our temporal-physical being and the Father. As a Foreman, when we enter Turiya, our conscious mind develops a new mode of awareness which parallels our perspective awareness within the mind. The Father provides this new mode of awareness.

U

Upanishads

The Upanishads are late Vedic and post-Vedic Sanskrit texts that document the transition from the archaic ritualism of the Veda into new religious ideas and institutions and the emergence of the central religious concepts of Hinduism. They are the most recent addition to the Vedas, the oldest scriptures of Hinduism, and deal with meditation, philosophy, consciousness, and ontological knowledge. Earlier parts of the Vedas dealt with mantras, benedictions, rituals, ceremonies, and sacrifices.

While among the most important literature in the history of Indian religions and culture, the Upanishads document a wide variety of rites, incarnations, and esoteric knowledge departing from Vedic ritualism and interpreted in various ways in the later commentarial traditions. Of all Vedic literature, the Upanishads alone are widely known, and their diverse ideas, interpreted in various ways, informed later traditions of Hinduism. The central concern of all Upanishads is to discover the relations between ritual, cosmic realities (including gods), and the human body / person, postulating Atman (Ain Soph) and Brahman (The Father) as the summit of the hierarchically arranged and interconnected universe.

Around 108 Upanishads are known, of which the first dozen or so are the oldest and most important and are referred to as the principal or main (mukhya) Upanishads. The mukhya Upanishads are found mostly in the concluding part of the Brahmanas and Aranyakas and were, for centuries, memorized by each generation and passed down orally. The mukhya Upanishads predate the Common Era, but there is no scholarly consensus on their date, or even on which ones are pre-or post-Buddhist. (Sourced from Wikipedia 2023)

Void, The

The Void and Nexus are central organizing points within the planetary group mind where the forces of consciousness, mind, and matter intersect. The Void is the central organizing point found at the center of the temporal group mind of the planet corresponding to the Earth in the physical universe. The Nexus is the central organizing point found at the center of the spiritual group mind of the planet corresponding to the Earth in the primordial universe.

The mythology of Hell is a metaphorical representation of the temporal planetary group mind and the Void. Both are very real. They are quantum realms of mind and consciousness. These realms have many levels as the mythologies of Hell suggest.

The levels of Hell are the bandwidths of the temporal group mind of the planet Earth. However, we do not have to die in order enter the levels of Hell. People resonate with these levels both during life and after death.

The nine circles of Hell are a popular historic mythological motif. The nine circles are representative of the bandwidths of the temporal group mind. The thirteen bandwidths profiled in the book *Song of the Immortal Beloved* can be easily reconciled with the number nine by collapsing all the trans-cognitive bandwidths corresponding solely to the vital temporal body and by removing the Void; the Void is not so much a bandwidth, but the center of gravity within all the temporal bandwidths.

The Void does not correspond to a body of the mind. The Void is devoid of bodies. The Void is the space within the cosmos which came right after the moment of creation but before energy-matter was organized.

V – Void, The

Our completion of the alchemical labor called Neptune in the second mountain of the three-mountain alchemical process of reconstituting the Monad, leads our focus of conscious awareness into the temporal core of our individual being. The temporal core of our individual being coincides with the temporal core of the planet - which aligns with the temporal core of the cosmos at large. All life and all things on a planet share the same planetary core. All life and all things in the universe share the same cosmic core. The temporal core at the center of our individual being is the same temporal core at the center of our planet and is the same temporal core at the center of the universe. This core is the "Void."

As we descend into the Void, we realize that there are no more temporal ethereal bodies to silence. Mysteriously, the initial cognitive feedback we receive as an echo recoiling from the depths of the Void is that of "oblivion." When the temporal mind renders the Void as a realm of oblivion, this perception arises as a result of the temporal mind attempting to comprehend something which it lacks the cognitive faculties to comprehend. However, the fact that we can gather any sense of the Void at all, and characterize it in some manner, even if the result is irrational, means we are at least partially aware of it.

During our initial engagement with the Void, if we continue to focus our inner sensory awareness on our sense of "oblivion" rather than just dismissing it, our sensory feedback response will eventually begin to reformulate into a more rational rendition of the Void. We must learn to listen with our inner cognitive feelings. When we start listening with our feelings, the Void begins to fill with a profoundly exotic knowledge. An entire new dimension of reality begins to unfold before us.

As we develop our super cognitive emotional awareness, the Void shares with us that its very existence, and its very nature, harken way back to an ancient period of the universe when the universe was newly formed.

Void, The – V

The Void shares with us that in the very beginning there was darkness, and this darkness was the Void. The Void also shares with us that this darkness has a profound story behind it which the alchemist unravels and learns all about in the Third Mountain. The Void shares with us that there was something which preceded the darkness and there was something which came after it.

But what? and why?

The alchemist discovers, for some profound reason, that receiving knowledge directly out of the underlying cosmic quanta of the universe is essential and fundamental to the integration process. Direct Knowledge, Awareness, and Integration are all interdependent.

Once we enter the Void, we never actually leave it.

To leave the Void would mean losing our conscious awareness of it. The entire alchemical journey of the Third Mountain unfolds inside the Void. This may surprise some readers who may be thinking of the alchemical process purely from a preconditioned mythological perspective. After all, Dante exited Hell before entering Purgatory and Heaven.

What actually occurs is that we pull our awareness of the divine source into the temporal core of the Void by expanding our awareness into the heavenly realms while remaining inside the Void. When we ascend the heavenly realms of the spiritual group mind of the Earth, the heavenly realms enter us just as much as we enter them. We must fill the Void with our awareness of the divine source.

The divine source itself exists inside another core which exists out of phase with the temporal core of the Void. The divine core is the spiritual core, which is called the Nexus. In the Third Mountain, the alchemist must integrate the temporal core (Void), with the spiritual core (Nexus).

Will of the Father

The mystery of human suffering is a question which many people attempt to reconcile with a belief in God. The will of the Father is to lift up creation into the light, to lift up the world out of darkness, to lift up all who suffer. The life of his will is the Human / Noetic Soul. You are not the subject of the suffering. You are the Father's answer and solution to the suffering. The forces of darkness attempt to come between the Noetic Soul and the Father. The darkness tempts us to question our worthiness of the Father's love and to question the very existence of God. The Noetic Soul is sent into the world by the Father to engage and save that which is in darkness. This is why we come to experience the suffering of the world. It is not that the Father does not love you. It is just the opposite. Your Noetic Soul is the Father's expression of his love for creation and his will to save it. The Noetic Soul is the only begotten Son of God.

> *"For God so loved the world,*
> *that he gave his only begotten Son,*
> *that whosoever believes in him should not perish,*
> *but have everlasting life." ...John 3:16*

Wuji – **W**

Wuji [Wu-Ji; Wooh-Shee]

In Taoism, the Wuji is the infinite, abstract, un-created realm from which all of creation comes forth. It is said to be the ultimate reality—or only true reality—which precedes all of creation. Everything else is a shade of gray or distortion of that ultimate reality. The wuji always was and always will be. The wuji is absolute because it has no correspondence or relativity to anything within creation. Only the original divine Monad, or cosmic singularity, from which all things come forth, resides in the absolute abstract space of the wuji. The original divine Monad has many names depending on the philosophical source. In western alchemy, and the Kabbalah, one such name for the original divine Monad is the term Ain Soph.

Similar or Equivalent Terms:

George Hegal:	Absolute, The
Erik P. Antoni:	Causal 'A'
Mahayana Buddhism:	Ārūpyadhātu (Formless Realm)
Hasidic Judaism:	Dwelling Place of Atzmus, or Atzmut
Hinduism:	Brahmaloka, Bramapura, Satyaloka
Sufism:	Noor-e-Ahadi, Haqiqa, or Haqiqat
Taoism:	Wuji
Theosophy:	Realm of Atma-Buddhi, Atman
Zoroastrianism:	Domain of the One Eternal Light

Y

Yang

In Taoism, Yang, is the masculine or magnetic positive force.

Yin

In Taoism, Yin, is the feminine or magnetic negative force.

Yuan

In Taoism, Yuan, is the balanced or magnetic neutral force.

Z

Zen Buddhism

Zen Buddhism is a fusion of Mahayana Buddhism and Taoism, practiced chiefly in China and Japan. It places great importance on moment-by-moment awareness and seeing deeply into the nature of things by direct experience. The name derives from the Sanskrit word *dhyana* referring to a particular meditative state. Zen tradition developed a rich textual lineage based on the interpretation of the Buddhist teachings and the sayings of Zen-masters. Important texts are the *Platform Sutra*—attributed to Huineng; the Chán transmission records, such as *The Records of the Transmission of the Lamp*, compiled by Tao-yün and published in 1004; the *Yü-lü Genre* consisting of the recorded sayings of the masters, and the encounter dialogues and koan-collections, such as *The Gateless Barrier* and *The Blue Cliff Record. (Sourced from Wikipedia 2023)*

Zietgeist

In eighteenth and nineteenth century German philosophy, a Zeitgeist is an invisible agent, force, or daemon dominating the characteristics of a given epoch in world history. The term is usually associated with Georg W. F. Hegel—contrasting with Hegel's use of Volksgeist "national spirit" and Weltgeist "world-spirit." Its coinage and popularization precedes Hegel—and is mostly due to Herder and Goethe. Other philosophers who were associated with such concepts include Spencer and Voltaire. Contemporary use of the term sometimes, more colloquially, refers to a schema of fashions or fads that prescribes what is considered to be acceptable or tasteful for an era: e.g., in the field of architecture. *(Sourced from Wikipedia 2023)*

Z – Zoroaster

Zoroaster

Zoroaster, also known as Zarathustra, is regarded as the spiritual founder of Zoroastrianism. He is said to have been a Persian prophet who founded a religious movement that challenged the existing traditions of ancient Persian religion, and inaugurated a movement that eventually became a staple religion in ancient Persia. He was a native speaker of Avestan and lived in the eastern part of the Persian plateau, but his exact birthplace is uncertain. He founded the first monotheistic religion in the world and also had an impact on Plato, Pythagoras, and the Abrahamic religions – Judaism, Christianity, and Islam.

There is little scholarly consensus on when Zoroaster lived. Some scholars, using linguistic and socio-cultural evidence, suggest a dating to somewhere in the second millennium BC. Other scholars date him to the 7th and 6th centuries BC as a near-contemporary of Cyrus the Great and Darius the Great.

Zoroastrianism eventually became the official state religion of ancient Persia—particularly during the era of the Achaemenid Empire—and its distant subdivisions from around the 6th century BC until the 7th century AD, when the religion itself began to decline following the Arab-Muslim conquest of Persia which became Iran. Zoroaster is credited with authorship of the Gathas as well as the Yasna Haptanghaiti, a series of hymns composed in his native Avestan dialect that comprise the core of Zoroastrian thinking.

In the Gathas, Zoroaster sees the human condition as the mental struggle between asha (truth-light) and druj (falsehood-darkness). The cardinal concept of asha is at the foundation of all Zoroastrian doctrine, including Ahura Mazda, creation, existence, and the conditions for free will.

The purpose of humankind is to *"sustain and align itself"* to asha (truth-light). For humankind, this occurs through active ethical participation in life, ritual, and the exercise of constructive / good thoughts, words and deeds. *(Sourced from Wikipedia 2023)*

BIBLIOGRAPHY

Andreae, Johann Valentin. *Chymical Wedding of Christian Rosenkreutz*. Edinburgh, UK: Floris Books, 2016.

Antoni, Erik P. *Concerto of the Rising Sun: Dialogues in spiritual Alchemy*. San Francisco, Noetic Press, 2019

Antoni, Erik P. *Song of the Immortal Beloved: A Contemporary Explanation of spiritual Alchemy*. San Francisco, Noetic Press, 2018.

Atkinson, William Walker, *The Kybalion - A Study of the Hermetic Philosophy of Ancient Egypt and Greece*, 1908

Atmanspacher, Harald, "Quantum Approaches to Consciousness," *The Stanford Encyclopedia of Philosophy* (Summer 2015 Edition), Edward N. Zalta (ed.), 2015.

Berne, Eric M. D. *Games People Play*. New York: Grove Press, 1964.

Campbell, Joseph, Bill D. Moyers, and Betty S. Flowers. *The Power of Myth*. New York, N.Y.: Anchor Books, 1991.

Chia, Mantak, and Michael Winn. *Taoist Secrets of Love: Cultivating Male Sexual Energy*. Santa Fe: Aurora Press, 1984.

Chia, Mantak. *Fusion of the Five Elements: Basic and Advanced Meditations for Transforming Negative Emotions*. Tuttle Publishing, 1989.

Darwin, Charles. *The Origin of Species*. Franklin Center, Penn: The Franklin Library, 1859.

De Chardin, Pierre Teilhard. *Le Phenomene Humain*. Paris: Editions Du Seuil, 1955.

Freud, Sigmund, and James Strachey. *The Standard Edition of the Complete Psychological Works of Sigmund Freud. Vol. 22. (1932-1936). New Introductory Lectures on Psycho-Analysis, and Other Works*. London: Hogarth Press, 1964.

Global Consciousness Project. "The Global Consciousness Project Meaningful Correlations in Random Data." Accessed July 24, 2018. http://noosphere.princeton.edu/homepage4.html

Hall, Manly P. *The Secret Teachings of All Ages: An Encyclopedic Outline of Masonic, Hermetic, Qabbalistic, and Rosicrucian Symbolical Philosophy*. New York: Jeremy P. Tarcher/Penguin, 2003.

Johnson, Obed Simon. *A Study of Chinese Alchemy*. Kessinger Publishing, 2010.

Jung, Carl Gustav. *The Archetypes and the Collective Unconscious*. Princeton, N.J.: Princeton University Press, 1980.

Kaku, Michio. *Parallel Worlds: A Journey Through Creation, Higher Dimensions, and the Future of the Cosmos*. New York: Anchor Books, 2006.

Levi, Eliphas. *Transcendental Magic*. Kessinger Publishing, 1942

Meyer, Stephen C. *Darwin's Doubt: The Explosive Origin of Animal Life and the Case for Intelligent Design*. New York: HarperOne, 2013.

Shah, Idries. *The Sufis*. London. ISF Publishing, 1988.

Steiner, Rudolf, and Christopher Bamford. *How to Know Higher Worlds: A Modern Path of Initiation*. Hudson, NY: Anthroposophic Press, 1994.

Wikepedia.com "Eschatology." 2018. Accessed July 25, 2018 . https://en.wikipedia.org/wiki/Eschatology

———. "Fourth Way." Accessed July 24, 2018. https://en.wikipedia.org/wiki/Fourth_Way

———. "Gog and Magog." 2018. Accessed July 24, 2018. https://en.wikipedia.org/wiki/Gog_and_Magog

———. "Hermes Trismegistus." Accessed July 24, 2018. https://en.wikipedia.org/wiki/Hermes_Trismegistus

———. "Osiris Myth." Accessed July 24, 2018. https://en.wikipedia.org/wiki/Osiris_myth

Winn, Michael. "Primordial Qigong." YouTube video, 08.18. Posted [Nov 23, 2009]. https://www.youtube.com/watch?v=rIP_ICLWpAs

Winn, Michael. *Daoist Internal Alchemy: A Deep Language for Communicating with Nature's Intelligence.*

www.ingramcontent.com/pod-product-compliance
Lightning Source LLC
Chambersburg PA
CBHW022113080426
42734CB00006B/112